genesis

Another Chance for Parents, Teachers, and Anyone Involved in Education

David J.P. Murray

Circle Press
PO Box 5425
Hamden, CT 06518-0425
www.circlepress.org

First published by murray books, 1988. This edition published by Circle Press, a division of Circle Media, Inc.

Book design by Melissa Hartog

Printed in the United States of America

ISBN: 1-933271-11-6

Dedicated with love to the original JP

and to the always loving Moo

MY THANKS TO THOSE WHO HELPED
THIS LITTLE DREAM OF MINE COME TRUE:

Joel López, Javier Fiz and Thomas Williams, Legionaries all three, who urged me on. Paco and Lindsay for being such great sounding boards. Máire for her help with the proofing, well, with some of it. Kid-Dog for not spilliing the ink over the manuscript. Diego for his marathon read. Tom, Tony, Bertha, Jaime, Patricia, Valerie, Owen, and Eduardo for their dedication. Claudia Volkman and the Circle Press team for being such great people to have on your side. Fr Evaristo Sada for his active input and Nuestro Padre for giving me something worth writing about.

RAVE REVIEWS

"Great book. Pity about the content."

BILL BOGGS, SALOON MANAGER

"More formative than the cane. It's heavier and hurts more."

MR SNEAKY SLEEZE, STATE CORRECTION CENTER

"Never has so little been said in so many words."

GREAT BOOK REVIEW

"A splendid read, or so I have been told. Couldn't get past the first page myself."

MARGARET FREDERICKS, AUTHOR OF THE JOLLY EDUCATOR

"This book's balance is superb. We use it in all our 'Walk Right' classes."

MME. SANSBRAIN, TRES RICHE SCHOOL, SWITZERLAND

"A prodigious accomplishment. Well worth the read. Don't believe what others say about it."

MURRAY

"Let us make man in our own image."

Genesis, the Book of Creation

Overview

Overview

Preliminary Notes

Before setting out, I am happy to tell you that this document does have a glossary (beginning on page 198) that contains a brief explanation of terms and concepts with which the reader may not be familiar.

For Whom

This book is intended as a basic personal formation tool for anybody working with children between the ages of seven and fifteen (the children, that is, not the educator). It is intended for both male and female educators.

What

This is not, nor has it ever tried to be, a complete manual. I apologize if you bought this book hoping to find the definitive treatise on all things related to the formation of young people. Some areas have just been touched in passing.

All I have tried to do is offer my personal reflections on what I consider to be the basic tools for an educator. Actually working with these tools hopefully will lead to another book that will cover such topics as habit formation, group management, leadership detection and formation, the role of the educator as a personal life-model and, of course, the spiritual dimension that is the real backbone of any worthwhile and lasting formation.

genesis is but a collection of personal reflections, nothing more.

Words

In these reflections, the use of the word "educator" refers to that person who has the responsibility of teaching or educating a kid, or a person who is in charge of kids. “Mother” or “father” could be used in a family setting and “teacher” in a school setting.

I speak of the educator and his kids, but the reflections are equally applicable to female educators and her kids.

The use of “kid” is intentional. I feel the word “student” and even “boy” or “girl” falls short.

Sorry

In some incidences I have used examples that do not speak highly of the people involved. I am at pains to point out that the people in such examples have been rendered unidentifiable in these examples, that in each and every case the situation was rectified, that in practically every case the person in question was a trainee, that each trainee in question learned positively from the cited case, and that at no time were any students ever in moral or physical danger or subject to abuse or neglect. Should any educator, assistant or youth worker, whether past or present, feel alluded to, he is asked to remember that kids and situations can be the same the world over, and that there is nothing that has happened to him that has not happened to others before him.

In any event, should anyone take even the slightest offense, may I extend my sincerest apologies. (In legal terms we call this a “disclaimer”—so you will not be able to sue me. I'm glad about that.)

Some examples are made up of individual events that I have strung together for the sake of illustration.

How to Read genesis

This is designed neither as a novel nor as a manual. You read a novel from cover to cover, and the start leads to the finish. To read a manual you usually have to have the computer, or whatever the manual is about, in front of you as you read. **genesis** is a mix between a reference book and a "how-to" book. The trainee/educator or the educator-to-be can read it from cover to cover and it will give him a fair introduction as to what his job will be. **genesis** can also be used as an on-going reference that an educator can dip into as he works.

The book has five parts. Each part is divided into various sections. Many sections will have "topics" that offer areas for discussion or personal thought. Some topics play the part of the "devil's advocate," and so the reader should be careful not to interpret them as statements that endorse what the preceding chapter has said. A footnote will refer the reader to a guideline for answers.

Parts Two and Four have additional "support" reading material at the end of each part that the educator might like to read through.

1
Background Concepts

Answers that Need Questions

Answers that Need Questions

In a renowned boarding school in Ireland, run by an order renowned for its educational expertise, on every hike day the students would receive five cigarettes along with their packed lunch. Since many of the students were not avid smokers they would not smoke their ration during the day's walk. They would wait until they came back in the evening when they would congregate (in the gym of all places) and puff away in a relaxed fashion recounting the adventures of the day. This was in the golden days when Bogart, Bacall, and all their Hollywood friends flaunted the glories of nicotine, and when it was fashionable for the hero, and even the heroine, to smoke. Today that boarding school is a smoke and drug-free zone. Things change.

But there are certain things that do not change: like a good education, human values, right and wrong, and the right way to do something. These things do not change.

Course introductions are usually more helpful after rather than before the course. However, I have placed this section on basic concepts at the beginning as I consider it important that the educator should have a grasp of them before he starts working. But I also feel that the concepts explained here will be more readily and more fully understood once the educator has started to work.

In this light, might I suggest a quick read-through of this section before going on to the other sections. Or you may skip it and return once you have a few chapters under your belt.

Focusing the Mission

An educator's primary and only mission has to do with formation. This formation has many areas but just one focus: to help kids acquire and master the tools for self-development.

Formation

Formation is not a nice word. People understand different things when you mention formation. Often what comes to mind is something quite negative or superficial. We may think of the sculptor chiseling away at a piece of granite trying to "form" something. Not nice if you're the chunk of granite. Or we may think of soldiers marching in "formation." One foot out of line and you get eaten alive by the sergeant. But we will use "formation" in a totally different sense. When we speak of "formation" we are referring to the kid's efforts at personal development. If education can be described as "giving the kid the tools he needs," formation can be described as the kid himself using these tools. We educate the kid; kids form themselves. If we wanted to use the above example of the sculptor to explain formation, we would say that the kid is both the block of granite and the sculptor. We give the kid the chisel (education), show him where and how to strike (guidance) and encourage him (motivation) until the work of art is completed.

So we can see that formation is more than just education. Not only does it require education, but it also calls for constant motivation, guidance, and even correction. Formation is the result of effective education.

In our work with kids we can, for simplicity's sake, categorize five interrelated areas of formation:

Spiritual – dealing with a kid's relationship with God
Human – dealing with the kid as a man-to-be
Academic – having to do with the cultivation of the intellect
Athletic – having to do with physical development
Cultural – dealing with a kid's place in the world

While many of these areas overlap, and while each one does have a definite influence and bearing on all the others, each area will have a specific focus. We do not talk of medical or of psychological formation, because doctors may be called in from time to time to help fix something, and these areas in themselves are not ones that a kid is expected to develop. In this document we will deal basically with human formation, but as the reader will see, we often treat overlapping areas in some detail, given their influence on human formation.

Virtues

Virtues are, so to speak, strengths. Much as muscle power is the strength needed to walk, human and spiritual virtues are the strengths we need to be real people. A man without loyalty, without a keen sense of his responsibility, without concern for others, without a clear awareness of his own meaning, can hardly be called a real man. If anything, he would be an animal in a man's clothing.

Values

Values are "something of worth."[1] We have two kinds of values:

Subjective values (what I consider to be valuable)

Getting up early in the morning might be something to which I attach a certain value. I might also consider smoking valuable, so subjective values are not necessarily real values. They are simply what I feel is good for me.

Objective values (what is valuable, whether I think it is or not)

Man is supposed to be a certain way, just as the human body is supposed to be a certain way. And as there are things that are good for the body (exercise, good food, rest) so too there are things that are good for man (honesty, loyalty, and so forth.) These things that are good for man, for any man, are gleaned from what man is supposed to be.

Everybody has subjective values. Our efforts, as educators, should be to get our kids to take on objective values as their own. It is easier said than done.

Values and Virtue Working Together

Values have much to do with virtue. After all, honesty is both value and virtue. Honesty is good for me, so I use the virtue of honesty to be honest. Value is, so to speak, the goal or what inspires. Virtue is the exercise or action we use to attain the goal or to do as we are inspired. Value and virtue are the two faces of the same lens, or the two sides of the same coin.

Interrelated Formation

All areas of formation head in the same direction: the personal development of the kid. They are so intimately related that a lack of one will irreparably damage, or at least stunt, the other. And yet each area is distinct.

I once had a great mechanic. He could fix just about anything. Very often his screwdriver and oily hands got my car up and running. Then I got one of these new-fangled cars. It had "electronic injection" and a "control center" and electric windows. One cold morning it wouldn't start. I called my faithful know-everything, fix-anything mechanic. He came up and had a look under the hood. He wiggled a few wires, shook his head and smeared his chin with grease as he rubbed it in defeat. "The control center's messed up," he groaned. "You need to take it to the specialists."

While not wanting for a moment to compare a kid to a car, the episode does prove the point that it takes more than four wheels and an engine to run a car. And wise educators know their limits. A teacher qualified in math, for example, may not be qualified in physical education. He may have a few notions about the theme, but he will not attempt to take on the role of coach. However, in his math class, he will insist that kids sit straight and not slouch. He will dedicate himself to teaching math without forgetting that he is not just teaching math.

Just as food gives the athlete energy, training puts this energy to good use. Good training leads to teamwork and teamwork to a good game. After a hard game the athlete will be hungry. Everything has its part to play... so too all aspects of formation blend together. Human formation will invigorate spiritual formation. Healthy spiritual formation will strengthen human formation. A kid with no will power will not be as good as he should be in academics, etc.

Blended Formation

I believe that there is a certain hierarchy within the various areas of formation and success will depend on the blend. The human sphere, for example, is the basis for the spiritual one.

Athletic formation is important, but without values such as teamwork and constancy, gleaned from human formation, any athletic skills would be lame. So there is a hierarchy, but it is not an exclusive hierarchy. Just as if we were to ask, what is the most important part of the body, we would answer: the brain. This does not mean that the heart is unimportant, or that arms and legs are accessories. But there is a hierarchy. And just as in the body, in formation all aspects work together. And the better the one, the better everything else, with the one making the other stronger.

However, we must be careful not to overemphasize any aspect.

Some national soccer teams sure know how to score goals. One team that comes to mind has been world champion a few times over. But when you see how they bad-mouth the ref and feign injury, you begin to wonder whether goal scoring is really what sports is all about.

Still on the soccer field: I remember seeing a player before going onto the field, kneel and make the sign of the cross. I thought that was nice. But when he came to shoot at the goal, he was quite useless, and not just once. I thought to myself that if this guy was being paid to be a professional player, he might like to spend a little less time on his knees and more time practicing his soccer. (Don't get me wrong – in this world, there is plenty of time for both prayer and practice.)

In our work therefore, we must be careful to have all spheres in mind, giving priority where priority is due, but knowing too that the secret of good coffee is in the blend.

Integral Formation

There is another term we must consider. It's what we call "integral formation."

When I heard the term first used I thought it had something to do with how to make brown bread![2] In fact we can all conjure up our own meaning for "integral formation." But in this book, integral means completely and harmoniously blended. We strive to ensure that each facet of formation is fully developed and that the kid attains his complete goal in each and that all are interdependent and well blended. The term "integral formation" doesn't sound too attractive, sounding rather like an "integrated circuit" on a computer motherboard, but what it means is indeed attractive.[3]

Human Formation as Such

As this book deals basically with how we can be effective in helping our kids attain solid human formation, let us now spend a few paragraphs going over what is meant by the term "human formation."

What do a dead-fish handshake, a frayed collar, and a messy bedroom have in common? They all denote a lack of human formation. What do an unfinished job, a sloppy copybook, and being late for an appointment have in common? They all denote a lack of human formation. What do an interesting business presentation, a pleasant evening out, and a serene smile have in common? They all denote the presence of human formation.

We could draw up lists and counter lists, but the fact is obvious: human formation counts, and we would all love to have it and have it in abundance. Human formation has to do with the acquisition and mastery of human virtues. Not only will a solid dose of human formation make us better people, it will make us more human, and it will also help us to be useful humans.

A friend invited me to take a ride in his newly purchased pre-owned car. It was a big car and rather sluggish. It was difficult to find parking for it and it used a lot of gasoline. But wanting to let my friend show off his new treasure, I willingly accepted the ride. As we maneuvered through the narrow, bumpy street, I felt that my own little car was just as good, if not better. "What do you think?" he asked me. "Not much, right?" He had read my mind. "Well," I said jokingly, "at least it moves."

We headed out onto the highway and my friend said, "Now, sit back and just listen." He engaged the fifth gear and brought the speed from the 60 kilometers an hour we had been doing until then, up to 120 km, well within Italian speed limits for highways. As the car passed through 110 km per hour, the whole engine dropped a tone. At 120 km my car would be revved up to an incredible pitch, making everyone aboard fear for their physical integrity. But this thing just purred along effortlessly.

"Something else, right?" And I sure had to agree. It certainly was something else. "And you know what?" my proud friend said. "At this speed it uses less fuel than at lower speeds. It was built for this." As the Tuscany countryside glided by effortlessly, I just wondered what my little car had been built for!

We can only be satisfied with ourselves when we are doing what we were made for. We can only be deep-down happy, when we are what we should be. We can only really help others when we be as we ought to be. And human formation is all about this: being what you are supposed to be.

Human formation deals with values and virtues, and the beauty is that human formation is exquisitely visible. Values and virtues are useless if not put into practice. In fact, if they are not put into practice they simply disappear, much like muscle tissue. But this "visibility" can fool us. A guy with clean shoes points to human formation, but then again it could just point to him being lucky enough to have someone who cleans them every day for him. The guy with the firm handshake might lead us to believe that we have a confident person in front of us when maybe all we have is someone who is naturally strong. And this then is the unfortunate tragedy: sometimes we might think that human formation is a series of externals and not the result of inner conviction. But having said this, we can state one thing for certain: when external manifestations of human formation are lacking, human formation is lacking. And this has a definite bearing on our work as educators.

A well-mannered person will not slouch down in his chair when listening to someone trying to explain something. He will want to understand what the person is saying and will put his body into "attentive mode" to do so. A person who values other people will polish his shoes, not only to help preserve the leather, but also because he wants to give other people something nice to look at. A conscientious worker will do a job to the best of his ability, not only because he wants to be paid for a job well done, but also because he knows that it is his responsibility to do the job well. So when we speak of human formation we are not referring to the mere practice of externals, but to cultivating the spirit or conviction that will spontaneously lead to these externals.

The kids were standing in a perfectly straight line and in silence. "I can keep them there for hours, if I wanted to," confided the trainee. "How's that for formation? That's what I call human formation!" he stated proudly and looked at me to confirm.

"I don't know," I said. "For me, it's just a straight line. In Ireland we have them at every downtown bus stop." It was a somewhat cruel remark, I admit, but as I was training the young man, I felt it my duty to point out the difference between "human formation" and a "formation of humans."

Habits and Formation

So what is an educator to do: dedicate himself to motivating the kids, to forming concepts and convictions? Yes, but not exclusively. He must work on the externals at the same time. Just as a mother will insist her five-year old finish his vegetables before he gets dessert, we too must work on getting kids into the habit of doing things right. As time goes on, we will be able to give the reasons behind the habits, just as the five-year old will grow to realize the importance of iron in his diet (albeit when he hits sixty!). Hopefully we can accelerate this "interiorizing" process and, given the age bracket of our kids, it is reasonable to presume that we can.

Some educational systems approach this from another angle. They say, "Let the kid do what he spontaneously feels like doing. Work on training his emotions and feelings so that good behavior will naturally flow." Maybe such systems were written by doting grandparents, but they certainly do nothing good for the kid. Basically what they are saying is that if a kid feels like punching another kid in the nose, he should go unpunished if he draws blood. Our efforts should be to help him love and respect others, and the assimilation of this love and respect cannot be forced. This is an exaggerated example, but you get my meaning.

Other systems will take the opposite approach: total and exclusive focus on the details. Clean shoes, crisp uniforms, politeness at all costs. These are the military schools. An exhaustive codebook will contain a detailed reaction for every conceivable occasion, leaving no room whatsoever for personal maneuver.

We, however, have a different approach inspired by the gospel. Christ was at pains to form the hearts of his apostles, but even from the earliest pages we see him correcting them. The morning after a hard day's work, the apostles said it would be best to stay put, but Christ corrects them and they all head off to another place. He didn't say, "I am leaving, you can come when you understand my mission." Nor did he say, "Move out!" Rather, he says, "Let us go elsewhere... so that I can preach there too because this is why I have come" (see Mark 1:38). Another example is the Gospel scene in which a bystander chops off a guard's ear. Christ rebukes him and fixes the poor guard's ear.

And so we must work on both areas at the same time: the cultivation of values and virtues in the kid's heart, and the fostering of external habits. External habits will never lead to a kid assimilating an interior value system, no matter how many details or habits you pile on, but interior human formation without the externals is pie in the sky. Externals without interior formation are as worthless for cutting it in life as a sword made out of foam rubber.

Tagging Along for the Ride

I often get the impression that in some schools and in some families, the kids are simply there "for the ride." It is as if the school or family was heading off in its own direction and the kids just happened to be there. It can be easily understood. A school has its curriculum and it's up to the kid to pull his weight and fulfill it. We could hardly expect a school to say, "Oh well, Jimmy, don't you worry. Just do what you can and you'll be fine." An educational institution has its standards and it is up to the kid to meet those standards or go elsewhere. A busy mom and dad have their lives to run and other kids to provide for. As parents, they have things to do and places to go. You can hardly expect them to stop dead in their tracks and put the kid at the center of everything.

One balmy Rome evening, I was having a late supper in a nice restaurant. I had been there many times and this night I was chatting with the elderly owner. As we sipped our digestivo, I asked him what he thought had been the most important thing in his life. (Italian after-dinner drinks do spur such philosophic discussions.) "My restaurant" was his simple answer. I congratulated him. And I felt sorry for his kids, now grown up with families of their own.

But let me state my case: families, schools, youth centers, football teams, etc. should all be aimed at, focused on, and lived for the kid. No other game plan is acceptable. No other agenda is worthy or worthwhile. Understanding this "kid priority" and balancing it with other demands (the day-to-day running of family, school standards, etc.) is, I believe, a key not only to successful education but also to life itself.

First Things First and Everything at the Same Time

An educational consultant was explaining why he thought it was best to teach English as a second language.

"A student cannot be expected to say a word, or a series of words, if he has not heard it and understood its meaning first. As the student uses the new word or phrase for the first time, after hearing it, he should be coached as to how it is pronounced. The student should also know how to read that word or phrase and practice how it is written."

A teacher in the audience raised his hand to make a point: "It all looks rather time-consuming to me. If I had to teach my students how to say a word and then how to read and write it, it would take me forever."

"Ah," said the consultant, "the trick is to practically do it all at the same time and throw in a bit of grammar as well." And he went on to give an example. He asked the audience to take a pen. On the blackboard he wrote Chi è Lei? "Chi è Lei? is an Italian phrase and means 'Who are you, sir?' Chi è Lei?" He motioned the audience to repeat the phrase. "And as you practice the phrase, please write it down. Notice that the word Lei, which means 'you,' is written with a capital L. It is a sign of respect."

Then he wrote Sono Paul on the board and followed the same drill, saying that sono is Italian for "I am." He then rapidly asked people in the audience, "Chi è Lei?" and the audience was quick to answer, each with his or her own name.

"You see, by using this 'everything at the same time method,' we have spent less than a minute to learn how to understand, speak, read, write, and communicate in Italian. And we've learned a little grammar too. What might be difficult to explain can often be easier done than said."

We can apply what the consultant said about learning a language to the apparently overwhelming task of education.

Wrap Up

Our mission, as educators, is to help the kid become a real adult. By this we do not mean that we want him to grow at an accelerated rate and become an adult before his time. What we mean is that we want to give the kid all the tools, skills, guidance, and encouragement that he needs in order to become the man he is supposed to become.

A kid is like many worlds, all together and all at the same time. Our work is aimed at all these worlds that, when orbiting in harmony, will become the microcosmos that is the complete and balanced adult. The purpose of human formation is to give a person the human capabilities he needs to function correctly—and therefore happily—as a human.

Human formation is a tool. We ourselves use it to get our job in life done. Formation is not the ultimate goal. It is an immediate goal. We want to help kids form themselves so that they can do what they have to do, do what they are called to do. Formation is like driving. Nobody learns how to drive just "to drive." They learn to drive because they want to be able to go places. In this sense, formation is like driving. We have to help the kids "learn how to drive," or form themselves, but not so that they can bask in the glory of "being able to drive," of being formed, but because now by "being able to drive," by being formed, they can "go places. They can use their formation to do what they have to do and be the people they are called to be. The parable of the talents (Mt. 25: 14-30) is where this concept comes from.

Sometimes parents may just be happy to see that their child has learned how to walk. They will even celebrate the occasion and tell their friends, "My child can walk!" Thankfully though, these parents will soon put this walking capability to good use. If we, as educators, were to content ourselves with our kids just being well mannered, responsible, orderly and punctual, we would be like an aging parent who still proclaims to the world, "Hey! My son can walk!" "How old is he?" "Forty."

Topics

1. The Amazon rain forest offers some of the most beautiful examples of trees. Without human intervention, these trees have grown to enormous heights and awe-inspiring splendor. These trees, left to grow naturally, have fulfilled their potential.
2. No one has ever been truly happy by simply following a book of rules.
3. To acquire deep-rooted and effective human formation, it is sufficient that a kid lives for a period of time (six to nine months) in a strict environment.
4. When kids keep their rooms tidy, are on time and are well dressed, we can be assured that they have a solid degree of human formation.
5. A kid does not believe in God and is averse to all things spiritual. Is his formation doomed to be unbalanced and unstable?
6. In-depth spiritual formation by itself is sufficient to allow a person to attain complete and true happiness in this life and in the next.

2

The Four Steps Towards Integral Formation

Introduction

If you've never gone scuba diving, you might like to try it sometime. It takes about a full week to qualify as an "open water diver" and the learning process is as exciting and as fun as going on actual dives once you've qualified. It comes as no surprise that the steps to becoming a diver are basically the same as those we will follow as we try to lead kids to adulthood.

First, the instructor knows what diving is all about. He knows what a real diver is. He knows, for example, that a real diver is a calm and relaxed person, an athletic person, although not necessarily a mile-a-minute kind of guy. He knows that a real diver is capable of caring for those on a dive with him. He knows that a real diver has no major respiratory problems. In other words, the instructor knows what it takes to be a diver.

Then, the instructor will size you up. He will see what you're like. He'll check you out and see what needs to be done to turn you into as good a diver as you can be. To do this he will even "try you out." He'll see if you panic when you're underwater and lose your breathing mask. He'll see if you are relaxed underwater. An interesting thing here is that if you are not relaxed, you will keep rising to the surface or simply sink to the bottom (it has to do with the amount of air in your lungs).

Once the instructor has a fair idea of how you match up to what a real diver should be, he will give you all the instruction that you need to become a decent diver. He will design a customized program for you. He will teach you all about "decompression" and "atmospheres"; he will show you how to get out of trouble underwater and how you can help others get out of trouble underwater.

But the best thing about a good instructor is being in his company as you go on your first dive. He will be right there beside you. If water leaks into your mask, he will remind you of how to clear it. If you start to sink just a little too quickly, he will ease over to you and lighten your weights, or he will indicate to you that you are breathing too fast and too short. If for whatever reason you feel a little panicky, he'll be right there for you. As you glide effortlessly along, he will show you the wonders of marine life. It is then that you really start to enjoy it all.

In the second part of this book, we will take basically the same four steps: first, we will define the ideal kid. Then we will see how we can get to know the kid we have in front of us in order to see how he matches up and what needs to be done. Next, we will create a personal program for him so that he can become the man he is supposed to be. Finally, we will journey with him, being ever present, as he ventures into life.

THE FIRST STEP: GOD'S PROTOTYPE

To be successful in our work as educators we must know where we are trying to bring our kids. This section discusses practical aspects of the "ideal kid."

Whether you are a parent, a schoolteacher, or a youth worker, there is always the first day on the job. What is the first thing we should ask ourselves when a kid is born or given over to our care? The answer is so obvious that quite often it never occurs to us. We almost take it for granted. But in this practical manual we will take nothing for granted. So what then should this first question be?

For parents, the most important question might seem to be, "What'll we call the kid?" For anyone else, it might be, "What's the kid's name?" But this is not the most important question. It might be the most urgent, but certainly not the most important. "Who's this kid like?" No. "What's this kid like?" No. "How can I successfully educate this kid?" No. "Do we have enough diapers?" No.

"What does God want this kid to be?" is the real question we must ask ourselves. Our overriding concern must be "What does God want of this kid?"

This is at once a simple and yet complicated question. It can lead to bland answers like "God wants him to be good," "God wants him to be successful," "God wants him to be happy"... but as educators our answer must be concrete and practical even down to the most painstaking detail.

The method we will follow is quite simple. First, we will see what God wants of the average joe. In other words, what is the ideal kid like in God's eyes? When God thinks "kid," what does he see? This will involve us understanding God's vision of man... and of kids. It will mean that we must have a firm grasp of what the human and spiritual virtues entail, for a kid in God's eyes must be nothing short of perfect. Of course, the "ideal kid" will be a rather general view. God has no intention of having everybody be exactly the same. But the basics will always be the same. Every kid is called to be generous. One kid's living out of his generosity will not be the same as the next guy's, but all are called to live generously. Every kid is called to be responsible, although every kid will have his own way of living out his responsibility. But the basic qualities (generosity, responsibility...) are the same for everybody. So we must understand what exactly goes into the makings of the perfect kid. This will be our first step.

Once we have clear in our minds God's prototype (step one), we will see with whom we are dealing. We will measure our kid against this prototype, see what's up to standard, and see what's missing (step two, pages 33, 41). From this analysis we can draw up our work areas for the kid (step three, page 45). Once we see what needs to be done so that this kid achieves what God wants of him, we must then help the kid get there (step four, page 59).

These four steps are at the core of all our work. Our effectiveness as educators will depend on how well we know what the ideal kid is, how well we know and comprehend the kid we have in front of us, how detailed we can be in bridging the gap between what is and what should be, and on how able we are to motivate this kid to attain what God is calling him to attain.

So, far from being a disciplinarian, far from being a babysitter, and very far from being an entertainer, an educator is an educator. So let us begin. Let us venture to discover what God thinks of when he thinks "kid."

> One meaning of the word "educator" can be derived from the Latin "ex" (or "e") which means out of, as in "exit," combined with "ducare" which means "to lead."
>
> **Thus, "e-ducation" can be understood as a "leading" someone "out" (of their ignorance, of their shell).**

Kid-Awareness

First of all, the ideal kid knows he's a kid. But not simply a son of his parents, but above all, a son of God. He was born of God, is God's child always, and is destined to return to be with his Father. This may appear to be a rather fussy idea but don't be overly concerned about it for the moment. This "kid-awareness" is the essential quality of our prototype. It is from this awareness that all other qualities will flow. It is this awareness quality that gives meaning to all other qualities. All qualities are an expression of this, and all qualities are fulfilled by this.

Kid Qualities

There follows a short and succinct list of simple qualities that are essential to the kid prototype. I have not listed them in order of importance. Many overlap and many are essentially interrelated. Some are more important than others.

Generosity

This means self-giving born out of concern for others. Not a total forgetfulness of self, but a realization that the other person is another "me," just as important and maybe just a little more in need than me.

Willpower

This means more than the guts to take a cold shower on a sub-zero day. It means putting duty before pleasure, always. It even means going beyond the call of duty... always.

Sincerity

When the Romans built marble columns or statues they would, if the marble was defective, cover in the holes or cracks with wax. Such workmanship was considered to be cheap. It meant that the column or statue was not made of good quality stone. "Sine" in Latin means "without" and "cera" means "wax." "Sin cera" meant that the statue was all good marble, one solid piece of marble. Sincerity as a quality in a person means simply that he is one person, and that he doesn't try to live as two. What you see is basically what you get.

Discipline

We can mean two things with this word. One is the external aspect: the simple, almost mechanical or military following of established rules and regulations. These rules and regulations have their meaning and "raison d'être" and range from traffic laws to bedtimes. Another is the personal or interior discipline that motivates us to do what is right because it is right.

Hard Work

Nothing comes easily, and most things of value are costly.

There is no substitute for honest-to-goodness hard work or personal effort, be it in the classroom, be it virtue acquisition, or be it on the playing field.

Constancy

Constancy is the doggedness to do again and again what we have to do. This quality is intrinsically tied up with fidelity.

Initiative

Initiative is the capacity to detect a need and come up with a workable response. It can even include the creation of a need and of the adequate response.

Self-Sacrifice

Generosity leads to self-sacrifice. Sometimes this will mean depriving myself of something (sleep, candy, comfort...) so that someone else may have what I could have had. Other times it will mean giving up me myself, as in the case of when you are working within a team and have to give up your ideas, your way of doing things for what you see as the good of the team. I might add here that self-sacrifice must never be an end in itself. We must never seek to be self-sacrificing, but at the same time we must never ever shrink from it.

Responsibility

This has two meanings. One is that of being able to answer for your actions. If something goes wrong because of me, I will own up to it and will not run from the blame. But it also means that I am, that all of me is "called into question." When I am asked to do something, I, all of me, will do my very best to get the job done. I will not go about it halfheartedly, but wholeheartedly. I will not take on the job and then, because of other pressures or demands, neglect it.

Respect

This means taking the other into account.

Good Manners

It may seem a rather unimportant quality, certainly not one that God would request for his prototype, but when we consider good manners as nothing more than an expression of respect for the other person, it is then that we begin to realize its importance.

Niceness

By "nice" I mean "good manners going the extra little bit." It is good manners to open a door for a woman at the supermarket. It is "nice" to go and get her a shopping cart. It is good manners to say "thank you" for a meal offered by friends. It is "nice" to send them a thank-you note.

Healthy Qualities

Beyond the above-mentioned basic or single qualities, there are some special ones. These qualities will indicate that other qualities are present, just as a healthy appetite indicates a healthy body. They include joy, serenity, drive, and optimism. These healthy qualities cannot be achieved as stand-alone units. In fact, were you to go off and search for "joy," you would not find it sitting somewhere all by itself. It would be surrounded by many other qualities. If you tried to pluck "joy" away and leave all the others, you would find that it simply disappears.

It is these "healthy qualities" that will be one of our measures of success. When we see that our kid is serene (serene, I say, not dopey), we can be pretty sure we are on the right track. And we don't have to wait sixty years to measure our success. Everything is so interrelated that a hardworking kid will usually be a happy kid, and an optimistic kid will usually be open to self-sacrifice. Kids are not born with all these characteristics (at least none of the kids I have known). Kids will be open to acquiring them, and some may be more open than others. It will be up to the educators to help the kid acquire them. But one thing is sure—the more honed the qualities, the greater will be the joy, the stronger the serenity, the more powerful the drive, and the more solid the optimism.

Can we say that Christ is God's prototype?

Christ is the embodiment of all virtue, the perfect man—as well as being God. In this sense we can say that he is without doubt the perfect fulfillment of God's prototype. However, when I speak of God's prototype, I am referring to that set of basic characteristics that the perfect kid, in God's eyes, should have. In this sense Christ goes way beyond the prototype—he fulfills it perfectly. This is just a little nuance, but you might like to keep it in mind.

So then, we can say that this God-prototype of kid has a good dose of "kid-awareness," has a firm hold on basic qualities, and is "healthy." But in practical terms, what does all this mean? How can I tell how generous or how self-giving the kid I have in front of me is? That's what we are going to see next.

The Second Step: Measuring Up

How does our kid compare to God's prototype?

A compass will have four major points: north, south, east, and west. The Aztec compass had five. The fifth told them where they were; it was the center of the compass. Knowing where you are is a good starting point.

Whether we are parents or work in a school or club, our contact with kids affords us the opportunity to get to know them. By "getting to know" the kids I mean getting to know, firstly, how they match up to the prototype and, secondly, what gets them to do what they do. Some environments give us more of an opportunity than others. Live-in situations however, such as the family or a boarding school are by far the most fruitful, but for an opened-eyed educator, all occasions are valid. Right now we will focus on the sizing up of a kid. What is the kid we have in front of us like, and how does he measure up?

As we work, we need to be careful not to read too much into any one detail. Our aim will be to search out patterns, rather than individual elements. For example:

> We see a kid on the soccer field giving a fellow player a well-placed kick in the shins. We might immediately conclude that the kid is vicious, a bad loser, or a hot-tempered individual. But maybe, as an adolescent, his coordination isn't exactly what it should be and maybe he simply missed, connecting with a shin instead of a ball. Rather than judge him straight off, we will see how he reacts and see if he apologizes. We will keep the episode in mind and see if in

other areas he continues to be vicious or just simply uncoordinated.

We can say that there are two ways of getting to know a kid—through preliminary knowledge and through working knowledge. Preliminary knowledge can help teachers and youth workers know something about the kid before they actually meet him. It can also be useful for adoptive parents or foster parents. Working knowledge (firsthand experience) is what we witness and is by far the more valuable tool.

Preliminary Knowledge

If we work in a school or youth group, there is some groundwork we can do even before we meet our kids for the first time. We can learn about the kids through such things as application forms and reports. These will not give us a total understanding of the kid by any means, but they will help us get to know him even though it is superficially.

First of all, a form or report will tell us the kid's full name. Boiling things down, there is little that we can learn about a kid just from his name. Christ called Simon "Peter," or "Rock," which would lead us to believe that the fisherman was a solid man. But when he was called "Rock" by Christ, he was anything but solid. He later became strong, but his name was more a description of his post rather than of his person.

We do well to learn the whole name by heart and match it to a photograph. In the weeks leading up to the beginning of classes, a useful exercise is to see if we can match a complete name to the students' photographs.

The application forms will also give us the student's age, although this won't tell us very much. Age differences have become blurred over the past decades. Whereas forty years ago the age of thirteen for boys and of twelve for girls was considered the onset of puberty, today we can register boys as early as eleven and girls as early as ten beginning to take the physical jump from kid to adulthood. And apart from the physical aspect, television and other media have shifted concerns in an alarming fashion. Boys of twelve feel they are not normal if they do not have a steady girlfriend (!) and grown men are enticed to buy cars as if they were toys! So it is difficult today to set "standard age characteristics" that differentiate age groups.

But there are other things that will help us a little more. If the kid has brothers or sisters, it will mean that he will be somewhat more balanced than an only child. He will have learned a little of the art of "give and take," he will be more open to doing things for others and more aware of their needs. If he is the eldest kid, he will be naturally more responsible. If he is the last kid, chances are he will be a little spoiled, or that he will be concerned about being different from his other brothers. Or if he is the last kid and only has sisters, chances are that his manners may be a little effeminate. If he is the middle of three kids, there's a good possibility he will be unsure of himself and maybe somewhat of a rebel, albeit a well-intentioned one.

Of course, the above are generalizations and we need to be careful not to build up our picture of the kid before we know him. Prejudice, which means to prejudge, is when we try to make a person fit what we believe he should be. Here's an example that will show just how ridiculous and dangerous prejudice can be:

Prejudice 1: A kid is selfish. You see another kid ask him for the loan of a pencil. The "selfish" kid says, "You should have your own. Ask the teacher for one." Very selfish kid!

Prejudice 2: A kid is truly concerned about helping others to be better people. You see another kid ask him for the loan of a pencil. The "concerned" kid says, "You should have your own. Ask the teacher for one." This is the fifth time that the same kid has asked our "concerned" kid for the loan of a pencil. On previous occasions he has willingly lent the pencil but now, after speaking about it with the teacher, he believes that the kid's laziness is not good and suggests that the kid speak to the teacher. What great concern!

Previous school records will also tell us something about the kid. We are not interested in high or low grades, but in patterns. Check over the last few years to see if the kid has been constant. If grades are on a downer, it means the kid is swimming in difficult waters. This may be due to family problems or to the kid's growth.

His interests also will tell us a little about the kid, although usually today interests will be somewhat the same for everyone.

Other forms, such as psychological and medical reports, will tell the educator rather little about the kid. Both such reports may help us later on, but in a school or youth group environment, they simply tell us whether the kid is fit (mentally and physically) to be in the school or youth group.

Medical and psychological reports, when all is said and done, help us determine three basic facts:

1. That the kid will not suffer from his stay in the school or youth group environment

2. That he is capable of living out his stay with positive results
3. That he will not harm either himself or others.

However, whatever the background information we have on the child, be it psychological, medical, grades, or other, we must remember that each piece of information is but a snapshot. And like any snapshot, it is not to be trusted. It gives us an idea, but not a certainty. Just think of your passport photograph. (Is that really you?) But this background information will give us a general idea of what is coming our way.

First Impressions

The only thing that we can say for first impressions is that they last, something like a weed—hard to get rid of and worth very little. When we meet a kid for the first time, let us not be too quick to be fooled by first impressions. The kid will usually be nervous, and he will more than likely be out of his normal element. This applies to kids coming to their first day at a new school or youth group and similar experiences. However, it may well be that it is you who are new and possibly nervous.

Working Knowledge

Personal appearance

Here's what personal appearance can tell us about a kid.

> **Personal appearance has little to do with taste but a lot to be with respect.**
>
> GAELIC BOOK OF WISDOM

A kid who tries to show off, either in his dress, hairstyle, or manner has something not quite right. It is often a simple exteriorizing of his belief that he is different—if not better—than those around him. Sometimes it is a feeling of inferiority that might lead him to show off. But we must be careful, as quite often designer label clothes or the latest hairstyles may be nothing more than a by-product of the kid's lifestyle. Wearing such clothes or hairstyles is not what we should look out for, but how he wears them, his manner.

If the kid is possessive of his things, if he doesn't lend them willingly, if he gets uptight about others handling them, then we have a defect. Watching a kid with his clothes (and his other possessions) will help us detect whether he cares for others, whether he is worried about them or only cares about himself.

Beware of those who proclaim to have understood a kid immediately. "I can tell by just looking him in his eyes" is something I have heard more than once. Very rare indeed is this gift and only one person I know has it—and he will claim that he doesn't.

While most kids will always try to look good to their friends, observe how much time each kid spends on his looks. Girls will normally spend much more time on getting themselves ready, taking this chore as somewhat of a pastime. A boy's long preparation time on the other hand will often be due to disinterest and laziness. Notice how the kid cares for his clothes and his shoes.

> **A boy has reached puberty when he carries a comb around with him.**
> GAELIC BOOK OF WISDOM

Virtues and Where to Find Them

We can divide the field of virtues into two large camps. The two camps are totally interrelated and any distinction we make here is only to help us define our work with the kids. There are human virtues and spiritual virtues.

What makes a virtue "human" or "spiritual" depends on the *why*. For example: A kid gives a beggar on the street a dollar. Is this human virtue (solidarity, care for other human beings) or spiritual virtue (charity)? By just looking, we will never know. It is only by finding out why the dollar was given will we know. If it was given because the kid felt sorry for the beggar and wanted to improve the poor man's lot, we still do not have the answer we need. Why does the kid feel sorry for the man? Because the poor man, just like me, is a human being and we're all in this together (human virtue); because this man, too, is a Son of God, and Christ has said, "Do to others what you would like them to do to you" (spiritual, or Christian, virtue).

As we can see from the example, the division between human and spiritual or Christian virtue is not an exclusive one. It is possible that the virtue is both human and spiritual at the same time. In fact, any human virtue is really Christlike, and every spiritual virtue can easily be seen lived out in human ones. Our role as educators, even more needy in this God-weak world, is to turn human virtues into spiritual ones—in other words, to get kids to do things for God's sake and not simply for human sake. But here we will deal with human virtues.

Now we are going to run through some virtues and measure a kid up against them. What are the telltale signs that a kid is, or is not, generous, obedient, sincere, caring? Let us see.

> **First the man, then the saint.**
>
> FR MARCIAL MACIEL, LC.

Care for others

Watch kids in the dining room.

Dining room	
Caring	**Non-caring**
Joe serves another first.	Jimmy digs in before the others begin.
Joe asks for something to be passed to him.	Jimmy stretches out to get something.
Joe will offer before he takes.	Jimmy will grab.
When finished, Joe will leave his plate and cutlery in an orderly fashion.	Jimmy will push his plate away from him.
Joe will make sure the table around him is clean.	Jimmy will not spare a thought for a tidy table.

And watch them in other places too.

In other areas	
Caring	**Non-caring**
Joe will let another use the door first.	Jimmy will barge through.

In other areas	
Caring	**Non-caring**
Joe will pass the ball without having to be told.	Jimmy will hug the ball and will always be calling for it when he hasn't got it, even though his position isn't good.
Joe will see where his companion wishes to sit.	Jimmy will make a dash for the place he wants and remonstrate if it is contested.
Joe will keep his eyes open when getting ready, maybe someone needs a loan of some polish, or a clothes brush.	Jimmy will have eyes for himself alone.
Joe will offer you his first and last candy.	Jimmy will only offer you something if he has a lot of it.

Willpower

This is the motor for many other virtues, such as responsibility, generosity, and obedience.

Will power	
Yes	**No**
Punctuality	Being late (and blaming others)
Correct uniform for everything	Mismatched uniform (and blaming others)
Up immediately when called	Needs an extra push in the morning

Will power	
Yes	**No**
No complaints about discomfort	Constant complaints
Getting the job done	Leaving things half done

Responsibility

Responsibility	
Yes	**No**
Joe, once he knows what he is supposed to do, will do it (getting up in the morning, homework, small chores, tidy locker.)	Jimmy will need constant prodding.
Joe will be capable of distinguishing duty from pleasure and ask for extra time for duty even at the expense of pleasure.	Jimmy will be timetable led and not objective-driven.
If Joe goofs up he will admit it and try harder.	When Jimmy goofs up, he will simply give up and say it's not for him or that he is not really supposed to be doing things like that.
Joe will do his best to do things right.	Jimmy will be rather mediocre in his results and slow getting there.

Responsibility	
Joe will try and do well even those things he doesn't much care for.	Jimmy will be one-track minded and only do well what he likes doing.

Discipline

Here we refer to external discipline, the first step towards what we are really after: internal discipline.

External discipline	
Yes	**No**
Joe will be punctual.	Jimmy will be late.
Joe will be well-dressed, properly groomed, and manly in his behavior.	Jimmy will be shabbily dressed, his hair will be badly combed, and he will slouch a lot (in class, in lines).
Joe will keep silence where and when silence is expected.	Jimmy will try and break silence any way he can (dumb asides to his friends in class or in lines, noise at night, questions out of order).
Joe will listen to his superiors.	Jimmy will play the line of minimum respect necessary to his superiors.
Joe will obey promptly and in good spirit.	Jimmy will be reticent to obey and oftentimes will obey grudgingly.

Hard worker

Hard worker	
Yes	**No**
Joe will be attentive in class and sports.	Jimmy will be distracted and even seek to distract.
Joe will sweat.	Jimmy will only sweat doing the sports he enjoys.
Joe will try, try and try again until he gets to where he wants to go (understanding a math problem, getting to grips with a virtue, overcoming a defect, getting along with a non-friend).	Jimmy will give up at the first available opportunity.
An educator might often come across Joe all by himself busily trying to finish up doing what has been entrusted to him.	If left to himself on the job, Jimmy will slack. If he is with others, if he is not wasting their time, he will certainly be wasting his own.
Joe will try to be doing something always, even when in recess he will be doing something.	Jimmy will tend to withdraw into himself and be sullen (alone on the bus, alone in recess, interested solely in his own little things).

Constancy

Constancy	
Yes	**No**
Joe's grades will stay relatively the same as before he came to the school and while he is with us.	With the change to a new school, Jimmy's grades may plummet.
Joe will be getting a little bit better every day	Jimmy will be quite content to be the same old Jimmy all the time, constant in his mediocrity (constantly getting worse, in other words).
Within the framework of the school or academy, Joe will maintain or better his position regardless of changing circumstances (if he is usually among the top five students, he will still be among the top five even if there is a surprise change to the timetable).	You'll never know where Jimmy will place, but you can be sure it won't be among the first.
Joe's copybooks will be tidy.	Jimmy's copies will be akin to a modern art gallery

Initiative

Initiative	
Yes	**No**
Joe will come to you with questions about things he does not understand (about school regulations and rules).	Jimmy will be quite content to more or less do what he is told.
Joe will try to respond to any project, suggestion, or concern that a superior mentions.	Jimmy will be oblivious to efforts made to help him.
Joe will look out for ways to make the school, the academy, his class, or his section better and suggest them to you.	Jimmy couldn't care less about his school, academy, class, or section.
Joe will not be put down if one of his initiatives is.	In the event Jimmy comes up with an initiative and it is not accepted, he will remain defeated.

It's hard to find what you're looking for if you don't know what you're looking for. (Although Aristotle did say that you do know when you found what you were looking for even though you didn't know it was what you were looking for... rather confusing, if you ask me.) But the point is that when you know what you're looking for, you stand a better chance of knowing when you've actually found it. Otherwise you could easily mistake what you've found for what you were really looking for.

But with the illustrations above, the trainee/educator will have some practical things to look out for and thus draw up a rather accurate picture of what the kid in front of him is like. Of course, this picture will come more and more into focus with time and with extended observation. And in the beginning we must be careful not to make a hasty diagnosis of our kid's needs. But at least the above does give us room for seeing objectively where the kid is at. There are however, a few more qualities that we have not mentioned yet: gift qualities and guardian qualities.

Gift Qualities

As we measure up the kid we have in front of us with the God kid, we will discover that he might well have what we could call an "extra" quality or two that we could consider a bonus. We will call these "gift" qualities.

A boy may be quick-witted, artistic, entertaining, creative, or "gifted" in some area. We are not talking child protégé here, but simply referring to that quality or those qualities that make a kid stand out. Sometimes these gift qualities might be quite dormant. As educators, one of our tasks will be to detect, boost, educate, and orientate these qualities in the kid. If these gift qualities are particularly strong, they can have a negative impact on our work as educators if we do not take them into account.

I remember the case of a thirteen-year-old who was definitely gifted as far as drawing was concerned. His ability to sketch a scene, or a person, with a few easy strokes was almost uncanny. This gift gave him high standing among his friends. He was, thanks to his artistic talent, a natural leader. And herein was the problem. He was quite happy with his lot and gave little or no importance to anything or to anyone else.

His grades were low, his personal appearance shabby, his concern for others nil. He had absolutely no desire to be anything other than what he already was. And what was worse, given the fact that because of this "gift" he was a leader, his behavior encouraged those around him to follow his lazy example. This is a tough call for even the most experienced educator.[4]

On the other hand, being aware of these qualities will enable the educator to help the kid not only make the most of them, but also to aid the kid in integrating this quality into a comprehensive character development program.[5]

Guardian Qualities

If a kid had all the above virtues in abundance he would still not be complete. In fact, without the guardian qualities that we are now going to speak about, the poor kid would end up sooner or later being a danger to himself and to the community. So we need to gauge his grasp of them.

We can take an illustration from our wardrobe. As with all analogies, our illustration will fall short, but at least it will give you an idea of what we are talking about. Let us say that you have a vast collection of fine clothes—everything from pajamas to evening dress, from beachwear to blue jeans. These items of clothing can be compared to the virtues we have been talking about up to now. (Indeed, tasteful color matching and suitable clothes can complement each other just as individual virtues complement one another.) But now the question arises, what to wear? Without a set of guiding principles we would be at a loss as to know what to wear, how to wear it, and when to wear it. If we are going to a formal evening dinner party, we can hardly go in denim, no matter how comfortable denim may be. The guiding principal of "formal protocol" tells us what type of clothes to wear to the dinner. If we are going to meet our mother at the airport, we will be casually but well dressed. In fact, if your mother is the type to put on fine clothes for traveling, then you might even consider arriving at the airport in as formal a mode as she will be in. On the other hand, if you are going off some afternoon to serve supper at a soup kitchen, you certainly will not dress formally, nor are you going to wear identifiable brand name casual clothing. You will want to put the diners at their ease. And here it is not a case of social protocol, but of concern for the other person.

In the practice of virtue we also have these guiding principles. I call them the guardian principles, or guardian qualities. Basically they guide our use of virtue, much in the same manner as a guardian will aid a toddler as he stumbles along a footpath. Unfortunately these principles have rather heavy and outdated names. They are prudence, temperance (or moderation), justice, and fortitude (or courage). They are old, but good.

Prudence

At school when I was a kid, if we wanted to say that someone was slow, unexciting, and inept, we would call him a "prude," short for "prudent person." And how often, as older kids, have we been annoyed by someone reminding us to "be prudent" as we took the car out. Imprudent driving, in our elders' opinion could be anything over fifteen m.p.h.! Prudence does not have a good name for itself. (But then, "discipline" doesn't fare too well either!)

Prudence is that guardian principle that basically tells us what to do and when. It involves weighing the elements in the light of the Gospel, taking into account consequences for ourselves and others, and then deciding. An example I like using is that of driving. Some believe that slower is always safer. These are the people you almost crash into on the highways. They will hug the middle lane doing a steady thirty m.p.h. They feel perfectly safe. They are, after all, well within the speed limit (65 m.p.h.). These people have caused so many accidents that now some lanes not only have a maximum speed but also a minimum speed limit. And large trucks are required to put on their hazard lights if they are traveling under forty m.p.h. So slow is not necessarily safer. If these thirty m.p.h. people were really prudent, many of them would end up having someone else drive for them.

Prudence is that quality that needs the global view of things. It will sometimes apparently sacrifice one value for another. Staying with the driving example, we have the case of a dad who has been on a twenty-hour shift at some remote location and is really tired. He is a father and should be home with his kids once work is over. But a ninety-minute drive home on icy roads might well bring the guy to that home in the sky rather than back to his family. Prudence will have him catch a good night's sleep before sitting behind the wheel. Or, if his family can afford it, he could call a cab.

I don't think a person is born with prudence. I believe it comes from experience. But it doesn't come naturally. The better you know the Gospel and the better you know how to weigh things and more things together, the better you can be at arriving at a prudent decision.

Moderation

Moderation is another guardian principal. We used to call it temperance, and you can call it that still if you wish. But here again, temperance, and even moderation, has a bad name for itself. And once again the bad name is due to a misreading of what the actual quality is. Moderation is not abstinence. Nor does it mean "moderate" as in "mediocre." In fact moderation is the key to getting the best out of everything.

Too little food is a bad thing. Too much food is also a bad thing. Say the same for liquid, salt, speed, luxury, and even sleep. For our purposes as educators we apply moderation to the practice of virtue. Moderation will be the guardian of our responsibility, of our joy, of our concern for others. It will help us distinguish what is necessary and good and what is self-indulgent and superfluous. Once again we refer to the Gospel as our measuring stick for this. Take concern, for example. While we must have an eye on the future, especially as educators or parents, we must also be concerned about what is happening today. Christ tells us that today has enough worries of its own, but we also see how his life was focused on his redeeming act of the cross in his future.

A moderate person is not just a person who doesn't go overboard, he is also a person who makes the best of his stay on the boat.

Justice

Justice is another guardian principle. I will not go into a detailed discussion of the three kinds of justice (commutative, distributive, and legal). For our purposes, justice simply means giving people, including oneself, what is rightfully due. What is "rightfully due" ranges from respect for other people's things to ensuring their opportunity for free speech, civil liberty, and privacy. Justice is way more than simple respect, however. We can respect a pauper's state of poverty, but justice requires that we do something concrete to help the person attain those living standards that he, as a person, has a right to. We might respect a kid's wish to be uninvolved, but when others depend on him, justice calls for us to ensure that he gets involved.

Kids will usually have a keen sense of justice. They may not be able to explain it, but justice is one of the first qualities they appreciate once they reach the age of reason. Their measuring stick may be somewhat vague at first (it may be based on their parents' authority, or on a personal experience). As justice is giving every person his due, injustice is when someone is denied what is his due. Egoism is the root of all injustice.

Courage

Courage is the fourth guardian quality that will guide us along the way of virtue. Sometimes called perseverance, fortitude, or endurance, courage is that quality that will fortify and sustain our quest for virtue. Sometimes it is easy to do the right thing and do it the right way. Other times it is not. Courage is unabashed persistence in doing the right thing, whatever the cost to oneself. Among its enemies are apathy, routine, and bravado. Courage keeps the fire burning.

Wrap up

Every educator should have a firm grasp of what each quality means, a series of ways to see if they are present or not in the kid, and to detect whether these qualities are growing.

A note worth mentioning here is that we need to be careful not to project ourselves onto our view of the kid. To give an example, if I am one of those overzealous reformed smokers, other people smoking will be my biggest enemies. The guy might be a liar, he might be a robber... but what really gets me is the fact that he smokes. Bringing the example down to kid level—if I had a brother who always annoyed me because he was pushy, then if I see any traces of pushiness, no matter how slight, in the kid I am measuring up, I will point out that he really must work on being less pushy. So we must make an effort to be as objective as possible.

The first step (God's prototype) gave us a good idea of where a kid should be. The second step has shown us where the kid is at present. We must now trace a route to get him to where he ought to be headed.

The Third Step: Mapping Out

Getting our kid on track towards God's prototype

Pointing a kid in the general direction is never really enough. What we need here is a MapQuest thing. For anyone traveling, a map has the principal task of showing you not just where you want to go, but more importantly where you are in relation to where you want to go. This knowing where you are, and what should be coming up next, is what has made GPS navigational aids so useful to us all. So we will draw up a detailed route for our kid. And we will be forever updating it for him and with him, just as a GPS is continually updating your position when you're on the road. We will be walking, though, not driving.

To start, pick out a behavior in the kid that is not quite right. Just pick one. Just make sure it's an important one. If the kid is going around insulting his granny all the time, don't select his untidiness as a place to start working! Then pick out something that seems to be good, no matter how small. A tip here is to pick out something positive that the kid himself is interested in.

Then we will search out two short-term goals that will start the kid off towards where he's supposed to be. Short-term goals will prove invaluable.

For example, let us say that among other things, we have found that the kid is lazy, but he is an enthusiastic soccer player.

If we have a lazy kid (negative), who is good at soccer (positive), we will not start with an immediate goal of being a totally not lazy kid who is very good at soccer. We will go step by little step. While total self-disinterest and excellence in sports may be our midterm goal for this kid, we need to give him something that he can attain every week, something concrete that every week will bring him closer and closer to his goal. And it is here that sometimes an educator will balk, as the constant setting of reachable and coherent targets is by no means an easy task and requires not only constancy but also imagination and initiative. But here are some ideas that might help.[6]

Setting Short-Term Goals

(See also "100 Short-Term Goals," page 335)

Pick any virtue. Let's pick the virtue of willpower. We can find "violations" of willpower all over the place. One of the most common among kids is laziness. Another one is lack of constancy. To find immediate and reachable goals it will be sufficient to see where the kid is slipping up in this virtue.

A lazy kid will, for example:[7]

- be late for most things, or at least for those things he isn't too keen on
- drag his feet when walking
- have his sweater sleeves down over his hands
- have shoes that could be better polished
- dillydally in study
- arrive at sports without the complete uniform
- have a room or locker that could be tidier
- have difficulty in avoiding candies between meals
- react slowly to commands
- have slumped shoulders
- be easily discouraged (in sports, or studies, for example)
- quite possibly have difficulty in getting to sleep at night

- not go out of his way to help others
- lose things
- have his school books in bad repair
- be sloppy in his homework presentation

We could pick any one of these defects and propose its rectification as a short-term goal. Such a meager detail may seem quite insignificant, but little by little we can bring the kid around. These small detailed short-term goals not only give the kid a measurable element with which he can record his progress, but they also give the educator a focus for his personal work with the kid for a short period.[8]

Spiritual writers will talk, in this field, of "dominant passion" or "dominant defect." Basically the dominant defect will be either "pride" or "passion." We are all a pretty unique mix of both these passions. Deep down we think we're great (pride) and deep down we are always after what our bodies like (passion). The deadly, or capital, sins can be reduced to sins of pride or sins of the flesh. Some of us are so bad that it is hard to determine which sins are out in front in the race for dominance. Some of us seem to have the appropriate sinful reaction to any occasion that comes along! But we do not have to worry about such things at this stage. Suffice it for us to work with the kid on those aspects of his personality that most come to light. If we are methodical in our work, deeper things will emerge as we go on.

As time goes on we will need to keep setting new short-term goals for and with the kid. There are two reasons for this— one is to keep him interested, and the second, and more important, is that hopefully the kid will actually be accomplishing the goal and will need to move on.

There is a hidden beauty in all of this. There is satisfaction in doing things right. And there is satisfaction in doing what is right. We don't have to go any further than our own experience to realize this. As the kid reaches each goal he will feel as if he's getting somewhere, and he is. Not only will this progress itself be satisfying but, when push comes to shove, doing things right is more satisfying than doing things wrong. And in time, doing things right, or being as we should be, is easier than doing wrong or being as we shouldn't be.[9]

Enter Personal Dialogue

One of the most effective tools, if not the most effective tool in the hands of the educator is personal dialogue. This is not the only tool in an educator's hands—his constant presence and ongoing motivation also play an important role—but personal dialogue is the most valuable.

> **A professional educator working with kids in a school or youth group environment who does not spend at least thirty percent of his every working day every day dedicated to personal dialogue with his kids has wasted not only thirty percent of his day, but his entire day.**
>
> **In the case of parents, no amount of so-called "quality time" can ever replace "quantity time."**

Personal dialogue is a regular, opportune, prudent, challenging, firm, objective, kind, positive, respectful, and confidential moment wherein the parent or educator speaks with the kid and together reviews progress towards formation and sets new goals. As we will see as we describe these characteristics, not everybody is up to having personal dialogue with a kid. Some parents might feel that their kid gets great formative input from someone outside the family, such as a priest, a scout leader, or a dean in a school. This can be beneficial, but it does not supplant the parents' role as their own kids' primary educators. It may however, be seen as a welcomed hand in a job that is, by its very nature, tough.

Personal dialogue gives us the perfect opportunity for having the kid take on board his own formation as he implements the map we offer him. He should see it as a natural consequence of our love.

We must remember that personal dialogue as suggested in Genesis is not a therapy session. Nor is it a "sit-down-now-with-me-and-we-will-discover-the-meaning-of-life-together" thing. It is certainly not confession. It is something that is not more complicated than speaking with (not "to") a kid about things that really matter to him and to us—about him being what he should and could be.

There are many modes of personal dialogue, ranging from the in-depth and serious spiritual direction to the almost casual concern an older brother might have for his younger brothers or sisters. But God has chosen parents to be the guardians of the kid and so it falls to parents to use all in their power for the good of the kid. And one thing available to practically all parents is personal dialogue with their kids. The mode of personal dialogue will vary according to the kid's age, sex, and personality and also according to the parents' personality and possibilities.

Qualities of Personal Dialogue

Our duty as educators demands that our personal dialogue with each kid be constant, prudent, challenging, firm, objective, kind, positive, respectful, and confidential.

Constancy

Gracie Fields, a wartime movie star, went to live in Capri in the twilight of her life. A reporter asked whether or not she felt gratitude towards her fans for having made her famous. "Not really" was her open reply. And with a marked degree of honest humility she hastened to add, for fear of being misunderstood, "Lots of people become famous. But few stay famous. I am forever grateful to, and deeply appreciative of, my fans for having kept me famous."

Constancy is the hallmark of formation. Formation without constancy is deformation. It is the destruction of a person. A lack of constancy betrays the innermost essence of our role as educators. Here's an example:

An educator worked hard at getting a small group of kids enthused about a project. The six girls in question were introverted and self-centered, always complaining and showing distain for, rather than appreciation of, others. An apathetic clique—these girls, beneath their shabby veneer of smugness, were experiencing the unease and deep self-discontent that is the immediate fruit of egoism. On an individual basis though, each girl was willing to try to be better. A definite way to break through this wall of egoism was to get each girl involved in a project that would benefit her larger group.

Initially the plan went well. The educator spoke to each girl of the wonders of altruism and how each girl could, with time and effort, break the bonds of egoism and become meaningful for others. The educator drew up a precise, detailed, and demanding program for each girl and skillfully blended the individual effort into a group effort.

Little by little, the small group began to open up, much as a small chicken pecks its beak through the eggshell that blocks out the world. The small group began to get involved with the other girls. After three weeks a twinkle could be seen in the eyes of the six, although breaking out of such hardcore and blatant egoism was not easy. One by one the girls began to feel the pressure of effort building up within them and sought personal guidance and support from their educator. But the educator, thinking that her job was done, had decided that personal dialogue was no longer that important and gave all her attention to the group project (the founding of a club where the six would be the leaders) rather than to the individual aspect.

Within another two weeks the six girls had lost all interest in the group project, the club folded, and the six reverted to their earlier state, but this time with a difference. Now their disillusionment with virtue was total. They knew that as bad as their egoistic state was, there was no real way out. After all, they had really tried to break free and had failed. All further attempts to help these girls break free were met with "Been there, done that, seen that, it doesn't work." It would have been much better had the educator never even started.

This is the harsh reality of the responsibility we have been entrusted with. Going halfway is far worse than going nowhere. It may not appear that way, but given the seriousness of our calling, a little reflection will prove the point.

If you were a basketball coach and only got as far as teaching the kids how to dribble, at least this would be something. They would have learned at least that and could find someone else to take them on from there. But if I tell a kid that I can lead him out of his mediocrity and precisely because of me he loses all confidence in being able to do so, then not only have I left him in his mediocrity, but I have destroyed his confidence in himself and in those who claim to be able to help him. We're not talking sports here.

This risk of doing such damage to a kid (by not being constant) is so great that it might lead us to opt for not doing anything at all, or to feeling that we are not up to really helping the kids in these areas. But this would be the devil speaking, for not only is there an awful lot an educator can do, there is an awful lot an educator must do.

And let not fear of failure daunt us. We will accomplish our mission if we just simply follow the rules. Just as a pilot has to ensure his aircraft is at the right ground velocity before he pulls the nose up, and that he simply has to reduce his airspeed before landing again, we too have simple basic rules to follow that will ensure we get our kids to where we are supposed to get them. And one of these rules is constancy in personal dialogue.

Constancy versus Drudgery

A little note here on keeping an eye out so that our constancy does not result in the kid seeing his "sessions" of personal dialogue as a heavy obligation. A kid must be willing to use this means of formation, and while sometimes he may not be enthused by the idea, we must make sure that deep down he appreciates it. We do not expect kids to always enjoy personal dialogue, but we certainly do not want them to run from it. If we make sure our dialogues have the qualities that we are touching on here, we can be pretty sure that it will never become a burden, but we must keep our eyes open nonetheless.

Should we detect that we are becoming overly burdensome in personal dialogue with a kid, we can either give the kid a holiday (skip a session or two) or better still, suggest a different person with whom the kid can have dialogue. Maybe it's not the actual dialogue that is burdensome for the kid, maybe it is you. It can happen.

Personal dialogue is quasi-sacred and should be offered to the kid at least monthly. Every two weeks is optimal. For this reason, the educator must keep his eyes open all the time or soon he will run into the rut of repetition and boring platitude.

Opportune Moments

This means that we must look for the right moment for personal dialogue. If the kid is upset because his team lost a game, or quiet because someone didn't say hello, or plain bored, we would do well to pick another moment. The morning rush to school is not a good time. During the middle of a movie is another bad time.

A friend of mine was telling me about when he was a kid. His dad would have "Special Outing Days." The kids could pick the venue, the dad the topic. And it was always along the lines of what we are talking about here. The kids loved it. The guy didn't turn out too bad.

> **Just as kids are God's blessing to parents, parents are God's gift to kids.**
> CELTIC BOOK OF WISDOM

Prudence

Prudence is well illustrated by the little prince in the book of the same name, The Little Prince, by Antoine De St. Exupery. He finds himself on a little planet and manages an audience with the King. "So you can do anything?" asks the little prince. "Oh, yes!" replies the King. "Have the sun come up!" requests the little prince. "But it's nighttime," retorts the King. "But if you can command heaven and stars," says the little Prince, "Can you not also command the sun?" "Most surely, but with prudence. A king must command with prudence," concludes the king.

They waited and waited and at sunrise the king commands, "Sun, rise!" and the sun rose. "But it would have risen anyway!" complains the little prince. "Oh, maybe," says the king. "But when you command you must be sure the order can be carried out. Prudence, my little prince, prudence!"

A silly tale, maybe, but a clever one nonetheless. We must never ask our kid to do something unless we are sure he is able to do it. Maybe he himself isn't sure that he can do it, but we must be sure that he can do it. He might leave something to chance, but we cannot.

We cannot, for example, set a kid the task of being at the table two minutes ahead of time if we know that he is the oldest in the family and therefore has to ensure that his kid brothers get there on time. We must arrange things in such a way that it is nearly impossible for our kid to miss the boat. We may, as in the proffered example, have to say, "From today on, the youngest in the family is in charge of making sure everyone's at the table on time!" in order to lay out the conditions for our man to meet his goal. This, too, is part of prudence. Never expect miracles, prepare for them. We have to do the groundwork.

In practical terms this calls for an acute sense of practical matters. What does this kid need in order to be able to reach his goal? We set the scene. The kid just has to play out the part. The kid just needs to be punctual. We will make sure nothing stands in his way. A kid needs to be kind to others. We would make sure the recipient is a willing "victim."

Prudence will also tell us to be wary about promising too much to the kid. A youth club in Ireland some thirty years ago had the slogan, "Rocklands offers what you've got to give." The club didn't promise miracles but simply stated that it would draw the best out of you. In our work, we need to be careful to "e-ducate," to bring the best out of people rather than simply fill them up. A bad teacher, for example, will throw data at his students. A good one will give kids data, show them how to use it, and have them assimilate it by using it.

In practical terms this aspect of prudence asks us to avoid telling the kids that we will make great men of them, that the school or the academy is what they have been waiting for, that a year with us will be a milestone in their lives. We will, if they help us help them, make better men of them, but our role is more of a signpost to greatness than that of a car that will bring them effortlessly there. And here we do well to remember that there is no "car" that will be effort free. There is no sidestepping personal effort and dedication. We will certainly make it our job to show the kid what is the best way for him to scale the mountain, but we will never promise to scale it for him, nor much less bring the mountaintop down to him.

Challenging

Being prudent goes, strangely enough, hand in hand with being daring. In our personal dialogue we must offer the kid a challenge. We cannot hope to form kids if our plans do not call for personal effort on the kid's part.

Were we not to challenge the kid, we would be like a circus animal trainer who has his lion walk lazy circles around him. In fact, prudence itself dictates that our dialogues, and all our work with kids, be signed with the bite of challenge. Only in this way will the kid feel personally involved. Only in this way will he feel that he is progressing. And this involvement and progress will also encourage the kid to be constant.

A radio psychologist stated that one difference between people who are mature and those who are not is that mature people know how to wait. If you say to a seven-year-old, "I will give you a dollar now or ten dollars tomorrow," he will take the dollar. The twelve-year-old will wait for the ten. While I do not agree with this concept of maturity, the idea is a valid one.[10]

Practical examples of how prudence and challenge go hand in hand can be taken from the annals of experience.

A youth club leader decided that it would be great to have a drink dispenser. So he bought one and had it installed. All club members could use the dispenser any time they cared to, but they were requested to leave a contribution of twenty-five cents in a cup beside the machine to cover the cost. Designed as a means of strengthening the members' principles of honesty, the project was a miserable failure. Within two days, the canisters were empty, paper cups littered the area and the contributions amounted to little less than two dollars.

Another case: an educator wanted to encourage his kids' spirit of responsibility. The kids had pooled their money and wanted to buy an ice-cream machine that was on special offer in a local store. The agreed upon idea was that only those kids who scored a certain average every week could use the ice-cream machine during breaks and could select to have ice cream instead of the normal dessert at lunchtime. The ice-cream machine was purchased, but the educator decided never to let it be used. He feared that the kids who were not entitled to use it would use it and cause a little war. He said that he "did not want to offer the kids the opportunity to get out of hand." The ice-cream machine stood idle for months as a monument to the educator's inability to form.

(After much encouraging from his fellow educators, the educator in question eventually allowed the machine to be used as planned during the Easter holiday period. There was no mayhem and weekly averages soared.)

During a visit to a boarding school, I was walking around one evening during study time. As I passed by the various classrooms I could see an educator with each group. Some were walking up and down; others were helping individual kids. There were the usual sounds coming from each room—a pencil dropping here, a teacher explaining something there, an educator asking someone to get down to work. Having passed the last "inhabited" classroom, I neared the end of the corridor where there was an empty classroom with its door ajar. Well, I had supposed it to be empty as there was not a single sound coming from it. I glanced in and was surprised to see a group of students earnestly at work.

From the door, I looked inside to see who the educator was who had been able to instill such diligence in his students. There was no adult there at all. Sensing somebody at the door, a student looked up and stood up, and all the others followed suit. Feeling somewhat ashamed at having interrupted them, I hastily motioned them to sit down and to continue studying.

As I turned back into the corridor, I came across an educator. "You'd think these were the brainy guys, wouldn't you?" he asked me in hushed tones. "But most of them are not. I offered them the challenge of studying by themselves if they took it upon themselves to do their very best and to be of absolute zero disturbance." Maybe the kids were not the brainy guys, but their educator sure was sharp!

Firmness

Firmness should be another characteristic of our work and of our dialogues with the kids.

> **Let your word be "Yes" if it is to be "Yes," and "No" if you mean "No."**
> JESUS CHRIST

This firmness must not be confused with dictatorship.

Not a good idea:

"Joe, your goal for the next two weeks will be to do an act of service twice daily."

The way to go:

"You're doing well, Joe. But there's still a ways to go. A sign of any great man is his concern for others. I was thinking that maybe you might like to try to make a special effort to actively serve others. And to keep it practical, what do you say to doing one, or maybe two, acts of service a day for the next two weeks?"

The motivational and suggestion approach of the second example has many things going for it. First, it puts the kid in the main role. We make a suggestion, we motivate a little, but leave the final word up to him. Once he accepts, then the suggestion is no longer our imposition, but his law. And we will hold him to it. Secondly, we give him a choice and the very act of the kid choosing either one or two acts of service a day will make it more his own.

The first, "not a good idea" way, will tend to have the kid rebel immediately. Nobody likes being told what to do, and even were the kid to accept, it is more likely that he would carry the task out to keep his educator at bay rather than to become a better person.

One should be firm not only in nudging the kid along, but firm also in calling the kid to attention should he fail to do what was expected of him. One should be firm, but not annoyed.

A kid was given the short-term goal of making a visit to the Blessed Sacrament every day. During this visit he would ask the Lord for the grace to be responsible. (This was proposed as a cure for his high level of forgetfulness.) During the next personal dialogue, the educator asked the kid how his visits had gone. The kid simply said, "What visits?"

The educator blew up, called the kid irresponsible, immature, and a waster of the educator's time. He told the kid to go away and come back whenever he felt he could be more responsible. The kid, of course, never came back.

Sometimes it is necessary to pretend to be annoyed. And sometimes telling a kid to go away and come back when he thinks he can be "more of a man" is a useful trick. But such educator behavior is always the result of prudently thinking the thing through, and never a spur-of-the-moment reaction. So firm always, dictatorial or annoyed never.

> **A spoon of credit does more good than a barrel of barks.**
>
> GAELIC BOOK OF WISDOM

Objectivity

Objectivity is another element of dialogue. By this we mean that we must know when to call a spade a spade. When a kid does something well, give him credit. When he slips, pull him up.

Kind

When we say that personal dialogue should be kind, we do not mean that it should be sloppy. It simply means that we must be gentle in how we treat the kids. This will involve more attitude than actions. And children are quick to sense attitude. When applied to personal dialogue this "kindness" must not be interpreted as "chumminess" or "Now-let's-just-sit-down-and-have-ourselves-a-nice-little-inconsequential-chat."

Kindness is that quality that stems from our deep respect and even love for the kid before us and from our concern to help him be the person he is called by God to be. It has little to do with cuddles or sweet words, although in other circumstances (such as a mother/daughter relationship) such cuddles and sweet words are an accepted way of expressing kindness. As educators, we must be kind, but careful. While not wanting to appear cold or aloof, we must be extra careful not to become real "shoulders to cry on."

Sometimes it may be quite necessary for an educator to care for a crying girl by hugging her. This would be a natural act of kindness and of warmth and, is in itself highly beneficial in a family setting or in the case of a girls' school. (It almost goes without saying that such showings of kindness are totally out of context in an all-boys school environment.) But personal dialogue is neither the time nor the place for such outpouring of warmth. Personal dialogue, as I have mentioned, is not a therapy session.

Our kindness can best be made clear in personal dialogue by showing the kid that we know him, have been following him along, admire him, and want him to be better because God wants him to be better. And when we draw his attention to his errors it is solely to help him overcome them.

See if you can spot the error in each phrase:

a) "I see you're still being very self-centered in games."
b) "Now, what have you been working on these last two weeks?"
c) "I really think you're great. You've come along so much. I wish all the kids were like you."
d) "What else?"

Answers

a) When noting errors, leave out superlatives. The error is bad enough by itself without blowing it up. (In fact, leave out superlatives every time you can.)

b) We should know what each kid is working on and not have to ask him. The only question slightly worse than "What are you working on?" is "What's your name?"

c) Admiring a kid must be an inner appreciation we have for him, not an outpouring of sentiments.

d) Rather less annoying in English than its Spanish counterpart ("¿Qué más?"), nevertheless this phrase smacks of "Give-me-the-bad-news-I'm-strong-I-can-take-it-and-anyway-up-to-now-you-haven't-told-me-anything-interesting-and-hurry-I-have-other-things-to-be-doing." The snappy two-word formula is far removed from the cordial tone that should characterize personal dialogue.

Positive

The tone of personal dialogue should be warm but professional, objective, and positive. What kids—and most people—need is a boost. Putting kids down is easy. Lifting them up is another matter.

> **Personal dialogue is much like "spiritual direction, a time for decision, not discussion."**
>
> PARAPHRASED FROM BISHOP FULTON SHEEN

While we may be in a hurry to get the kid along the road to human perfection, we must remember that it is not the educator who calls the shots. A kid's voyage towards virtue acquisition quite often does not follow the exact course we might have mapped out for him in the beginning. His progress, the kid's very life, is a book in the writing, not the fulfilling of an already written manual. The educator must be flexible and not try to constrict the kid to follow a neatly made up series of dialogue contents. Emphasis will shift, and new and unexpected areas may open up as time goes on.

Respectful

An uneasy Michele could not sleep. He had been in the boarding school now for quite a few days but as time went on he saw with ever more clarity that he certainly wasn't fitting in. The other guys were happy, enthusiastic, and hardworking. He was lazy, confused and, for a twelve-year-old, had an all too heavy baggage of conscience. One of Michele's classmates, upon noticing his increasing unease, suggested that he speak to the director, but until now Michele had not found the courage. But as he tossed in his bed, debating within himself whether to run away or go see the director, he decided that the bravado he had for doing evil should give him the strength now to be a man and go see the director.

He timidly knocked on the director's door. He wanted to be able to say that he had gone to the director, but hadn't found him. This would justify his running away. But to his surprise, for it was very late and everyone had been sleeping soundly for hours now, the door was open.

"Come in, Michele. I've been waiting for you."

All strength left Michele and, for a moment, he was more confused than ever. He wanted to run, but he wanted to stay. The director went over to his desk and Michele had the chance to run away without been seen. But the director's openness and total lack of coercion gave him the encouragement he needed. He stepped inside.

He began by saying that he couldn't sleep, that he knew the school wasn't for him, that he had come to say good-bye. The director listened quietly.

"But are you not happy here, Michele?"

"I want to be happy, and the others are great, but I am not like them. I would love to stay, but…."

"But you're confused."

"Yes, no. I don't know what to do. Yes, I'm in a mess."

"Tell me about it."

"I don't know where to start."

"Say the first few words and I'll help you finish. Give me the keys to your heart and we will settle everything."

As the cold Turin wind blew through the rafters in Valdocca on that night almost a hundred years ago, Michele laid bare his soul and his new life began.

This story about Michele Magone, taken from the life story of Don Giovanni Bosco, is an exquisite example of the respect that an educator must have when dealing with kids. Although the example here has to do with spiritual direction and not the personal dialogue we are talking about, it does help us focus the tone. We must not force our way into a kid's heart or into a kid's life. We can only venture in upon his request, or at least, with his consent. The door to a kid's heart cannot be forced.

Confidential

We have all heard of the "seal of confession," almost a vow a priest takes never to reveal what he has heard in confession. The history of Mother Church has ample examples of priests who have suffered and even died to defend this seal. Dialogue should never be mistaken for confession, but nonetheless, the content of dialogue is covered by a professional seal that prohibits the educator from speaking to others about it. When we speak of parents, it is always helpful that the kid sees the mom and dad as being totally on the same side, something not always easy to attain. We all know of cases when the kid will play the dad off the mom, or the mom off the dad. "If mom denies me permission, I will ask dad. He always says yes." Educating a kid can be rather educational for the educator too!

However, there are some cases when an educator (parent or other) will have to speak about his kids to someone else. A mother might find out from her daughter that she, the daughter, is going through a tough time because of a boyfriend. The mom may want to tell the teacher so that the teacher will be understanding towards the kid. An educator might be told by a kid that he, the kid, actually listens to music in his bedroom instead of doing his homework. The educator may well want to tell the parents to be on the lookout. In such cases, we must be careful to respect a kid's trust in us. So we may speak to another educator, but let us be careful. In the case of the daughter going through a rough time, there is no need for the mother to explain to the educator the reason why. In the case of the kid listening to music, the educator will tell the parents that he is not altogether happy with the kid's homework. In both cases confidence is not betrayed. In fact, any educator worth his salt will have noticed that the daughter is not herself, and any parent should monitor a kid's homework to see if it is acceptable.

There are times when an educator, when confronted by a certain case, might feel out of his depth. Or the kid might ask him a direct question that the educator is not quite sure how to answer. In such cases there are two things the good educator can do. One is to ask the kid is it alright with him if he, the educator, consults someone on the matter. Another is to suggest to the kid that he, the kid, talk with a priest or someone more experienced in the field. In this instance, the educator could also suggest that he, the educator, could let the priest or another qualified person know what the problem is so the kid would not have to go through repeating it.

This applies to parents too. "I had to tell your mother about what you told me for your own good," simply does not wash. A dad should not tell the mom something the kid has said without the explicit or implicit agreement of the kid. If he does not have this agreement, the dad is not being faithful to the confidence his son or daughter has in him. Once you lose a kid's trust, you will never ever get it back. In time the dad might be forgiven, but rarely again trusted.

But respecting confidence is not as tough as it may seem.

This also applies to cases when the kid tells you, the parent or teacher, about being abused. Such cases, thank goodness, are rare, but not nonexistent.

If you prepare the ground well, by speaking well of those who work with you, and if you have gained the respect and real confidence of the kid, the kid will only be too glad to have you consult with someone about the particular case. After all, if the kid has mentioned it to you, it means that he is worried about it and wants it fixed. Just as when you go to a doctor and he suggests you see a specialist, maybe you don't accept the suggestion gladly but you accept it nonetheless.

However, if our dialogue has "dragged" something out of a kid, something he didn't really want to mention, then he is not altogether sure he wants to solve the problem and may object to your suggestion of consultation or referral. Apart from respect, we should be careful never to force a kid in dialogue. Never force him to open up and much less force him towards a certain way of doing things.

Here is a specific case. What to do if a kid, in confidence, tells you that he has been physically abused? Now read this carefully, and should you wish to quote me, please be kind enough as to quote this and the following three paragraphs.

When told, first, do not looked stunned. Second, do not panic. Third, do not jump for the phone. Fourth, do not try to get details of any kind. That will get you through the first minute. What we do next is dictated by who we are.

If we are educators (as distinct from parents) we must remember that matters related to abuse do not fall within our direct authority. We are, however, obliged to help the kid. Our course of action is a simple one and in total keeping with confidentiality. We must endeavor to have the kid give us his consent for a referral. And this is not at all as difficult as it may seem. After all, if the kid told you it is because he wants help. And he will certainly not want others to suffer the same fate. He has trust in you, otherwise he wouldn't have told you, and so he will also trust you when you seek his consent for a referral.

If we are parents and are told of abuse, we should also ask the kid's consent for a referral.

Don't make a big thing of the kid giving his consent for referral. Don't draw up a paper for him to sign or anything like that. Make it easy for him. A nod as an answer to a very specific but simple question is quite sufficient. "Let's get some help on this, alright?" or something like that is enough. What is important is that the kid knows that you are going to tell someone else and that he does not disagree with that. He might well say, "Please don't tell so-and-so," but on this you will have to have him trust you.

And who should we tell once we have the kid's consent? If we are educators, (as distinct from parents) we should tell whoever is in charge of the school or youth group under whose authority we are working. That's it. This person in turn will carry out his duty. If we are parents, local law can inform us. The point I make here is that confidentiality is essential and at the same time, it is in no way opposed to fulfilling the legal obligations that may govern cases such as the one in question.

Having said all this, there are some cases when we have to "betray trust." Thankfully such cases are very rare, but you may come across one. Such cases arise when we cannot get the kid to agree to refer the case, or when the kid will not, or maybe cannot, mend his ways.

When, for example, state law, or even simple common sense, dictates that certain issues must be reported to the police or other authorities, and should the kid refuse his consent for you to take action based on what he has told you in confidence, the educator is not left with much of an option. If we have found out that there is a drug dealer or sex offender roaming around the school, we have a duty to the other kids and not just the duty of confidentiality to the kid who has talked with us. Or if we have learned in personal dialogue that the kid has been stealing money from his mother's purse and just keeps doing it, then we have the duty to tell the mother.

In all of this we can use the rule of thumb—confidence needs confidence. If the kid wants us to have confidence in him, he must show he has confidence in us. Nonetheless, we will do our utmost to respect a kid's trust.

Personal Dialogue Subject Matter

What themes belong to human formation dialogue, a dedicated educator area, and what themes belong elsewhere? This is a good question.

One thing to consider is the educator's area of expertise. Dedicated spiritual direction, for example, is best left to those who are trained for this particular purpose. This does not mean that we cannot use spiritual motivations or help the kid along the road to being a good Christian, but such things as helping the kid find an appropriate prayer method or explaining the simple and yet intricate workings of grace may be beyond our area of expertise. If a kid is mentally unbalanced he needs dedicated professional help. Sometimes a kid with minor traumas can benefit greatly from seeking dedicated professional help for a short-term period.

Another thing to consider is what the kid feels comfortable with. Many kids won't feel comfortable talking to their parents about sex, for example. Other kids may not feel comfortable about talking to an outside-the-family educator about problems within the family. Now, a lot of such unease is usually generated, sorry to say, by our inability to instill sufficient confidence in the kid about our knowledge or understanding. It's what we call a lack of "moral authority" in a certain area. None of us feel comfortable when we are told by a smoker how to stop smoking in three easy lessons. If we are told that by a guy who smoked four packs a day and gave them up and is now, at sixty, a model of health, that's a different story. So, we have to accept any of these limitations we may, and will, have and not barge in where we are not welcome.

Dialogue will cater to those aspects of formation that have to do with a kid's relationship with himself and with others (character, human virtue formation). Spiritual direction has to do with a kid's relationship with God (grace, or friendship with God, and the opposite, sin). So it will usually turn out that a kid with difficulties in obedience, for example, will treat one aspect of the problem with the educator (the practical side) and another aspect (the spiritual side) with his spiritual director.

While it has proven beneficial for a kid to have an outside-the-family educator for personal dialogue (some schools and youth groups do offer the service although they may not call it "personal dialogue"), parents would do well to have their own personal dialogue with the kid.

There are times when a kid will start dealing with spiritual themes with his educator in dialogue. Although this is not the appropriate forum for such themes, the educator should not cut the kid off, but should respectfully suggest that a spiritual director would be in a better position to help the kid in these areas.

Dynamics of Personal Dialogue

Personal dialogue should cover these three areas:

1. Review of last time's short-term goal (How did that go? Was it easy? What helped?)
2. Formation bite (Encourage the kid about the virtue being sought. Explain a little, not too much.)
3. Set up a further short-term goal (Suggest a new goal, set a new task for the kid.)

This basic scheme will never really change, although sometimes the formation bite will not be as the educator has planned, but come out of a special need the kid will have in that particular session. The kid may well have "something on his chest" and want to speak about it. However, when this is the case, the educator must be aware that the kid may just be distracting the educator from what the kid himself doesn't really want to talk about.

Personal dialogue should be cordial but serious, dotted with constant referrals to concepts the kid can grasp and that are in keeping with his program, and interesting.

Three notes on confidentiality:

1. There is much to be said for teamwork, and the good educator will never feel that he knows it all. He can and should draw on others' experience. You might have a kid who has an affectivity problem. You can consult someone on the case, but you must be careful not to identify the kid or to give information that might lead to his identification.
2. We must also be careful never to give the kid the impression that we have betrayed confidence. This is particularly important when dealing with girls.
3. Confidentiality forms a special bond between an educator

and a kid. The danger is that the educator might be tempted to use this bond power for his own advantage. An educator might feel that this power makes the kid his property. Throughout this book we have been saying that an educator must see the kid as "his" but the danger we refer to here is that the educator may feel that he possesses the kid.

Personal Dialogue—Friend or Foe?

Some educators are afraid of dialogue. They may feel they are not prepared or that they have nothing they can give to the kid. Or they may feel that group work is sufficient. Maybe they are self-conscious. Maybe they are too busy and just cannot fit it in.

The spiritual explanation of this fear phenomenon is that evil fully realizes the good that can be brought about by a determined dialogue plan and will try to thwart any progress.

But another explanation rests in the fact that dialogue does put the educator to the test. It requires preparation, brainwork, courtesy, determination, and a clear understanding of the educator's mission. So it cannot be taken lightly, but neither should it be taken too seriously. After all, it is not the educator who will guide the kid's steps, but the Holy Spirit. The educator is merely the instrument. An irreplaceable instrument, to be sure, but nonetheless an instrument. When we discuss the qualities of an educator later, we will touch on this point again. For now, let it suffice to say that should an educator feel afraid of dialogue there is no better remedy than to take a deep breath, invoke the Holy Spirit ("In Nomine Domini") and get to work.

Topics

1. The best way for a kid to develop is to have him live in a normal and healthy atmosphere. His conscience will tell him what to do. An occasional chat with those entrusted with his care is all well and good, but treating the kid as a patient, with regular checkup sessions (personal dialogue as suggested in the above chapter), is a little exaggerated when dealing with normal kids.
2. How many great people do you know? I mean, people who you consider to be real, fully mature persons? Quite a few, I'm sure. Now, ask yourself how many of these had regular "personal dialogue" as they were growing up? None basically.
3. "In theory, I find no fault with the preceding chapter. However, putting it into practice is unrealistic. And even were it feasible to put it into action, kids would soon tire of the routine."
4. It is unhealthy for anyone to have the control over kids that is implied in this chapter.

THE FOURTH STEP: MOVING PEOPLE

Motivating Kids

We have seen what the ideal kid is like. We have seen how our kid matches up, and we have plotted a course for him to follow. Now we have to help the kid get there. We will find positive motivation to be our best weapon. Positive motivation must be one of our educational secrets. But in practical terms, what is "positive motivation"?

Put quite simply, positive motivation is getting someone to do something because he "wants" to do it. The outcome, or the goal, is something positive. In other words, we "move" (motivate) someone towards something they see as good (positive). Put in yet another way, when we hold up something positive as a goal, we are talking about positive motivation.

"*The first five kids will receive a prize*" is positive.

"*The last five kids will have to clean up the classroom*" is negative.

The immediate result in both cases might be the same. (Everybody will dash to be on time either to qualify for the prize or to avoid having to clean up the classroom.) So we could say that on the face of it, both ways are equally as effective. And if getting kids to class on time was our only goal, we could use either form of motivation. However, our goal goes far beyond getting kids to class on time.

In essence, our formation project is geared at forming life habits in our students. And possibly the most important basic habit is that of "trying to be better." *Semper altius*. Negative motivation only leads to the habit of doing things to "avoid negative results."

To avoid being caught, in other words.

However, there is an important aspect to consider--what is the actual "prize"?

In the beginning, positive motivation will require concrete and almost edible prizes.

Let's take outing days, for example. Most kids love the idea of going somewhere, so we can use this as a "prize."

An example of negative motivation is:

"If you do something you shouldn't do, you will miss the outing."

(If you mess up your room, you miss out on the outing.)

An example of positive motivation:

"If you want to go on the outing, you must do this and this."

(If you keep your room tidy, you get to go.)

One immediate advantage of positive motivation in the case above is the educator's image. With negative motivation, the kids that miss out blame the educator. They are, in fact, being punished. And what is more, leading up to the outing day, the kids will try to avoid committing an error. With positive motivation on the other hand, punishment isn't an issue. If a kid wants to go, he proves it. It has little to do with the educator and a lot to do with the kid. He doesn't focus on not having his room messy; he focuses on having it clean.

Another example would be the actual distribution of practical elements of motivation. Let's say we are in a school and each member of the staff can award positive and negative points to the students.

Negative motivation will lead to the staff distributing more negative points than positive ones, or to the negative point being worth more than a positive one. Both of these outcomes not only inhibit the poor kids, but also leave those who distribute them in a rather negative light. Positive motivation, on the other hand, will lead to a member of the staff giving out more justified positive points than negative ones.

This will stem from him searching out the good in kids rather than zooming in on the negative. He will not shy away from distributing negative points, but he will emphasis the positive. A simple rule of thumb for staff in such a school would be that before they give out a negative point to a kid, they have to give out three positive ones either to the same or to different kids (assuming, of course that the points are of equal value).

The Four Stages of Positive Motivation

We can divide positive motivation into four stages:

The *first stage* is when the kid is offered a positive and almost edible reward for his compliance. Many "point" systems work on this basis. The kid who is the first in, or who has the tidiest room, will receive points that will put the kid in the running for a special outing, his choice of movie, or a special activity. We could call this stage the "edible" stage. The educator will dangle the reward in front of the students and they, wanting it, will be encouraged to get it.

The *second stage* is when motivation remains positive although no "edible" reward is offered. The edible reward will be replaced by a nonmaterial reward.

This type of nonmaterial reward might be a simple "Well done!" or another sign of appreciation of the kid's effort. This prize is still an "external" award. The kid does something right because he wants to be in his educator's or his parents' "good book." We call this an "external award" because the student still looks to something outside of himself as a reward.

The *third stage* goes a little deeper and implies a substantial change. A student will do something not because there is an edible prize, or even an external advantage to be gained, but because he finds that doing what is right, doing what he is expected to do, or doing what is asked of him "feels" good. This is not the good feeling that comes from taking a warm bath, but the deep down satisfaction that comes from knowing you are doing right. The student, for example, will be first or second in class, or at least on time, simply because he enjoys and feels good when doing what is right. And here it is nature herself who lends us a helping hand.

We were born to do things right. Just as a car when in perfect working order is a pleasure to drive and a well-prepared meal a delight to eat, so too there is great satisfaction to be had when we behave as we are supposed to behave. It's a case here of "Virtue is its own reward."

The *fourth stage* of positive motivation is when we manage to create the habit in the student of doing what is right, or what is expected of him, simply because it is right. And he wants to do what is right. This is what we often call "interior discipline" or "conviction." The motivation in the previous stage was the "good feeling" that the student gets out of it. However, with time this "good feeling" will be replaced by, or educated and elevated to, more than a mere feeling and will become a guiding life principle, not just in one area, (punctuality, for example) but as a lifestyle.

The Dangers of Superficial Positive Motivation

When I speak of superficial positive motivation I am referring to first stage positive motivation, where motivation proposes an immediate and concrete, almost edible, reward.

While necessary in the beginning of our formative process, it must always be used as a beginning and not an end. Some elements of this type of motivation will be necessary all through the year—and throughout life—but as time goes on, we must strive to wean kids off this type of motivation in those essential elements of human and spiritual formation. If not, the formation will be as superficial as the prizes we offer them.

Progressing from One Stage to Another

How can we move our kids up through the various stages of positive motivation?

During stage one, we must ensure that the prize we offer is really attractive for the kids. This may be done in two ways.

One way is to offer something that is, of itself, attractive. A good movie or an exciting outing will be attractive to most kids. A visit to a museum will have limited appeal and cannot be considered a valid prize for most. Nor can a kid's weeklong effort be rewarded by a single candy bar.

Another way of ensuring our prize is attractive is by building it up. The prize, for example, might be a simple pin or medal that the kids hang on their sweaters, or the right to sit in the front seat (if the kid is twelve or over). If the educator explains that this pin or seat is given to a selected few, that this shows the world that the kid is special, that such a prize is hard to get, then little by little, the kids will want the prize.

Moving up into stage two is a little more difficult. It means passing from edible to nonedible prizes. It must be said immediately that passing through this stage is not always necessary and, in fact, quite often we will see kids jump from stage one to stage three. But here we will discuss stage two, as much of what we will say is applicable on a wider scale.

For a kid to value another person's opinion about him, the student must value that other person. In other words, should an educator be a gruff and unjust authoritarian, or an "everything's fine by me" type of person, or an insecure and incapable person, it will be difficult for the kid to look up to him and even more difficult for the kid to care about what the educator thinks of him.

And so, we, as educators, must always try to ensure that the students see the best side of us. If an educator is no good at sports, let him limit himself to encouraging the kids on their effort and performance from the sideline. If he is good at sports, let him in recess show the kids how to dunk. If an educator is no good at organizing competitions, let someone else do it. If a mother has difficulty in getting the kids to bed at night, have the father do it.

A point to consider here is that speaking well of others will be of enormous benefit.

A dean of studies was having a hard time in a Mexican school with the teaching faculty. A dean from another school visited one morning. In casual conversations with individual teachers, he spoke highly of the two educational degrees that a person as young as their dean of studies had managed to obtain in such a short and unheard of time frame. The teachers admitted their ignorance of their dean having such qualifications, as he himself had never mentioned them. From that day on the teachers saw their dean in a different light and previous problems were refocused. Speaking well, in practical and real terms, of your fellow workers not only is Christian, but also extremely effective (like most things Christian!)

There is a possible problem with having kids do things because they seek an educator's approval. Naturally anybody will enjoy having people do things just to please him and would be content to leave things on this level. He feels that he, the educator and only he, has control over these people. It is, if you will, a temptation of power. So we must be careful. When we find that we have kids at this stage, doing things because they seek our approval, we must hurry along and get them higher up the ladder of positive motivation. And don't worry. The higher kids go on the ladder, the more they will admire and respect their educator.

From stage one ("edible reward") through stage two ("appreciation") to stage three, where virtue is its own reward, requires formation on the student's part. He must be educated to see what is expected of him. Virtues must be built up for him. Highly beneficial for reaching this stage is conscientious use of personal dialogue (see pages 70-94), good reading materials, solid friendships, positive role models, and a healthy family or school atmosphere.

Good reading materials, especially books, can give the kids livable, attractive, and believable examples of virtue. Solid friendships will help the kid realize the good things in the friend and encourage him to follow suit. Positive role models will inspire virtue. A healthy family atmosphere—a joyful dedication to duty, a keen competitive spirit, a fast-paced but not rushed schedule, good food, tidy facilities, projects that call for team work—all these elements go together to make up an environment that will encourage the kids to appreciate virtue and to want to be better.

Getting students from stage three, where a kid does something because he wants to, up to stage four, where a kid gets into the habit of trying to do all things right because it is the right thing to do, is basically a matter of practice.

We must be careful not to expect students at stage four to work on autopilot. Even when they do things because they know it is right to do so, and therefore they want to do so, they may easily get lazy, lose focus, become bored, or even dragged down by contrary forces. And so we must continually recognize the good attained, on a personal and group level, and be constantly aiming the kids higher.

And no matter how virtuous a kid may become, he will always be open to attack from those forces that want to drag him down. These forces may be present at school and even in the neighborhood. They are certainly present in the media. And so there is a place for "testing" in our formation work. We must not be afraid to test a kid. Overprotecting a kid can be just as harmful as overexposure. If a kid is able to attain an acceptable level of apparent internal discipline at home, the able educator will prudently put this to the test. This testing works much in the same way as does temptation in the spiritual life. Temptation can knock us down or strengthen us. In human formation, thank goodness, we are not dealing with "temptation" but with testing. We are responsible for the student's spiritual well-being, and it is totally illegitimate to deliberately expose him to an occasion of sin. Life itself will take care of offering the kid sufficient temptation in this sphere.

But as far as being punctual, responsible, generous, we can put the kid's virtue to the test without in any way compromising his spiritual well-being.

Testing

It is difficult to gauge a kid's grasp of internal discipline by just monitoring him. The reasons behind his actions may not be those of interior discipline, and he may well be much lower down the ladder than we would wish to think. Having a tidy bed, being on time, helping out his friends, being obedient, or even visiting the chapel may be motivated by many factors other than that of interior discipline. There is a way, however that will help us measure or verify his degree of internal discipline, and this is through testing.

In personal dialogue, you can set goals that will challenge, or test, the kid's virtue. Here's a practical example:

A kid has acquired an acceptable level of punctuality. Now we'll put it to the test. Before we test it, however, we must be certain that what we are about to ask the kid to do is indeed feasible. It is convenient that the test be in addition to the normal short-term goal we set.

Let's say there is a five-minute time slot between classes. We will ask our student, during this slot, as well as getting his books and being on time for the next class, to visit the game room to ensure the place is clean—and to do this everyday for the next two weeks. During the previous class, we will or have someone else visit the game room and make sure that it is acceptably clean. But some days we will drop a candy wrapper here, a plastic bag there. We will apparently pay no interest to the kid's performance during these two weeks. But we will of course monitor it. We will visit the game room during the second class and collect anything that the kid may have left behind. And we will check with the teacher to see whether or not the kid is being punctual.

During the next personal dialogue session we will make no mention of the test. Should the student himself mention it, we will be sparing in our praise. In fact, we will just grunt, tell him to keep it up for another two weeks, as if we were not really interested and pass on to something else immediately. Every experienced educator will have a series of tests from which to choose.

But in the next personal dialogue session you will definitely mention it. If the kid has done well, we will praise him to the hilt. If he has not done it, we will hand him all the rubbish we have collected. He will be left in no doubt as to our interest in him. And this may well cause a rethink.

Such testing can be a very effective educational tool. It shows us objectively where a kid is at. We must, however, be prudent and not overtax a kid's ability. Such testing does require a lot of constancy on our behalf, and so we must be careful not to dish out tests left, right, and center, forgetting who we're testing with what.

An ending note on this testing stuff—let us never seek to humiliate a kid by setting ridiculously hard tasks. Our testing must have all the characteristics of the true educator.

Time Scales

Passing up through the four stages of positive motivation may take some time. The interiorization of discipline (and that's what we've been talking about) does indeed call for time, effort, focus, and constancy from everybody. Patience too is important. While we must be "in a hurry" to interiorize discipline, we must never rush it. Some kids will get there faster than others. Some kids may never get there, either because they are completely seized up, have a deep emotional or other psychological problem, or because they haven't found adequate direction from their educators.

Once the external discipline is working well in a family, school, or group, the temptation sometimes exists to feel that an educator's job is done. But it most certainly is not. It has just begun. An educator must elevate the motivation continuously.

A Skillful Blend

There is no substitute for an educator's skill in this area of positive motivation. It is, and let no one doubt it for a moment, an art form. I feel that, dealing with kids as we are, there is always the need for a blend of both positive and negative motivation. A family or school where only positive motivation was implemented and negative motivation banned, would be on the short list for auto-destruction. The educator's art is precisely in finding that mix, that blend, of both forms of motivation so that priority is always given to positive motivation without letting discipline slip. At the beginning of the school year, or as kids are growing, the mix might be fifty-fifty. But as time goes on, positive motivation will increase as negative motivation decreases. With some kids the mix might end up being a hundred to one, but on an overall level there will always be room for a little negative motivation. That's the way we humans are, after Adam and all that. The skilled educator however will be constantly searching out ways of substituting the negative with the positive and will always be willing to run the measured risk.

Help from the Wings

No doubt about it, an educator's life is a busy one. If he takes his job seriously and does it well, he will be totally engaged trying his best to get the best out of his kids. If the educator, on the other hand, is only learning, or if he has not grasped the real meaning of his mission, he will also be busy, but with other things. He will be running around after the children much as a worried hen cares for her newborn chicks. So whether he is good, great, or hopeless, an educator will always have his time full. But as these notes aim to be practical, there is an activity, a "tip" if you will, that I have found to be of irreplaceable value for an educator. It is a simple and yet difficult thing to do—prayer.

Educators will spend a lot of time with their kids. This means that if there is Mass, the educator will go to Mass. When the kids pray before lunch, the educator will pray too. But when I talk of prayer as a "tip of the trade," I am not talking of this kind of prayer. As well as the above-mentioned, a skilled educator will always search out a secret moment every day to be alone with his Lord and speak to him about every single kid in his care.

An educator I had the blessing to work with in a boarding school, and from whom I learned many of these tips, once told me that at night, after the kids were asleep in their dorm, he would make a visit to the Blessed Sacrament. His prayer would be very simple. He would simply kneel down in the chapel and ask God to bless all "his kids." But he didn't just say, "God, please bless my kids," he said, "Lord, bless Johnny, bless Jeremy, Philip, Stuart..." until he had gone through his whole group. The educator used to call his little prayer his "litanies."

On this stage that is education a little glance into the wings every now and again helps keep things on track.

Keeping Motivation in Perspective

"Give me a support point, and a pole long enough, and I will move the earth." This famous statement of fulcrum physics is as exact as it is ambitious. A little downward push at the end of a very long pole would indeed shoot our terrestrial globe way off course. The fulcrum, that magic point on which you would balance your long pole, is a fascinating concept and one that is at work whether you're changing a tire or breaking into your garage.

In our work as educators, the ***fulcrum*** is ***motivation***. If we get the right fulcrum, or support point, we can move not mountains but men. The interesting thing about a fulcrum is that it is, in itself, nothing special. If you want to move a very large rock off your back lawn, you simply get a strong pole, put one end under the rock and use a log as a pressure point, or fulcrum. But you could also use another rock, or a strong metal box. The fulcrum in itself is nothing special. In fact, it is very simple. But it will have to have one key characteristic. It must be at least as tough as the rock you want to move. Otherwise, when you bring pressure to bear, your fulcrum will crumble. Try using a cheap brick as a fulcrum to move a rock of granite and you'll get the idea.

So applying this "strength" principle of fulcrum physics to motivation, we can immediately see that whatever you use to motivate must be at least as strong as what you are trying to move. "If you wake up and get out of your warm bed, I'll give you a candy bar at lunch." If the kid is any way normal, and especially if he's an adolescent, an extra five minutes in bed now is worth more than a box of candies later, so our motivation will simply crumble.

And we'll end up shouting the kid out of bed--pushing the huge rock off our lawn with sheer brute force. No brains at work here.

If we want motivation to be successful, it is therefore obvious that we need to know what we're up against. We need to know what we are trying to move. In other words, we need to know where such things as *psychology* and *experience* make an entrance.

Basic Psychology

The beauty of psychology is that you don't need to have a university degree to use it. A good mother will know more about practical psychology than many seventh-year university students. When we talk of psychology, we are not talking of dream interpretation, or of reading significant meaning into ridiculous inkblots. (They always look a bit suspicious, don't they, or is that just me?) Here, we simply mean understanding our kids, why they do things, what they are looking for, what they like, and what they don't like. It's no good asking a kid why he does things, because usually he doesn't really know. That is to say, maybe he'll throw a reason at you, but he will not usually be able to dig a little deeper and tell you the real reason.

A kid hits another kid. The victim responds by punching the aggressor's nose. "Why did you belt Jimmy's nose?" "Because he hit me (and, to justify his action, he will add) first." But deep down, we all know that there is more to the retaliatory action than just a simple tit-for-tat. The kid hits back because if he doesn't he will receive more of the same, or because he feels he has to prove his manhood, or because he hates the other guy anyway. It's normally this deeper reason that will help us understand our kids.

Movers

Boys will be boys, and girls will be girls. In many ways all kids are the same. What moves one kid might well move another. But there are other things that will move one kid and leave the other totally cold. But here are some general things that move both boys and girls:

The need to be recognized: This is something that kids will never lose. It's enough to call to mind how we ourselves are often annoyed when someone gets our name wrong. But this need in a kid to be recognized goes beyond knowing his name (although knowing his name is a great start). Kids want others to recognize what's good about them. If a girl thinks she has lovely hair, she will be moved if you recognize it, if you compliment her on her hair. If a boy thinks he's good as a goalkeeper, telling him "That save was really something!" will usually get him on your side. Here girls can be a little different. They will sometimes be content to be a little more vague about things. "I like being with you" makes a girl feel good, and she'll leave it at that. Say this to a boy and he'll usually ask you, "Why?" He'll want something a little more concrete: "Because you're strong" or "Because you really know how to score goals." But recognizing practical, positive points is well accepted by both girls and boys. As educators, we do well to take note. A simple rule of thumb would be for us to make a special effort to get into the habit of complimenting the kids at least three times a day for something we know they are concerned about.

On a more theoretical plane, we can talk of our being "born to love and to feel loved." This need to be recognized ties in with our yearning to know ourselves, to know others, and to be known.

Its fulfillment is in the conviction that we are recognized and known by God, and that we know ourselves as creatures of this loving God. Its total fulfillment comes only in heaven when we see God as he is.

Just a point here: I have said that kids want to be recognized for what they think they're good at, or for what they think is good about them. A young kid might naturally be a very happy type of person. We might want to compliment him on his being so joyous, but maybe the kid is not particularly interested in this aspect of his character. Our praise will not really get us anywhere. (When he's older, such a compliment will be much better accepted.) So we need to tap into what is of concern for the kid. Of course, we will also have to educate the happy kid so that he sees that his joy is a gift from God and that he can do a lot to help others by sharing this happiness with them. But at the beginning, as I said, he may not be concerned with this.

Our goal is to help the kid to get an ever more exact knowledge of himself. Usually we have an inflated image of ourselves. John Paul I spoke of the three "me's": the "me" I think I am, the "me" I'd like to be, and the "me" I really am.

To be challenged: Kids love a challenge. However, for a challenge to be effective, we must have recognized a kid first. In other words, if a girl is overweight, the challenge to do five laps of the field faster than other girls will certainly not be effective. It will turn her against you. But, following the same case, if you challenge the girl to lose a pound in two weeks and make an enthusiastic deal about it, and suggest how, she'll love it.

But having said this, we can safely say, especially for boys, that a good competition will be successful. Italian boys, for example, will react extremely well to academic competition. Their Mexican counterparts will not see it in such a positive light. But it can nevertheless be an effective mover. A challenge can make or break a kid.

As educators, we do well to challenge not just the physical or intellectual abilities of our kids, but also the kid as a person. In other words, let us not focus exclusively on getting our kids to be better at something (tidier, faster, more accurate in football, or more fluent in their second language). Let us primarily focus on getting them to be better kids.

"You are certainly improving," says much more to a kid than "Your math is certainly improving." If kids enjoy a challenge, it is not because deep down they want to know more math or know how to shoot goals. They enjoy a challenge because they aim at being better people and the challenge will help them do just that.

"You're getting better at swimming" and "Your swimming is getting better" may appear to say the same thing. But they don't. "You're getting better" speaks of the person. "Your swimming is getting better" speaks of something "outside" the person.

Deep down, we are more interested in being than in having. If our society today is more "have" than "be" orientated it is simply because having is easier to sell than being. But in our approach, better swimming skills and better grades will help kids become better swimmers, better students, and better persons. Here we have used examples of sports and school subjects to get the idea across. But our focus should be more on aspects such as being humble, generous, responsible—human virtues.

Before challenging kids, make sure they are up to it, whether it is applied on a group level and more importantly when it is on a personal level. Be careful not to overestimate a kid. And be even more careful not to underestimate him.

Doing the right thing: This is a motivational recourse that is not sufficiently valued. Kids will naturally want to do the right thing. They may find a hundred and one excuses for not doing it, but deep down they want to do the right thing. This goes deeper than any education—or lack ofvthat the kids have. No kid in his right mind will want to kick a teacher to death. He knows that to do such a thing is wrong and he wants to do the right thing. Of course, other forces may be at play and he may indeed, while not kick the poor teacher to death, at least insult him. And the kid might even enjoy it. In such cases we can safely say that the kid has lost his mind, at least temporarily. It's really hard to go against what we call the basic human law—do good, avoid evil.

It is our task to educate the kid as to what is right. And here we need to be careful. We must avoid at all costs having a thing be right just because "I say so." If things are right, there is a reason for it. While kids may not always see or accept the reasons, it is necessary that they see there is a reason—and that I am not that reason.

We must also show the kids the right way. "That bed is not made correctly. I want it perfectly straight." This will set the kid against you. Rather, show the kid a bed well made and say, "That is a well made bed." Don't add, "Why can't you make yours like that?" Don't attack the kid. Show him what is right and well done. Show him that he too can do it. Help him the first few times until he learns how to do it. Bed-making is not an inborn talent.

The kid should be able to point to his family or school or youth group and say, "Now, that's the right way to do things."

The trick here for us as educators is not to confuse the wrong-*doing* with the wrong *doer* and to make sure the kid recognizes the difference. The kid must see that we are on his side, with him, against any negative thing that may be trying to get to him. "You're a lazy individual" and "You've got a laziness problem" seem to say the same thing, but they don't. The kid may indeed be lazy, but saying it that way, in an accusing manner, shows only that we identify him with his fault. We should be careful. Let the kids see that we do not confuse the issue. (In the United States, some people try to be politically correct, so instead of saying that a guy is "slow on the uptake," they would say "he is intellectually challenged." This seems to be a nice way of saying it, but if we look at it carefully, we can see that they are still associating a facet of the guy's faculties with the guy himself. But then again, I guess those people who invent such terms are themselves "politically challenged.")

Anyway, that is why saying "Well done!" can be so very effective. It ties in perfectly with this deep-rooted desire to do what is right. It also ties in with the kids desire to be a better person (challenge). He has met the challenge. The "Well done!" proves to the kid that he can do it. In fact, it proves that he *has* done it. It also ties in with his desire to be recognized.

In these three aspects, (the need to be recognized, the need to be challenged, and the predisposition to do the right thing) kids are basically the same. And our motivation effectiveness is guaranteed to the degree we tap into them.

Experience—Knowing What Works

While basic psychology will help us know kids a little better, to know what moves them, *experience* will lend a hand by telling us how exactly to apply what we know, or think we know, about the kid's psychology. Ideas without experience are dangerous.

Most of us will have come across the new guy who thinks he knows almost everything. And while he may indeed know a lot, his lack of experience in a particular area will greatly hamper his work. He might work, for example, on the idea that basically all kids are good by nature. This may well lead him to trust too much in the kids. Ronald Reagan, after many years in power, had learned the trick, "Trust, but verify." Don Bosco's experience led him to write, "Treat them as angels, but know they can be devils." Or the new guy might work on the other wavelength, "You can't trust the kids an instant," an approach which will, in the long run, wave good-bye to all hope of interior formation (responsibility, sincerity, honesty).

It is experience that will help us reach the balance in practical terms. Experience will show that kids, while basically good, will oftentimes behave quite badly.

There is, in short, no substitute for experience. But just as you don't have to have a degree to understand basic psychology, you don't have to have worked with kids for twenty years to have experience. You can use other peoples' experience. Seeing how other good educators work, how they treat the kids will help you get experience. Talking to them and sounding out your ideas with them will be of great help to you. When you begin working with kids, be prudent with ideas or motivational strategies. Try them out in little doses. If they are good and work, keep them. If not, drop them.

Perspective

But we do well to keep motivation in perspective. There is no magic key. Positive motivation is not a magic wand. Kids are kids, and it is impossible to trace out a perfect blueprint of exactly what moves a kid in every instance. Only God has the blueprint. In this book I have given some basic guidelines and even some tips regarding motivation. Our work requires that we know as much as we can about effective motivation. Only in this way can we do what we are supposed to do.

Positive motivation is of the utmost importance. But it is not everything. If we gave the guy who wanted to move the earth the fulcrum he needed, he would still have a hard time finding the pole. We will never be able to completely dominate the theme. And if you ask me, it's just as well.

A Question of Worth

As important as it may be for us as educators to know what a kid is called to become, it is even more important for the kid to ask himself the question, "What does God want of me?" Or at least, "What am I expected to become?" or "What should I be like?" Our work as educators will be ineffective if we give the kid the answer without him first asking the question. We will know, at least to some degree, what God wants of each kid, but our main concern must not be to get this answer across to the kid. Our main concern must be to get the kid himself to ask the question. Then we can help him with the answer.

When I was learning to be a sound engineer, the instructor sat me down at the audio console and told me how to cue up records (CDs hadn't been invented). He showed me how to balance microphones, how to "pink noise" space, and how to connect decks. All this took about ten minutes. We flew through the theory. It was great. "You are now ready to record," he said. I started playing with the controls and found everything to be so smooth. There was nothing to being a sound engineer. "Easy, isn't it?" said the instructor with a smile.

Just as I thought he was going to leave me alone so I could get down to playing with the impressive equipment I had all set up in front of me, he said "Before you start, would you go down the hall and get me the charts I left in my office?" As I went down the corridor to the front office I couldn't get over how easy everything had been. I had been expecting the regular boring sessions of talk and theory, but here I was now, after just ten minutes of expert talk, a sound engineer.

In two minutes I was back in the little training studio. "I'll leave you to it," said the instructor as he thanked me for the charts and left the room. I sat down, put my headphones on, hit play on one of the decks and faded in the volume. But nothing happened. My phones were dead. The tape wasn't even moving. I had a moment of grief as I thought I might have pushed some "self destruct" button by mistake. Then I saw that the little LED lights on the consoles and on the various sound levels meters were not on and that the whole unit was dead. I summoned up courage and went to find the instructor, willing to confess that I had blown it big time.

"Excuse me, sir," I said timidly as I found him bent over a

degutted amp. "But it seems I may have...." "Try turning it on," he interrupted. I did a double take and only then realized what was going on. He wanted to see how well I had listened to his ten minutes of dense theory.

I hurried back to the studio and looked for the "power" on the console. I found it, pushed it with relief, and sat down. But everything was still dead. It took me thirty minutes to trace the power cables to the wall socket and found that the plug was out. I plugged it in. But things still didn't work. Instead of feeling defeated, I began to enjoy the challenge. I rooted around for the tool kit, pulled out a small screwdriver, and opened up the main plug. Sure enough, the instructor had disconnected one of the wires in the plug. I reassembled it, and plugged it in triumphantly. But the thing still didn't power up.

It turned out that not only had the instructor fiddled with the plug, but he had also removed the main fuse, ensuring that no power was getting to the socket. And not only this, he had also shifted the internal break fuse in the main console so as it would appear to make a connection, when in fact it was disconnected. I didn't even know there were internal fuses! It took me almost two weeks to get the console connected again and up and running. I had never asked so many "whys" in all my life. And I had never savored each individual answer so much.

Answers are useless unless we ask the right questions. Getting kids to ask important and meaningful questions is our prime task.

The Role of Questions

In our work with children and especially with adolescents, there is much to be gained by asking questions. And the questions we ask say much about what we think of the kids. There are easy questions, useless questions, useful questions, stupid ones, and clever ones.

1. How many New Age people does it take to change a lightbulb?
2. Why did you do that?
3. In the movie you've just seen, can you point out three things the main character did that go against what Christ says in the gospel?
4. Is anybody willing to give me a hand?
5. What do you all think we should do now?
6. Why do we have eyebrows?
7. Sammy, what do you suggest?
8. Why can't you keep your room tidy?

Well, we can set aside number one since it is simply a joke, and besides I could be labeled something nasty for using it.

Number 2 is a useless question because a kid will hardly ever be able to give you a correct answer.

Numbers 3 and 7 are clever questions because they require the kid (as an individual) to think and to come up with an answer.

Number 5 is another useless question, since whoever asks the question will more than likely have his mind made up even before asking the question.

Number 8 is a dumb question.

Number 6 is another clever question.

Number 4 is a useful question.

If you glance through the Gospels, we can see that Christ uses the clever question technique quite a bit.

When he was just twelve and was found in the temple by his

worried parents, he asks them why they had been worried about him.

When he meets a woman by a well, he asks her where her husband is.

When confronted by a repugnant group of self-righteous Pharisees, he asks them whether it is easier to cure a man's physical ailment or to cure his soul.

And when a woman caught red-handed in sin was brought to him for judgment, he told those in the crowd without sin to throw stones. Nobody threw a stone, so he asked, "Did no one condemn you?"

All these, and many of the other questions recorded in the Gospels, are clever questions in spite of what may appear from a quick initial reading. Each question calls upon the person to think. And in each case, the answer is the beginning of discovery, or at least throws new light along the way.

When he was twelve, "Why were you looking for me?" might be interpreted as a stupid or even bad mannered retort. After all, he had been missing and it was only right that his parents should be worried. So why such a question? It sparked thought in his parents, and it helped them understand his mission and their mission too. In fact, the Gospel tells us that his mother would think about this for many years to come.

The woman by the well was kick-started into life by the question Christ asked her. She felt the question deep in her soul.

When Christ asks, "Did no one condemn you?" he is not only speaking to the woman, but to the angry onlookers who realize, to a man, that the question had torn away the veil that up to then had hidden their innermost sins.

His many parables were often preceded by, "What do you think about this?"

Christ was an educator. He was The Educator, the One who brought, and who brings us out of darkness. And he used questions as part of his technique. How then can we imitate this aspect of Christ's teaching?

First, know what we're after. In other words, we must know where we want our questions—and their answers—to bring us. A simple, maybe too simple, example would be that we want the kid to think about heaven. The line of questions could be something like this:

"What are you going to do when you leave secondary school?

"And when you leave university? And then? And then? And then"...until you hit death, "And then?"

Then we must be pretty sure that the kid can give us an intelligent answer. He must be able to answer. "What will you be doing next year, on this day at four in the afternoon?" is a pointless question, and the kid will not be able to give the correct answer. But ask him what he was doing yesterday at four in the afternoon, and there's a pretty good chance you'll get a definite and precise answer. We can apply this concept to the kind of questions we ask. We should be careful not to make our questions too obscure. The more precise our question, the better chance we are giving the kid to give us a precise answer.

Compare:

"If you divide an integral multiple of the square root of seventeen by the number of deems in an Indian loaf, how many canoes are you left with?"

with

"Ten divided by two, multiplied by six, divided by thirty is equal to?"

Challenge the kid. There is nothing as boring as a simple, silly question. Ask him about what he knows, about what he is good at, about what he would like to talk about. That is why personal questions are effective. In fact, rather than ask, "Did Willy do right or wrong?" ask "What would you do in that case?"

Accept the answer and work with it. Quite often a kid will not answer according to your script. Be flexible enough to take his answer into account and work with it without forcing the issue.

You want to explain to a kid why it is wrong to run in the corridors. (We wouldn't ask this question as we stop the kid hurdling down the hall, but rather in a more serene moment.) You ask, "Why should we walk in the corridor?" "To get to the classroom" might be an answer. "Because we can't fly" might be another. So double back and ask, "Why should we not run in the corridor?" "Because we would make a lot of noise" might be an answer. "But let's say, you were wearing sneakers. You wouldn't make any noise, but still it is wrong to run in the corridor. Why?" "But sometimes I have to run, otherwise I'd be late." "But even if you're going to be late, running in the corridor is still wrong. Why?"

The kid will eventually hit upon the fact that running in a somewhat confined space can easily lead to bumping into people and other such accidents.

Popping the Question

Knowing what the ideal kid should be like (Part Two, Step One), knowing how our kid measures up (Part Two, Step Two), knowing how to draw up a program that meets the needs of the kid's development (Part Two, Step Three), and being able to motivate the kid so that he will want to attain what is expected of him (Part Two, Step Four) are all essential tools for an educator. However, and although we have mentioned this point in passing, it is worth stressing here: Any educational effort on our part must be seen as an answer to questions that kids ask themselves ("What should I be like?" "What does God expect of me?" "How do I get there?" "How do I overcome this difficulty?") Getting the kid to ask himself these questions is the real secret of successful education.

While it appears easy to get a kid to ask the question, "How do I make my bed properly?" (show him once, undo the bed, and let him try it), it may not appear to be quite so easy to get the kid to ask himself the more important questions about his inner formation. How then can we help a kid to burn within with the question "How can I be better?" As we have said, if the kid does not have this inner quest, all our effort will be akin to the Chinese man who gave fish to the hungry instead of teaching him how to fish. (The recipient died of hunger when the Chinese guy went on holiday.)

Ways to Stimulate the Question

Confidence

One way of getting a kid to embrace a personal quest for self-betterment is the confidence way. You show a kid how good he is and suggest he might like to be better. This can be extremely effective. It is not the "You're-good-but-Johnny-is-better. Try-to-be-like-Johnny" approach, which will only get the kid annoyed as you fail to recognize his effort. It's the "You're-good-and-maybe-you-could-be-even-better" approach. It works like this:

Jimmy is very fashion conscious. Unfortunately, his hair is always messy. "Wow, Jimmy! You're looking good today. Nice sharp press on those trousers. Good." Let the compliment sink in. "You know, I was thinking, if you're interested that is, that maybe if you did something with your hair... I don't know, but I think if you did something with your hair, you'd be the sharpest guy around. Yeah, maybe that's it."

Take a kid who is halfheartedly trying to be on time. Pick one occasion that he is punctual and compliment him sincerely on it. And then, "You know, I'm pretty sure that you could always be on time if you set your mind to it."

The trick in this approach is to suggest improvement only when you see the kid is open to it. And to avoid having your "suggestion" sound like an order. The important thing is not to get the kid to comb his hair or to be on time, but to try and spark an inner question: "Can I be better? How can I be better?" I am not saying that we should allow kids to run round with unruly hair and to be late for everything. What I am saying is that there are many ways of rectifying a fault, and that some ways are much better than others.

This confidence approach also has a bonus side effect. As well as stimulating an inner question, it can quite often lead to the kid accepting you as an educator.

I remember one Spanish kid on a summer course in Ireland who was a difficult kid to get through to. One day he bought a new pair of expensive Reebok shoes. He was getting ready one morning and he was putting on his new shoes. "Nice boots," commented the educator. "You know, in the States, the kids wear them without fastening the laces. They just shorten them." Up until then the kid had been lacing them as any normal shoe. He just grunted as the educator left the room. But later on, that evening, he came up to the educator, somewhat timidly. "Do these jeans go with these shoes?"

Example

Another way to get a kid personally interested in self-betterment is the model way. You show the beauty of some virtue and indirectly let the kid know that such beauty is within his reach. This is the "I want to be like him" line that gets kids to behave in the fashion of their hero, or wear a certain style of clothes, or use particular words.

The whole secret, in my opinion, is not to oblige the kid to follow the example, but simply to lay it out in front of him. Most of us have an internal shutoff switch that turns us off when we are told that we must (imperative) be like so-and-so. It is example, and not words, that really move people.

Self-examination

Yet another way of interiorizing self-betterment, in the case of thinking kids, is to get them into the habit of self-examination. This is not to be confused with the conscience exam that a kid will run through before he goes to confession, which all too often is sadly reduced to a list of the rules he has broken and not a review of those aspects of his life where he will ask for God's forgiveness and help.

This self-examination will introduce the kid into the joy of self-knowledge. It will help him see why he does things and it will challenge him to search out ways to overcome what he messes up and to do better what he already does well. I just indicated that this way of getting a kid to ask the important questions is for "thinking kids." Please do not try it on superficial kids whose thought span hardly covers a pop video clip. You will find that the approach is good for intellectual kids, and it is surprising effective in the case of practical-minded kids as well. Girls love it.

Don't Worry about Words

As educators we must not be overly concerned initially about the kid phrasing the question in the exact way we phrase it. In a strange paradoxical kind of way, getting the kid to pop the question is both the starting point and the arrival point of our mission with them.

Initially, we should search out that area in the kid's life that he wants to improve. And there will always be something. It might be "How do I make myself more acceptable to other kids?" It might be "I want to make my parents proud of my grades, or "I want to be a good soccer player," or even "I want to be more handsome." If we search carefully, we will find some area that expresses a kid's desire to be better. We should use this spark and fan the flame until it focuses in on the important questions: "How can I be a better person? How can I help others more?"

Virtue, Just the Beginning

Let us suppose for a moment that you were an educator in a small community school two thousand years ago. And it just so happened that there was a kid there who pretty much matched the God prototype that we have just outlined. In fact, you would say that this kid was God's prototype, so perfect was he in every way. Let us suppose then that you had Christ as a kid under your care--a daunting responsibility and almost impossible to imagine. But as you see this kid, a perfect embodiment of all virtue, you also find something else that goes beyond all virtue. What would it be?

The first recorded words of Christ in the Gospel leave no doubt in our minds as to what this something extra was. He was twelve at the time, just the age of many of our kids. And here are those words that open up a whole new world for us: "Didn't you know," he asked his parents, "that I have to busy myself with the concerns of my father?"

Mission. Christ, even as a kid, knew that he had something to do in life. And this something was not just "to make a living." It was a definite something. He had a mission in life.

Now, it could be argued that Christ discovered the nitty-gritty of his mission as his life went on. When he was twelve, he didn't say to his parents, "Didn't you know that I have to save the world?" He simply said that he had to take care of his father's concerns, as if this was just the beginning. During adolescence he would crystalize the meaning of his mission. This could be argued with some degree of success, but the point does not interest us here that much. Suffice it to say that the kid Christ, even at twelve had, and knew he had, a mission.

Every one of us, and every kid under our care, has a mission in life. Not a slogan, not feel-good-about-yourself-therapy, mission is the reason we are here. If God expects us to have certain qualities he does so because he has something for us to do with them. He has a plan for us and we will not be able to accomplish this plan if we do not have the means to do it. When we talked of God's prototype we were simply sketching the tools, the virtues a kid will need to do what he has to do in life.

Our task then, as educators, is, on the one hand, to help the kid prepare himself by acquiring the virtues that he will need. And, on the other hand, we must help the kid discover his mission in life.

When touring Detroit with a group of Irish kids, we visited a famous car museum. Al Capone's car was there and countless others that were famous for one thing or another. But there was also one so-called "car" that had never gone anywhere on its own four wheels. A carmaker had made it for himself, just to look at. It had plush red leather seats, a pearl (or was it ivory?) steering wheel, huge chrome fenders and a convertible top made of hardened white leather. Its motor was a sixteen-valve, sixteen-liter, masterpiece of mechanics said to be capable of a hundred-eighty miles an hour (great going for those days). But this car had never been driven anywhere and never would be. As one of the kids read the information he said, "Why build such a thing, call it a car, and then never drive it?" We agreed that the carmaker had been a nutcase.

Building character, forming personality, without a focus on mission is as dumb—and as useless—as the eccentric Detroit car manufacturer's "car" that was built to go nowhere.

Wrap Up

The above are suggestions as to how we can help the kid to get involved in his own formation. An educator's task is not to "form" from without, but to spark the interest within the kid for his own formation and have the kid form himself from within. There will be one overriding concern for us—to show the kid that we care about him. We care about him and accept him as he is right now. We will not give the impression of loving the kid he could be. We love the kid as he is, but we also know that he is called to do great things. And we love that vision too, and this is hope, for hope is the love of things future. And we will have faith in the kid too, knowing that if both we and the kid are determined and constant and patient, the fruits of our labors will not be long in coming.

Topics

1. A lovely chapter, but the author is oblivious to what real children are like in the real world. Sometimes the only thing young adolescents understand is a dire threat and if you have to carry out this threat, it only means that the kids needed it.

2. Come up with positive ways of encouraging the kids to do the following:
    - Keep the bathroom clean
    - Polish their shoes well
    - Be polite to a not-easy-to-get-along-with teacher
    - Do an act of hidden service
    - Avoid punching on the soccer field (boys)
    - Avoid speaking behind someone's back (girls)

3

Matters Related to Formation

Introduction

The educator's mission encompasses myriad facets. In this section we touch upon what I consider to be some issues related to our work. Some of these issues may appear a little theoretical and some less so. However, in each instance I have tried to explain a basic idea with practical examples.

Supervision

You have educators and you have babysitters and you have policemen. An educator is not a babysitter and certainly not a policeman. Supervision—being there, watching, monitoring—is part of the educator's job. It is a tool we will use, but we must never feel that supervision is an educator's most important role. It is an essential role, but not his principal role by any means. Together with the educator's own example, personal dialogue, the following of a personal program of formation, and the fulfillment of other educator duties, supervision is a must. An educator who does not supervise at every moment is, simply put, not an educator.

The reason for an educator's supervision is fivefold:

- to make sure his group and each kid is OK
- to know the kids
- to prevent accidents
- to instill serenity
- to ensure things go well

> There are two things a kid should see always and everywhere: an educator and a trash can.
>
> GAELIC BOOK OF WISDOM

Some Things that Have Happened

Kids have the tendency to write their script without letting us go over it before they start acting it out. They can, in other words, get into mischief. Sometimes this mischief can be quite innocent, other times it can put the kids in danger and even sometimes be criminal. Knowing what kind of scripts kids in the past have written will serve to keep us on guard. Here are a few examples:

Microwaved cat

While on a weekend away with a youth group, three kids put a cat into the microwave oven and turned it on. The cat died a painful, albeit a quick, death.

Runaways

Two teenagers, equipped with credit cards, sneaked out of the boarding school one night and "hit the town."

Bullets in a fire

While on a sleepover, the kids found a box of bullets. Finding no gun, and wanting to do something with the bullets, they threw them into a fire.

Missing

On a late night walk, the educator in a boarding school noted that one bed was empty. After checking the bathrooms and kitchen, the eleven-year-old was not found.

Backfire

The educator came upon a noisy classroom only to find the teacher standing outside. "They sent me out."

Nothing short of murder

Although not an example from any school or organization that I know personally, this case from England is rather extreme, but it did happen. Two boys, one ten, the other eleven, kidnapped a seven-year-old and murdered him. They left the body on the train tracks.

Overdose

Again not from the annals of any school or organization I know personally, but there is a case of an eleven-year-old girl found dead in her bed after taking an overdose of ... Tylenol.

A powerful drink

A boy was found lying on the floor in a garage. There had been a dare to see who could drink the most of a special concoction some kids had made—sugar and paint remover.

Flying

And then there is the case of the nine-year-old boy who, after seeing a movie, leaped from his fourteenth-floor window in New York convinced that he could fly. He couldn't.

Each kid is a powerhouse. Each kid is capable of the best and of the most base. We must not be surprised by what they can get into to. Treat them as angels, but know that they can act as devils. And let's keep our eyes open out there.

Supervision and What to Look For

With time, experience, and guidance, the educator should develop a professional skill for supervising. To explain this, I will use a poor example, but it gets the point across.

You buy a car, a Volvo. You jump in, start it up, and away you go. It runs. It works. The steering is a little heavy and the engine is a little noisier than in your last car and maybe the seats are not as comfortable... but hey, it's new to you and you'll get used to it. But you have noticed that the speedometer is not working right and so you will definitely get that fixed.

Now, give the same car to a Volvo technician. In he gets, and even before starting the engine he tells you that the lower springs of the driver's seat are dead and could use a replacement. He starts the car up and immediately notices an odd click-click-click in the engine. "Distributor cap is loose." Then says, "Power steering is gone. A faulty hose connection, more than likely." And then, "The brake system is strained." Even before driving the thing, he has detected an almost infinite list of things that are not quite right. Trying to save face, and not give the impression that you are totally stupid, you venture, "And I think the speedometer is busted." "Yeah," grunts the technician, "that too."

So what should we be watching out for when we supervise?

1. Ensure that the kids are doing what they are supposed to be doing.

If it's recess, everybody should be in recess. Recess is not a time for doing homework, nor is it a good time for personal dialogue. It's recess. Let everybody recess. In Ireland, it's called "recreation," and this is what recess is all about.If it's class time, everybody should be in class and paying attention. If it's shower time, kids should be taking a shower. If it's movie time, make sure that everybody is enjoying the movie (or at least watching it). If it's bedtime, everybody ... you got it!

2. Ensure that things are running smoothly.

   If it's recess, ensure that the kids have the means to enjoy themselves—a competition, a stimulating game. If it's time for a meal, make sure the food and the dishes are ready. Check and make sure the kids are eating well and with manners.

3. Anticipate disaster.

   If the kids are playing, make sure they are playing safely. If the floors are being cleaned, make sure the kids take a detour to avoid the wet floors. If a kid comes to you complaining of a severe headache, get professional help. If, at school, the kids are getting the stage ready for a show, make sure they are not climbing up ladders or working too close to the edge of the stage. If the kids are on a long bus trip, invent games or start some sing-along songs. And know where the rest areas are along the way.

Danger Signals (schools)

Here are some things that signal something is wrong:

- You do not know where a kid is. Maybe he's in the bathroom, maybe he's not. You don't really know. Check it out.

- Kids wander off on their own, either by themselves or in twos or threes. They might be distracted, they might be going off to have a cigarette, or maybe they just want to talk in private. Call them back.
- Kids whisper among themselves. Maybe it's secret-sharing time, or maybe they are saying something they would rather you didn't know they were saying. Cut out whispering.
- A small group of kids is always together and act secretively (they see you coming and they "look innocent" or they suddenly start speaking loudly about something totally innocent; or they see you and discreetly move off somewhere else). Don't hound such groups, but keep them well monitored.
- A kid takes longer than necessary to do something simple (like going to the bathroom, like getting things from his locker, like looking for some chalk, like bringing down the laundry). Check it out.
- A kid is constantly by himself. Be sure he stays involved with the others.

Not-to-Be-Forgotten Areas

There are some areas that are more hazardous than others.

Restrooms

Restrooms should be perfectly clean, well-supplied, and well-aired at all times, and supervised. A terrible thing to say, almost an invasion of privacy, you might think. But there is no doubt that this area lends itself to wasting time and to other more serious temptations. There is nothing wrong with restrooms, but they have a function and they should be used exclusively for that function. In this area supervision does not mean that we have to monitor everything that is going on, for this would certainly be an invasion of privacy and totally indecent of us. It is sufficient that the kids be aware that they are not totally alone, that, while not in view, there is an educator nearby.

It is a good practice to encourage silence in this area.

And please note that should you deem it necessary to be present in the actual restroom area (school) when kids are present, always have another adult with you, or at least within talking distance.

Dressing rooms (for sports, for showers)

Here again we have a perfectly normal activity that can, unfortunately, deteriorate. The general rule here is to ensure that the kids, out of respect for themselves and for others, can shower or change clothes in natural decency. Should the showers be for a group (as opposed to individual curtained-off stalls,) the age of the kids might suggest the use of swimwear. However, for reasons of hygiene, individual shower units are certainly to be preferred.

Bathrobes are an excellent invention as they allow a kid to dry himself off in public with decency. Because of the age of the kids, the physical factor may be cause for some embarrassment. Added to this is the all-too-natural tendency of curiosity, particularly accentuated in the preteen age group. So all serene measures we can take will be gratefully accepted.

Our role of supervision in this area should consist in "naturally being there." It is not a good idea to be actually standing with the kids as they change, much less be talking with them. Rather walk about, speeding things up, or calling out the time remaining. If you choose to stand at the door, which is a good practice, you might like to be checking your timetables, jotting down ideas for a class or speaking with someone who is ready. Avoid watching the kids. Just be there and be seen to be there.

So as not to let things go unsaid, let me say that girls and boys should not share the same dressing room areas, or at least, not at the same time.

And once again, supervision of this activity requires that there be two adults present.

Bedrooms (boarding schools and youth groups)

Bedrooms, or dorm areas, should be respected for what they are. They are not areas for chatting, for playing computer games, or for doing homework. Bedrooms are for sleeping in. Bedrooms may often be used for getting dressed, and in this respect I would ask you to apply what we have just mentioned about dressing rooms. Our supervision in this area calls for us to ensure that everything is in its place—and that includes "kids in bed" when it's bedtime.

On short-term events, a retreat or summer course for example, it may be convenient to let the kids speak to each other for a few moments once they get to bed. You could say that once everybody is in bed, they may speak quietly for five minutes should they so wish. Then when the time is up, you call for silence and make sure there is silence. This is a practical way of avoiding whispering, giggles, and noise. But please note that this is only a suggestion for short-term courses.

When it's bedtime, supervision calls for us to make sure that every kid is in his bed and making an effort to get to sleep and respecting everybody else's intention of getting to sleep.

Our supervision here prompts us to ensure that the sleeping quarters be "sleep-able." If there are mosquitoes, or if it's very hot, or very cold, we should do whatever we can to minimize the difficulty beforehand. (You can underline "beforehand.")

The good educator will remain on the floor until one half hour after he is sure the last kid has gone to sleep.

The good educator will be on the floor again one half hour before the kids' body clocks wake them up. Please remember that when away from home kids will tend to wake up earlier than usual on the first and possibly second day.

In these three "potentially dangerous areas" there is nothing better than prevention. An educator's discreet and yet visible presence is essential.

Before we leave this aspect of supervision, I think it's a good idea to always keep in mind the axiom, "Think the best, prepare for the worst." Always assume that the kid is doing something that is totally acceptable, but be prepared to react if you discover otherwise. If you discover four kids huddled together looking at something, believe that they are reading a great book, not filling their eyes with a "not-a-good-idea" magazine. But check it out all the same. If a kid takes thirty minutes to find a piece of chalk, believe him. But next time, see if he isn't going off to have a snack. Think the best, prepare for the worst.

I remember I was walking down a corridor and saw two kids duck out of sight. Then I saw a little head sneak a peek from the end of the corridor and when he saw me coming, he disappeared.

As I approached the end of the corridor, I heard muted whispers, "Quick! He's coming! Hurry! Hide that!" As I turned the corner I noticed that the lights were off. Thinking the best in this case was pretty hard to do.

As I entered the room, the lights went on and a song broke out. The kids had organized a surprise birthday party for me! And what were they trying to hide? The cake wrapper!

Supervision in Different Situations

There are two moments that offer the educator a privileged view of his kids—mealtime and playtime. In both areas, the educator will be able to see with great detail what his kid is like. He will be able to pull out examples from watching the kids that he can use to great effect in his dialogues with them.

Hints on Supervision (schools)

1. Be involved in, or at least pretend to be interested in, what's going on.

If you're supervising recess, walk around and encourage the kids in what they're doing. Take advantage of the moment to talk to them about sports or their collections or to complement them on yesterday's game. While supervision here is indeed a formal affair, keep the tone informal. Try not to hamper the kids' enjoyment, keep commands to a minimum. And never ever use recess or other things they really like for doing chores or for personal dialogue. The kids need their break.

If you're supervising a study period, study yourself. Set the example. You may like to sit up in front at the teacher's desk, although you might try sitting down with your book and note pad at the back of the class. Dig into your book, but keep your eyes open. Every now and again, get up quietly and walk softly around and check the kids' work. Respect the silence and should you need to talk, whisper.

If you are supervising a meal, sit down and eat as well and discreetly show that you are enjoying the food. But keep your eyes open. Rather than get up and go over to a noisy table, politely ask one of the kids at your table to go over and have one of the troublemakers come over to you.

2. *Constant head count*

Whatever the activity you are supervising, have your group in view. Get into the habit of doing a rapid head count. If you find your numbers fall short, do a more detailed name count in your head. Should you find that you are effectively short a kid or two, have two kids go off to find the missing guy (applicable only when on campus). When the missing kid turns up, remind him firmly about the rule of always staying with the group and of letting you know should he need to leave for a moment.

This head count is all the more important when away from the facility with the kids. In such circumstances, unless you're on a bus or plane, you should do a head count every fifteen minutes at least. If you have your group divided up, establish rendezvous points and times throughout the time you are visiting.

Count heads at night, too, when the kids are in bed if you are with them (academy, retreat). And as you do so, you might like to ask God to bless each one as you count.

3. Top and tail

"Top and tail" group movements consist of having one educator (or an older kid) lead the group, another taking up the rear. Do not allow kids to lag behind. Move the group as a unit. This does not mean that you have to have them walking in single file. Usually it is more humane to have them walk along together as a group.

4. Anticipate movement

Make sure things are ready for the kids before you send them there. This requires a lot of foresight on the educator's part. If the kids are going to see an in-house movie, make sure you have the movie beforehand and that the projector and audio system is actually working. If the kids are going to the dining room for lunch, make sure things are ready. If the kids are going to a sports activity, make sure the instructor has arrived. Never send kids "into the unknown." You might like to think everything is ready ("it always is"), but check anyway.

The Importance of the Why

For an educator the why is as important as the what. Being overly concerned with the why will lead us to becoming pseudo-psychologists, while being overly concerned about the what will turn us into drill sergeants. We need to strike a balance.

By just observing a kid, we will get an idea of what he's really like and how he measures up to our prototype. But given the fact that the why a kid does something is not always obvious, it may oftentimes be necessary to put virtue to the test.

A kid may be well-mannered at table because it has been drilled into him since early childhood. The fact that he is well-mannered is all very well, but maybe it isn't really his concern for others that motivates him, and his educated behavior may just be mechanical actions and reactions. On the face of it, this would not appear to be important. After all, the kid is well-mannered, and we should leave it at that. But no, we shouldn't.

> We don't want kids to be good.
> Our job is to have them **want to be better.**

The reason being that if a kid's good manners at table are motivated by a conscientious concern for others, this concern will spill over into other areas of the kid's life. If his good manners are just mechanical, he may be well behaved at table and a beast on the playing field.

Mechanical habits (saying "please" and "thank you," having a shower every morning, saying Grace before meals) are all well and good but our primary aim is not to drill these mechanical habits into the kids. After all, we are not boot camp drill sergeants, but educators. We want our kids to have good habits most certainly, but only as an expression of something deeper.

Some Tips on Controlling Kids

Our work with kids is sometimes reduced to getting kids to behave as they should. This section deals with some practical ways of getting this done effectively and in keeping with our principles.

Sometimes "being there" is simply not enough. When we spoke of supervision (see page 133), we mentioned that optimally our very presence should be enough to bring out the best in kids. But sometimes, especially at the beginning, just being there may not be enough. In such cases our supervision has to take on a more active role. Here are some examples, some taken from family life, others from school life.

Keep Things Low-Key

The kids are attending a conference in the school. Kids being kids, they may quite easily get bored. They will tend to slump down in the chairs, much as a tired airline passenger will recline in his uncomfortable seat and do his best to stretch out. In these cases, an educator's supervision will have him walking up and down, calmly letting the kids know he is there but also giving little signals to those who are slumping down.

The kids are in recess. Shirts slip out from the boys' pants. Until the kids get into the habit of always fixing their shirts, the educator will have to be continuously reminding them. Simple gestures should do, like looking at the kid and tapping your belt.

In class, you might see a piece of paper drop to the floor. Simply point to it.

At mealtime, you may have to gently remind the kids to keep their elbows off the table, not to stuff their mouths, and to keep their knives pointing in an inoffensive fashion. Avoid words.

You might be in the corridors and see a kid running. Slow him down.

In all of the above there are two general tips to be observed:

One, never make a big deal out of this type of correction. Try and keep the correction between yourself and the kid it is intended for. If you are walking up and down during a conference, move quietly and do not distract the kids. Don't go barging through a row of kids to get to one who is asleep. Stand there for a moment at the end of the row. The other guys will see you. And it usually happens that they will wonder what you're there for and immediately detect that you are looking at a guy who is asleep. It will be the kids themselves that will pass on your unspoken message and prod the sleeper. Then move on.

Two, use simple and discreet sign language. A simple and discreet "stop" or "slow down" sign with one hand will be sufficient to have the kid stop running. Gently and discreetly rubbing your elbow as you walk by a table will get the message across to the kid who thinks he's in a saloon. If you're teaching a class and you notice some kid speaking to another kid, stop everything for a moment, cock your head ever so slightly, put your hand to your ear, and you'll see how quickly the kid stops.

The thing to keep in mind here is that most of the corrections will be needed not because the kids want to behave badly, but simply because they are kids and just keep forgetting.

On one occasion I remember, a director saw that the boys always came running down the stairs. He asked the educator why this was happening. "We told them to walk, but they just keep running. What else can I do?" "Tell them again." "But we told them at the beginning of the year, and I have reminded them on numerous occasions," pleaded the educator. "But if you say so, I'll remind them again." And so he did. That night, after supper he addressed his group, reminding them about the dangers of running on the stairs. But ten minutes later, when the kids were coming down to study, they were running again. "See?" he said to the director. "How many times do I have to remind them?" As the guy was a trainee, the director invited him to the stairs just before the kids came down for their evening snack.

The stampede could be heard as the kids came running down the corridor to the stairs. And down they clattered. Halfway down the stairs, they saw the two adults. The director simply held up his hand in a "slow down" signal, and the running stopped immediately. The next day, the same thing happened every time the kids used the stairs. By the evening, no more signals were necessary.

Kids forget. You can tell them, but you must tell them exactly when they are doing it wrong. In this aspect, active supervision can be beneficial as far as getting kids into the habit of doing things right.

Don't Wait for the Crisis

It is this "active supervision," this constant, discreet, and respectful correcting presence that will prevent you from having to face a major crisis later on. My dad always used to repeat a wise saying to me when I was a kid. "Look after the pennies, and the pounds will take care of themselves." If we pay attention to the details of formation, the bigger issues will indeed take care of themselves. This is gospel.

"Active supervision" also has wonderful and seemingly unrelated benefits for the educator. If managed correctly, with discretion and constancy, and even sometimes with a smile, this active supervision can convince the kids that the educator is on their side, that he really wants them to be better. In this way he can win them over and he can be someone important for them. But if managed incorrectly, with shouts, constant public reprimands, and unquenchable demands, active supervision will turn the kids against the educator for life.

An educator in a school was having a terrible time getting his kids excited about a new sports tournament that was coming up. They just were not interested. The director, keenly aware of the advantages of a dynamic sports program, had asked the educator to recruit three teams from his more than one-hundred-twenty boys, and the poor educator was getting somewhat frustrated at not being able to meet the director's request. But two minutes with these kids explained why the educator was having such a hard time:

The kids' shoes hadn't been polished in months, or if they had, it wasn't done well. The boys' hair was relatively short, but the cuts were obviously intended for weekend use and during school they just plastered it down with gel and other substances. Trousers were more like combat uniforms, stained and creaseless. The classrooms had papers on the floor.

Put in simple terms, the educator had not been putting into practice the "active supervision" concept. The educator was a virtual "nobody" for the kids. He had not been demanding with the kids in the details. He never did get the three teams for the tournament, and the kids never really cared.

Topics

Sometimes an educator will come upon situations that could and should have been avoided. How would you handle these cases?

a. You enter the dining area to find a food fight in progress.
b. You are waiting in the car for your kids to come along. They don't show up.
c. You've just been to the mall with your kids and as you count heads, you find that one kid is missing. You wait five minutes and he doesn't turn up.
d. During what has been billed as a holiday activity, the kids simply refuse to get involved.
e. You're running a small talent show at school. One act takes on a line of dangerous innuendo and stifled giggles can be heard from the kids watching the show.
f. You find obscene writing on a campus wall.
g. (Boarding school) Parents visit and it's time to say goodbye. A group of kids and their parents are reluctant to part. A spokesman for the group of parents comes to you and asks permission for the kids to be allowed out to stay with them in a hotel for the night.

Study

Study is one of those essential chores that kids must do. This section offers some ideas that can make study more productive.

To be good at something you have to enjoy it. And the opposite is also true—we are not likely to be good at something if we don't enjoy it. Not a watertight principle, but as a general rule of thumb, it holds.

When we apply this simple principle to personal study, and

kids' personal study in particular, we can understand why many--if not most—kids do not make the most of the time they dedicate to study. They obviously do not enjoy it and therefore will hardly do it well. If we could only get the kids to enjoy study we would be well on the way to making better students of them. But is it possible for kids to actually like and enjoy study in a real sense? Yes.

Kids, being kids, will always much rather be playing football or working on their computer games. They enjoy these things. We certainly do not aim at making study so enjoyable that they will opt to study rather than to go and play. But we can make study acceptably enjoyable and thus more profitable for a kid. What we are about to see now can be applied to family life, schools, boarding schools, and even to youth groups. We will look first at group study method and then at personal study.

Group Study

There are basically three approaches we can take in an effort to help kids study better: study hall, teacher assisted study, and directed study.

Study Hall (or Study Center)

This is where a group of kids will come together to do their personal study in a quiet, well-equipped area. An adult is present to ensure respect for silence and timetables. The method may be applied in youth centers, boarding schools, to selected students in a day school and, with a few slight variations, to small group study at home.

Study hall helps create a study-oriented environment by eliminating distractions and by basically obliging the kids to buckle down to study. Over time, it will also help create a study habit in the kids so they will get used to dedicating a certain block of their time to this activity. It also ensures that kids do not spend too little or too much time studying. When study hall is over, it's over and the kids can relax. They've done their duty.

The disadvantage can be that it does little to help the kid find and develop a personal method of study and it does practically nothing to help him overcome subject-related difficulties that he has been burdened with to date. It also can consolidate bad study habits. And if a kid does not like study to begin with, he can come to hate study hall and all it stands for.

Teacher Assisted Study

This is when a group of students will come together to study one particular subject in the presence of a qualified teacher of that subject. This method is applicable on a periodic basis to day schools and youth centers especially when exam time approaches. The teacher will be able to go around to each individual, monitor the kid's work and guide him through any difficulties the student might be having. Should the teacher detect a group deficiency, he can address the whole group for a short period of time.

There are advantages of this method over study hall. It gives slower kids the chance to catch up and it gives the faster kids the chance to go ahead at their own pace. Kids will understand better. And this "understanding-things-better'" immediately leads to the kids enjoying the subject.

The disadvantage is that it requires a qualified teacher to be present outside normal hours. Another possible disadvantage is that it can make the student lazy, much in the way private classes do (see page 162). And all too often the session can turn into just another class, so care must be taken.

Directed Study

This study method is akin to the previous two in as far as the kids come together to study and there is an adult present. The difference is that the adult here does not have to be a qualified teacher as such, although he must be an expert on behalf of study itself and he must be well respected by the group. The main aim of directed study is to help the kid find and develop a personal study method. It may be effective in any youth study environment at the beginning of term for a couple of sessions to allow time for the kids to learn how to study, especially in boarding schools. It is not recommended for daily use.

Personal Study

To help a kid study well, we have to help him enjoy it. And as personal study is an intellectual activity, the more a kid *understands*, the more he will enjoy. Each "click" of understanding is like a little light that blinks on and gives the kid a little thrill. Let us not expect the kid to learn the art of study through some infused gift. We will need to help him at the beginning, sometimes a lot. Here are three ways we can get the lights to blink:

- Accomplishable challenge
- Controlled procedure
- Active study

Accomplishable challenge

Some kids thrive under pressure; others get squashed. When we speak of "challenge," we are not talking pressure. All kids, without exception, will rise to a challenge if the challenge is well presented. And not only will they rise to it, they will enjoy it. In other words, they will want to accept the challenge. And this is our first point: to make study an "accomplishable" challenge.

Here we are going to tie in with another concept—that of treating kids as adults, or at least as intelligent beings. (See "A secret deep within," page 309).

A language teacher, who obviously knew more about languages than about teaching, had us copy pages and pages of text so that we would get used to writing in French. This was not challenging, (most of us could write in secondary school!) and the exercise treated us more like photocopiers than human beings. We always dreaded these classes and we finished secondary school without knowing French.

Study must be presented as a challenge, and most homework should be too. But what I feel is important is that the kid feels, knows, that he has the ability to accomplish the challenge properly. By asking a kid to show you how he got this or that answer, and then saying "Well done!" or by giving a kid a little help to get over a math problem, we will boost the kid's confidence and help him feel comfortable with study.

When giving homework, teachers should keep this in mind. Parents should encourage their kids by complimenting them on the challenge accomplished.

Basics for Study

Here are some basic ideas that lead to good study habits.

1. Wherever study is to be carried out, the area should be well lit, well ventilated, spacious, and orderly. Not too hot, and not too cold.
2. Where the kid is expected to sit should be comfortable, but not soft. As a simple rule of thumb, the kid's back should be straight and the table or desk surface level ought to be the same height as the kid's elbow (when his arms are down by his side). Such a posture prevents slumping, aids respiration, and avoids cramping of hand and arm muscles.
3. For kids under the age of thirteen, any continuous period of study should not last more than sixty minutes. Should more study be required, a ten-minute break is a must. During this break, the kids should leave the study area. It is not necessary to organize games, or have the snack shop open. Just give them a little break to get the blood flowing, the air in the room renewed, and to give the eyes a rest.
4. Older kids can be expected to go a full ninety minutes, but never more than that without a little break.
5. All study areas should be areas of silence.
6. Study order
   a. It is beneficial to teach kids to "schedule" their study. In other words, say that they will spend twenty minutes on this, thirty on the other, ten on this, and encourage them to stick to this timetable as they study. If they finish something ahead of time, they can go on to the next thing. If they run out of time on a particular task, they can try and get the other things done earlier than sched-

uled. But with a little experience, they will get used to how much time a certain task will need. If kids find that they cannot fit everything into a respectable study period, tell them not to worry. Either they need to develop workable study habits, or they need to schedule more time for study. However, usually it will be the former.

b. It is also good to get the fast things out of the way first. If, for example, kids have some simple grammar exercises to do that will only take ten minutes to finish, get this out of the way first. It will free their minds for the more difficult things.

c. Once they get the fast things out of the way, head for the difficult. Leave the enjoyable until last.

d. Some people find it a good idea to segment their study. By this we mean, for example, breaking up the forty minutes a kid will need for a "brain burner" (writing an English essay on "ten good reasons to drink milk") into two twenty-minute slots separated by some other subject. This gives the mind the chance to keep on working, subconsciously, as the kid does something else. It can be quite amazing what they can come up with when they go back to something.

e. Leave time for a review check near the end of the study period. If the study period involved active reading (see number seven below), see if the kids can remember all the correct answers, or see if they still know that poem they knew so well an hour ago. This review helps consolidate the data in their minds. And if they get stuck on some math point, maybe now, in the review, they will come up with the way to do it correctly.

7. Active reading: Kids should "examine" a text and not just read it. They should grab it, shake it as hard as they can and see what falls out.A simple way of doing this is to jot down questions that might be made from the text on a separate piece of paper as they read. Once they have finished reading the text, they will close the book and take out the questions they have just written down. Then, on yet another separate piece of paper, they will try and answer. Like this:

Text to be studied:

"The King of Spain, Jorge VI, who reigned from 1610-1672, was one of the great builders of early European alliances between Mediterranean countries. After the Battle of Las Colinas, he signed a treaty with Prince Hugo of Naples which guaranteed peace for all countries of the Union and which put an end to rival faction fighting between the Bluegots and the Yellowgots. Jorge believed that only by making individual agreements with foreign powers, would he be able to consolidate Spain's trade routes with the East."[12]

Questions that the student could have written down on a separate piece of paper as he read:

1. Who was the King of Spain in 1622?
2. What happened after the battle of Las Colinas?
3. Who did Jorge sign a treaty with?
4. What did the treaty guarantee?
5. What effect did the treaty have?
6. Why was Jorge interested in building alliances with for eign powers?

Now, without opening the book, the kid will try and answer his own questions. It might run something like this:

1. Jorge IV
2. A treaty was signed
3.
4. the end of the war
5. opened up trade routes
6. to open up trade routes

Then the kid will open up the text again and check his answers. In the example we are following, he only got numbers two and six correct. So he will then take his questions and find the correct answer. Then he will close the text again and start answering his questions again on a new page and without checking previous attempts. The kid will do this until either he has all the answers right, or until his allotted time is up.

This technique of active reading can also be used to learn things by heart (poems, scripts, formula), but instead of writing questions down, the student will close the text and try and write out what he thinks he knows.

Alongside the in-text questions (questions that are answered within the text, Who was the King of Spain in 1622? for example), the student can also jot down research questions (answers that are not included in the text, What were the countries of the Union in times of Jorge VI? or, Where were the Bluegots from? for example). These research questions can call for investigative study that can be interesting and rewarding.

8. The capacity to relate: Our intelligence is made up of various sectors. And while memory may be one of the more important sectors, it is by no means the most important. And yet, we see all too often that certain types of study encouraged in some schools is totally memory based. This is hardly study in the human sense of the word. Parrots do the same. Whether it be in mathematics or language learning, science or history, it can be sad to see how much weight is given to the accumulation of mere data and to see how so much time is wasted. Far more important sectors of our intellect are the capacity of analysis (see the bits) and of synthesis (put the bits into a whole) and the capacity to relate.

   The capacity to analyze simply means the capability to individualize and weigh components. This art of analysis is so widely applicable in our everyday life that, if we want to be successful, be it in a professional or in a personal forum, a firm grasp of the basics is essential. Why a football game was lost, what went into Jorge VI's trade agreement, why one marriage is successful and the other flounders, why one product sells and the other stays on the shelf, why one person can be so happy and the other so depressed, are all examples of being able to analyze. And the sharper a person's analytical skills, the sharper his success can be. The art of synthesis, on the other hand, consists is being able to see many things at once and come to a precise and correct conclusion.

I was at a conference in Italy and although I understand Italian, I was interested to see how the English interpreter was doing with such a flowery Italian discourse. Nearing the end of his talk, the speaker (in Italian) said, "Having reviewed the eloquent and even mind-boggling events of the first twenty years of this accelerated and sometimes breakneck-speed century, when man was often at odds to keep up with himself, and having gone over the various factors that have gone into the makings of our company, elements that range from personnel difficulties to their successful and happy solutions, from the challenges of the times to the eagle-eyed vision of our leaders, from the attention to minor marketing ploys to the overall and global possibilities of the market economy, and then having remarked upon the enormous advances of science and technology in these latter years, I think it is obvious that we can conclude that...."

The English interpreter, after having been silent for all of the above paragraph, finally translated and said, "And so...."

This is a supreme example of the capacity to weed out the essential from the repetitious, the grain from the weed. It is a good example of synthesis.

And so, in our study, we should be constantly analyzing and synthesizing. Prodding everything with a why, and pulling everything together into a conclusion. Kids do have a natural tendency to analyze and to synthesis. A kid's inquisitiveness is a manifestation of the intellect's need to grasp the individual elements (typical of the early, or "why" years of life). Kids, especially as they grow into their teens, develop the art of synthesis and are perfectly capable of commenting on an entire day's event in one simple phrase. When a parent asks, "How was school today?" they will simply say "OK." Or when asked "What did you do today in school?" they will answer, "Stuff." Applying and developing these skills in study will greatly advance a kid's enjoyment of study.

Study and Homework

It is not a bad idea to make a difference between study and homework. Homework is an assignment the teacher gives a kid to do, an assignment that will be checked in the next class. The subject matter of homework is essential to grade curriculum. Homework is something you have to get done for the next class. Whereas study, putting it rather simply, is "feeding our brain." A good teacher will give homework that develops a kid's intellectual capacity rather than just his finger muscles. But it is beneficial to make a difference between study and homework. Our focus as educators should be study and not homework. All too often kids can get through their homework without even studying (without feeding their brain). And especially in earlier grades, it is all too easy to obtain acceptable scores in school without too much personal brain activity.

Knowing how to study, how to feed the brain, will help the kid do his homework better, and help him to enjoy doing it. Homework, when a kid knows how to study, is exercise for his brainpower, and can be food for his brain.

A study of various national education systems shows certain priorities at odds with one another. The American system is geared, in theory at least, to developing a kid's study ability, whereas some Central American state educational systems, notably Mexico, aim at more tangible, practical results. It is said that a Mexican can tell you what two plus two is, whereas the American will tell you why he thinks you can add two and two. While there is no clear-cut difference (spelling may be bad in Mexico in spite of the practical focus, although it is just as bad in the United States), basic tendencies do stand out. And so without going into too much detail, let it be enough for us to say here that our kids should know what two plus two is and why. We want them to be able to recite Shakespeare and to enjoy its beauty. We want them to know what the biggest city in the world is and why. We want them to know the Ten Commandments, how they are to be applied, and why.

To this end, developing solid personal study capabilities is essential. Why and how a wheel goes around, why and how smoke rises, why we must go good, avoid evil and how.

Private Classes

Personal tuition (tutoring), or private classes, is when there is one teacher per student. As a general rule, they are to be avoided since usually they are of little real help to the student. This is not because private classes are worthless, but because they lend themselves all too easily to misuse.

Many who had constant private classes openly admit that apart from actually hating the classes (because they took time away from other, more enjoyable activities), they benefited little from them. And these same people will be the first to admit that it was not the teacher's fault, but their own. In fact, private classes subconsciously encourage the kid not to worry about the normal class and to leave things for the private class. And some see private lessons as a crutch—being bad at a subject is covered over, or excused, by saying, "Oh, yes. I'm not much good at that, but I am taking private lessons."

So rather than help the kid make the most of the normal class, private classes make the kid more dependent on the private at the expense of the normal.

Private classes, however, can be very helpful in limited situations, much as caustic soda is useful for freeing up drainpipes. However, use of caustic soda on a regular basis points not only to a blockage but to bad drains. If a kid hasn't grasped a particular point in math or in chemistry, a private lesson or two should be able to free the blockage. Or if a kid has been under anesthetic for a few months (very sick), then a few private classes should bring him up to speed.

But as I said, as a general rule, private classes are to be avoided. There is also another aspect. When doing research for a certain project, I decided to see how a school attained its guarantee of what it called "academic perfection." Tuition fees were rather high and the student/teacher ratio was one to nine. I pretended I had a kid who was good, never repeated a year, but who nonetheless was a bit slow. I asked the school if it was capable of getting academic perfection from my kid. The answer was a definite "Yes, of course." "All needy students receive daily personal lessons." "Is this included in the tuition fee?" I asked. Then the sting, "Of course not. Each thirty minutes of personal lessons comes at forty-six dollars plus tax. Most of our students have regular personal lessons." I could get no definite bottom line figure from them for a year's tuition ("depends on the student"), but it was well in excess of thirty thousand dollars. What good was an educational system that relied so heavily on extraordinary means?

Another aspect:

If a kid gets into fourth grade, it means he qualified by getting through third grade. If fourth grade teachers then think private classes are needed, or that the kid is not up to the work, who's at fault? The previous teacher? The present teacher? Rarely, hardly ever, will it be the kid who needs help.

And another:

A gloating mother boasted at a party of just how many private lessons her daughter was taking. "She does piano, ballet, and painting. And of course she has her math tutor and her linguistic tutors, and then of course there's Mr. Sym who coaches her on her science projects." "Lovely, my dear," was the dry retort from her listener. "Yes, but our daughter goes to a good school."

And another:

In Ireland, I was speaking with a mother of two children who was telling me just how dedicated the teachers her children had and what a good school it was.

"Nancy called me the other day. She's Jennie's teacher. She asked me if it would be alright if Jennie got out of school a little late for a couple of days as she wanted to give her just a little extra coaching in math. I thanked Nancy for her offer, but candidly told her that I could not afford private lessons for any of my children. "Oh, no!" Nancy said laughing. "These aren't classes, just a little boost for Jennie ... I'm a teacher," she said."

Any teacher worth his salt will take his students seriously and should be willing to go a little out of his way to help them over the little obstacles. This applies also to any educational institution worth its salt. It should have a built-in mechanism that allows for this. Directed study can cater to this need for periodic boosting admirably.

The quality of a school is inversely proportional to the number of private classes given.

GAELIC BOOK OF WISDOM

THE WORKINGS OF A GOAL

A little healthy psychology can go a long way. This section speaks of how we can tap one of man's deeper desires.

When all is said and done, the fact remains—we all like getting something done. We have a built-in mechanism that aims us at getting things done and that clicks when we actually get something done. This affects—and can be seen in—our everyday life. The satisfaction of a day's work done, a good game played, a tape well compiled, a meal eaten, or a letter written and posted. Sometimes it is simply getting something small done, like tidying your desk or sorting your socks. Other times it may be a little more ambitious: painting, refitting a car engine, or decorating the house. Sometimes these goals can be long-term and very ambitious: a happy marriage, a solid career, or educating a child. But the constant is there, the pattern set—we are made to get things done.

I am sure that there are many explanations for this, but we will not busy ourselves with them right now. It will be enough to say that just as eating is necessary—and is many times pleasurable—so too is fulfilling our mission in life. The value of this drive can be illustrated by its effects. And here are two:

First, the world will usually be a better place for it (even if it's just a letter to your mom, a tidy desk, or a nice painting). The second effect is the human satisfaction element. We feel good when we get something done, when we do something right. And this "feeling" goes way deeper than a full stomach or a good siesta. It is a "value" feeling. Our bodies may complain—house decorating can be a tiring task, a happy marriage is tough going—but deep down our spirit breathes and grows stronger.

As educators, we do well to tap into this inborn instinct and to use it to educate. We must train our kids in the art of goal achievement. We must be careful not to project ourselves or our kids too far into the future, but rather we should busy ourselves and our kids about today. Christ teaches us this when he says that we have enough to do today and that we shouldn't worry too much about tomorrow. With the following example, this will become clear.

An educator in a boarding school was concerned about preparing his kids for the future, for their life as good parents. And he was convinced that the fruits of his labors would not be seen now, but later. His main concern was to embark his kids on the road of "final formation." He didn't worry too much about the present, but he was totally focused on the future. He wanted to give the kids values that would make them men of character in later years.

His talks were always about the need for adult maturity, his dialogues always aimed at being responsible men. He was aware that he would have the kids for just nine months (he worked in an academy) and that in a few years the kids would be men. "I give them values that will bear fruit in years to come," he would say.

But the present was a mess. The kids' dorm was always untidy. His kids were lackadaisical. Their grades were generally poor. "You must be patient. They are only children now, but they will be men tomorrow and my patience will triumph," was a favorite line. He was not respected, and his kids did more or less what they wanted and when they wanted. He was more a bad grandfather than a good dad. As time wore on, his group got more and more out of hand. Two months prior to the end of the year, he was relieved of his position and another educator was put in his place. There was little this newly appointed educator could do. He basically got some semblance of order into the group but that was all. Used to loose living, the kids didn't look kindly upon anyone who wanted them to get things done in the present tense. Basically it was a year wasted. The educator had not realized that the present is the only time we have.

The opposite can also happen. An educator will focus exclusively on the today. Bedrooms will be tidy, classrooms neat, uniforms in order ... all good in themselves, but without an eye for the future, they will lack what is most important—the backbone of conviction.

It is unrealistic to believe that our kids will be men of character tomorrow if they are not kids of character today. Kids of character are forged today. Today they must be made and put to the test. Only this way can we help straighten out the buckles and bumps. Only this way can we be anyway sure that our kids are ready. No mother will give her child a cookbook and tell her to read it when she is married. The mother will take her daughter into the kitchen and have her help her cook as a child. No father worth his salt will extol the virtue of honesty without demanding that his kid be honest here and now.

So, if we want our kids to be goal achievers tomorrow, we must train them in goal achievement today. And as the time we have with kids is short, our training them must be oriented at the future but practiced in the present. Short-term goals are perhaps the most effective human formation tool an educator possesses.

Whys and Wherefores

Knowing the reasons behind the rules makes compliance a lot easier and certainly more human. We do not necessarily ask that kids understand and accept the many reasons behind what is asked of them, but we would do well to help them understand. Even if a kid has heard an explanation and maybe does not agree with it, we will still expect him to follow the rule in the hope that some day he will want to understand.

Here are some ideas that come to mind. I am pretty sure that the reader, once he sets his mind to it, can come up with more and more valid reasons, but in the meantime here are some. It is important that the kids see that there is a reason for each rule, or way of doing things, and that this reason is part of the "bigger picture."

Why do we ask the kids not to put their hands in their pockets? (Good manners do require that we, as adults, and kids do not go around with our hands in our pockets.)

- In olden days, if you wanted to attack your enemy, you would hide what you had in your hand (a knife) by putting your hands in your pockets. Having your hands in view was a way of saying, "Hey, I'm friendly!"
- If you fall with your hands in your pockets, there is little hope of you protecting your face.
- A man is not afraid of a little cold. Having your hands out

always is proof of one's virility.

- Having your hands in your pockets puts your trousers out of shape.

Why is it not correct to pull the sleeves of your sweater down over your hands to keep them warm?

- First, it is a bad reflection on your parents who have not been able to provide you with a pair of gloves.
- Second, it stretches and disfigures your sweater.
- Third, it shows that you are not clever enough to dress correctly for the weather.

Why do schools ask their students to wear uniforms?

- Far from trying to "level out everybody," a uniform brings an identity. A uniform stands, or should stand, for an ideal. Give me a kid with a uniform and I'll show you a kid with an ideal. It also gives a sense of working together towards the same goal.
- On a practical note, although there is nothing impractical about a good ideal, having to wear a uniform frees the student from having to worry excessively about how others see him. This is especially true for adolescents, girls as much as boys. And a uniform will be the most fitting attire for the specific activities within a school.

Why is it not a good idea to whistle indoors?

- By its very nature, the pitch of a whistle is high and therefore penetrating, allowing it to travel further than the spoken—or hummed—word. A whistle will go far beyond where the spoken word will, and it will disturb others who are distant.

When setting the table, why should we place the blade of the knife towards the plate?

- We do not want to offer a jagged edge to our neighbor.

Why is it bad manners to wear a hat, or a cap, indoors?

- We should trust the guest's roof to protect us from the sun and from the rain. Wearing hats or caps in the house is the same as saying, "I don't trust your roof."

Why should a man open a door for a woman?

- The very act of pushing a door requires force that we should not expect a woman to exert. It's basically charity—doing something so that someone else will not have to.

Why should a man open and close a car door for a woman?

- It is not a case of a woman not understanding the mechanics of how a door opens and closes but rather a desire to save a woman from exerting her physical powers to open and close a door.

Why should a student stand when a teacher enters the room?

- Basically one stands to show respect. But what does respect mean? Simply put, it means that we take the other person into account; we are willing to "lend him our ears." We stand, as a sign of respect, to show that we are ready to do whatever he might ask of us. Standing up shows our readiness. If we were sitting down, we would waste time in getting up.

Why should a student go to bed in silence? (on outings or at boarding schools)

- It stops the kids from messing around.
- It helps the kids to reflect upon the contents of the night talk (or camp fire talk).
- It calms the kids down for sleeping.

Why should women "go first?"

- Well, they shouldn't. It's simple but true. A man should go first. When a man opens a door to a restaurant for a woman, he should first make sure that inside the restaurant there are no thieves or mad people waiting to pounce upon the woman. Once he has done so, or once he has proven the safety of what lies beyond, then he should open the door for the woman and let her through. If he doesn't want to get in her way, he will obviously have to let her through first. However, we can usually suppose that the man has checked out the restaurant with the necessary foresight and thus acquired the security that the place is reputable.
- But women should go first because, if they are going into a restaurant, a man must show that although he is hungry, he respects the woman enough to let her in first, putting a hold on his hunger. If they are going to a cinema, although he wants to see the movie too, he shows that he wants the woman to enjoy as much of the show as possible, even if he misses a half a second.
- As well as that there's a psychological aspect to be considered—a woman, or anybody really, will feel more protected when the person looking over them is slightly behind them

Why should you not cut your nails in public?

- This is a simple rule of common decency. We do not want bits of ourselves all over the place. While this rule may appear unnecessary to mention, it is broken again and again by kids and by adults alike. Kids will bite their nails. Adults will use nail clippers. But the end result is always the same—little bits of unhygienic us all over the place. That's why it is not correct.

Why should a kid be quiet when an adult is speaking?

- This rule of respect has its root in the fact that usually the adult will have something important to say. Unfortunately many adults have little contribution to make, but good manners require that we give them the benefit of the doubt.

We know it is not correct to interrupt someone when they are talking, but why is it not correct?

- Basically, when we interrupt we are saying, "My idea is better than yours. Be quiet and listen to wisdom speak." In other words, I'm better than you. We are all here to serve, not to dominate.
- This is not applicable, of course, to those lively conversations that invigorate any friendly discussion. In these, sometimes it is impolite not to join in the general mayhem.

Why should kids not go into some stores?

- Even toy stores can have novelty toys or postcards that are vulgar. Visiting such stores may be seen as a lowering of oneself to a level of cheap vulgarity that befits no man or woman. But whether it is vulgar novelty toys or soft-porn magazines, the kids should be told clearly why they are requested not to enter certain stores.

Why do we kneel in the chapel?

- Kneeling is a sign of submission, a sign that whom we kneel before can do what they wish with us. Have you ever tried to run away on your knees?
- It also implies a certain sacrifice and thus shows our willingness to suffer, to do something that is a little costly in return for the privilege of being allowed into such august company.
- This same reason is behind our kneeling down correctly. Some might kneel on one knee only. This is a halfhearted way to kneel. Rather than be a position of submission it is almost one of an athlete on a starting block! And some will slouch down and sit on their heels. This is a sitting position, not a kneeling one and is more associated with a desire to be entertained or fed rather than an act of submission. And then there are those who will kneel but slump over whatever is in front of them. This is not the correct posture in chapel as it simply says, "I am kneeling because I have to, but I really don't care much for the person I am kneeling before."

Why is "soap and water" the preferred scent?

- In bygone days, our medieval—and not so medieval—ancestors did not have a liking for water and would, could they afford it, douse themselves in perfume. This perfume was not meant to enhance their presence, but to hide the stench of body odor.

- Nowadays, perfumes, deodorants, and lotions are not usually used to cover up bad smells, but rather have the intention of making our presence more agreeable. And there is no doubt about the need for a simple antiseptic after shaving. However, what should be avoided are perfumes—be in it on women or on men—that invade another's space. Your perfume may be another's poison (in fact, there's a widely used woman's perfume with just that very name). Out of respect for others, and also to show that you are as you appear and are not trying to hide what you really are, "soap and water," as well as being the most healthy for you, is the safest scent. Having said this, a discreet aftershave for men or a delicate perfume for women can be tasteful.

Why should people walk and not run indoors?

- Given the fact that corridors and other indoor facilities, with the exception of a gym, are usually restricted in size, there is a lack of visibility and reaction spaces needed to avoid a crash.
- The same could be said for the use of stairs, with the added element of gravity—if you slip or fall, you stand a good chance of banging your head.
- There is also another reason that is worthy of consideration. Someone who runs, unless it is for reasons of sports, usually does so because he is late. Being late shows that a person has not yet managed to organize his time. He is, in simple language, not a responsible or dependable person. Or, if the

run is directed to the dining room, it shows an unattractive animallike side of the person, much as a group of hungry dogs dash to the scene of a kill.

Why should kids avoid using portable music devices?

- The question is somewhat erroneous. Portable music devices, such as Walkmans and iPods can be useful. Their use, however, should not exclude people's company. In other words, if kids are together, it is bad manners to use these devices as they block out people and say, "I'm not interested in you."
- Similarly these devices should not be used when riding a bike or horse, or when driving, as they distract you from hearing what might be a warning or even a greeting.
- Such devices, over a long period, may induce self-centeredness and a lack of sociability, just as overdoing the computer can. But if we follow what we have just mentioned, there is no real danger of this.

Why it is not right to drag your feet?

- It marks the floor.
- It makes noise.
- It also shows that you are incapable of dressing yourself correctly as quite often foot-dragging is due to footwear that is too big for you.
- It also shows that if you cannot even control your own feet, how are you going to be able to do more important things?

Why is it wrong to put your elbows on the table while eating?

- The simple reason is to avoid invading the other person's space. With your elbows on the table your radius of action on the table is much larger. Keeping your elbows down helps you to avoid knocking over things (glasses and the like) on the table.

Why is it incorrect to use your fingers to bring food to your mouth?

- First, it is incorrect because of the hygiene factor. But even supposing you thoroughly washed your hands before a meal, it would still be impolite to use your fingers. It is to be assumed that your host has gone to the trouble of setting out knives and forks for this purpose. Not availing of them is simply to snub him. No cutlery has been invented for bringing bread to your mouth, so fingers do not contravene this rule. In such places where cutlery is not provided, fingers are totally legitimate.

Why should shoes always be well polished?

- It is nice to see clean shoes. But it also tells the person you are with that you care and that, just as you have taken care with the top or visible part of your shoes, they can be sure that the underside is also clean.
- It also shows that we are, or at least try to be, above the dirt we might walk in. And besides, real polish—not the self-shining liquid sold in many stores—helps care for the shoes and thus they last longer (and the longer they last, the more comfortable they are!)

Why is physical contact between out-of-family educators and students limited to handshaking and the occasional pat on the back?

- The easy answer is that anything other than that could land an educator in court on charges—ridiculous as it may seem—ranging from child abuse to sexual harassment.
- But that's not the real why behind this rule. There are many "real whys" and each one is directly tied in to our mission as an educator.
- There are three situations when an educator might wish to go beyond the physical contact allowed: sentimentality, anger, and retribution.
- What can be more natural than an affectionate cupping of a kid's face in your hands as you tell him he's great? Nothing, if you're the kid's mother or father. Or what can be more natural than sitting down beside a kid and giving him a hug to help him through a rough moment? Nothing, if you're the kid's brother or sister. An educator is neither father nor brother to his kids. He is their educator. The urge to become a father or brother figure can sometimes be strong, but yielding to such a temptation is nothing short of waving good-bye to your mission and responsibility as an educator. There's something wrong with a dentist who starts doing brain surgery.
- Another situation is anger—the kids are unruly, will not listen to you, and are generally running amuck. The immediate response is to control the situation by lashing out. At least this will get their attention. An educator, however, must be a man guided by principle and not by passion. We are educators, not sergeants.

- Or, a kid has done wrong and you feel that a slap, or an old-fashioned whipping, would be the just retribution for his evil acts. But slapping or whipping is not just, because it matches the evil done with a physical equivalent. And this is not correct. Let's say a kid has stolen another guy's rollerblades or a girl has spoken badly about another girl and you find out. How can we equate a lack of respect for another person (or his property) with something physical? We cannot. We are talking two different spheres here. It's like the Mafia boss who builds a church for his local neighborhood, thinking that with his money he can buy into heaven. We're talking different currencies here.
- So in order to be true to our mission as educators—educators not parents—men of principle not passion, just and fair men, we do well to avoid any physical contact that goes beyond the handshake and the occasional pat on the back.[13]

Why should we treat timetables, or schedules, as quasi-sacred?

- There are two main reasons behind schedules. One is so that everybody knows where he is supposed to be and what he is supposed to be doing. The other reason is that people work better when they know they have only a certain amount of time to do things. "Murphy's Law" states, "Work expands according to the time available."
- When dealing with more than one person, schedules are essential. But schedules, an element of discipline, must never be confused with discipline in its deeper sense. Wanting to do what is right and doing it by one's own volition, inner

discipline, is as far removed from schedules as calculus is from cheese.

- But once a schedule has been established by the competent authority, it takes on an almost God-like authority. It is, put clearly, what God wants us to be doing. This does not mean of course that if we are late we have sinned. But as Saint Augustine put it, God may not necessarily want you to do what you are told to do, but he does want you to do as you are told to do. In other words, he may not want you necessarily to be in class at nine-twenty in the morning, but he does want you to be doing your duty (which at nine-twenty in the morning, for you, means being in class).
- So from this we see that schedules are more than just a time management option. It is what you should be doing. And if you're not doing what you're supposed to be doing, you'd better have a pretty good reason.

The Question of Punishment

When and how should we punish our kids? This sounds like an absolutely terrible question to ask, but I bring it up fully aware that the reader has read through the chapter on positive motivation and fully aware too that sometimes kids will not react to this form of motivation as we would wish.

If some time is spent on talking about punishment, it is only to ensure that when it is necessary to punish it will be formative.

You might find it necessary to go over this chapter again as this topic can easily be misunderstood—especially with the way I write!

We should punish our kids when they break a rule that they

know and that they know they should have and could have done right. This "something they could have done right" is important for emphasis. It is rooted in our role as educators. We are not policemen waiting to ticket any infringement of the law. Nor are we scientists in a lab where mice will run through an electrified maze and eventually find their way out or be executed in the process. Nor are we talking about punishment such as whipping or bread and water rations. We are educating people.

Here are some examples:

A kid forgets to do his homework. He should be punished. The very fact that he forgot means that he knew—you cannot forget something you didn't know.

A kid is caught in the kitchen having a late night snack without permission. If he's a new kid to a boarding school, maybe he doesn't know the rules. He should be told the rule. But if he knows the rule, he should be punished.

A kid "borrows" something from another kid without permission. This is basically stealing. Unless the kid is mentally challenged, he will know that taking other people's things (even if the other person is his brother or sister) is wrong and should therefore be punished.

You ask for volunteers to help you clean up the dining area after an impromptu snack. A kid offers to help. You leave him at it and return ten minutes later only to find that he has been messing around instead of clearing up, or that he has not really tidied up properly at all. Strange as it may seem, because after all he did volunteer, the kid should be punished. Not because he volunteered, not because the place is not tidy, but because he could have done better and he didn't. (Yes, this is a tough one.)

So punishment must be considered a logical result of not having done something right that could and should have been done right. But the "when" of punishment must also take into account another element—we should only punish when it will be beneficial. This isn't as easy as it seems as there are two elements that we must take into consideration: one is the immediate action required by the educator to halt bad behavior, and the other is the actual punishment that must be dealt out.

Signal, Evaluate, Punish—The Steps Toward Punishment

Here are six examples:

1. Johnny has been misbehaving all month. Basically, he cannot tolerate authority. He has been disrespectful and has been repeatedly punished. But he just keeps getting worse. The punishments are making him more obstinate in his wrongdoing. He considers himself a martyr for the cause and glories in punishment (or at least he pretends to). And now, in private, he has just insulted you.
2. Andrew is having a hard time. His parents are going through a divorce, and he has been sent to the academy so that he wouldn't see all that was going on. And he knows it. A good kid at heart, Andrew however has just hit a guy over the head with a tennis racket. The victim of the blow laughs it off and is not hurt. You saw it all from afar.
3. Jimmy has just received his monthly grades. Not a particularly bright student, he has made an effort but his results are miserable. He loses all interest in academics and is totally distracted during class. His teacher asks you for action.
4. Tom is one of those guys who takes his game seriously. With

just minutes to go before the end of a game, his team is one point down. He tries to encourage his teammates not to lose heart and to give their best in these dying moments of the game. The ball goes to one of his teammates. But the player starts laughing and doing silly tricks with the ball instead of playing the game. Believing defeat to be inevitable this player is obviously making fun of the game. Tom runs over to him and calls for the ball. The dumb player kicks it into the sideline with a "Wheeeeee!" Tom punches him in the nose.

5. Ted is doing his best to be just as he should be. He is making a real and constant effort, but he is wild. One morning at breakfast, he knocks over the jug of milk, and it spills all over the table and onto the floor. A passing kid slips on the milky floor, bangs his head, and lies unconscious.
6. Bill is very quiet. That's the way he is. He keeps to himself. He's a loner. He thinks he's quite special. He looks down his nose at the other kids and obviously feels superior. One afternoon, someone asks to borrow his hockey stick, but he refuses to lend it.

Sometimes to signal a wrongdoing, it will be enough for the kid to see the educator looking at him (ex. 1). An educator's look should be one of his most potent weapons. Other times it will be necessary to call the kid over, either immediately or a little later, and mention to him that what he did was wrong (ex. 2, 4, 5).

Apart from signaling the wrongdoing, oftentimes we must take immediate action to stop the wrongdoing. This is very obvious in example four. We should intervene immediately—if the referee does not—to stop the kid from punching the kid again in the nose.

And in all the other examples too, we must signal the wrongdoing so that the kid knows that we know he has done wrong.

But signaling is not punishment. It is, if you will, the first step towards punishment. There are even times when the actual signaling will make further punishment unnecessary.

Each punishment must be evaluated. In other words, we must take into account the kid's actual status (what external factors led him to behave this way, how much could he have avoided it, is it normal or exceptional behavior for this kid), the gravity of the wrongdoing, an effective and formative punishment, and the kid's receptiveness.

Kid's status:

In example one, where we see constant disrespect, an external factor to be taken into account would be the kid's actual age. Most teenage kids hit a point in their lives where authority is extremely uncomfortable. Another external factor might be that we, as educators, are coming down too hard on this kid, treating him as a ten-year-old when in fact he may be thirteen or fourteen and will resent us for this (so we are part of the equation). These external factors do not make the bad behavior any "less bad," but they will have a bearing on the actual punishment. Then, if this wrongdoing is normal for the kid, we must evaluate our previous handling of such incidents. Quite possibly we have not been formative in our prior punishments. We must take these things into consideration.

Gravity of wrongdoing:

When evaluating a punishable situation, we must take into account the grievousness of what the kid has done. This must have a direct bearing on the punishment we will deal out. And here we are called to educate, to teach the kids a correct value scale.

Here is a question: What is the most grievous offense a kid can commit?

Seriously injuring an educator? No. Insulting his mother? No. (Sorry, moms!) Burning the building down? No. Leading kids into sexual misconduct? No. Speaking badly about others behind their back? No. To find the answer we must turn to the Gospels. The only sin without forgiveness, and therefore the most grievous, is the sin against the Holy Spirit. Theologians tell us that this translates into despair, a nonacceptance of God's mercy. It's the "I'm-so-bad-not-even-God-can-save-me" syndrome. That's the worst thing that a kid—or anybody—can do,[14] to believe he is useless and unable to be saved. Having noted this, we must say that there are degrees of gravity.

This answer leads us to an interesting conclusion regarding our role as "punishing" educators—we are not called to punish every bad deed. We are not called to punish a kid having bad thoughts about another person. We are not even called to punish a kid for not being as good as he could be (the sin of omission, a hideous crime all the more dangerous as it often goes undetected).

Moralists talk of the internal forum and the external forum. The internal forum is what goes on inside a person (thoughts, daydreams, ideas, fantasies, decisions). The external forum is what happens on the outside (the way a person behaves, what he does, how he speaks). Here's our rule:

An educators' punishment should be concerned exclusively with the external forum in as much as it affects the external discipline (or running) of the family, school, or club. An educator's educational efforts, however, are aimed at the internal forum.

Here then is a list of things that educators should deem punishable:

- Any action that harms or puts other people in either physical or moral danger (fights, speaking badly of others, telling lies, sexual misconduct)
- Any incompliance with their responsibility as a kid (chores, respect for siblings and friends, attention in class, healthy concern for good grades, conscientious study)
- Any incompliance with established rules of conduct (schedules, silence, dress code, respect for others)
- Disobeying legitimate authorities (parents, teachers, coaches, bus drivers)
- Any action that could result in harm to the property of others (theft, vandalism, bad usage of equipment or school facilities or property)
- Fostering any of the above in others

Punishment Qualities

The qualities of punishment should be remedial, formative, effective, just, and prudently immediate.

Remedial

Now, after signaling the wrongdoing, and after having evaluated the situation, it is necessary to come up with an effective and formative punishment. Both adjectives are important: effective and formative. We must distinguish between punitive punishment and remedial punishment.

Punitive punishment is when someone does something wrong and must pay for it, like getting a parking ticket. Punitive punishment does absolutely nothing to help you to be a better person. It just makes the "getting caught" painful. No matter how many parking tickets you get, you will never be able to park your car any better.

Remedial punishment, on the other hand, seeks to right what was wronged. Sometimes a convicted vandal will be sentenced to hours of community service. An example is the recent case of an American drunk who totally wrecked the gardens of a neighbor by driving roughshod over the lawns and flower beds and was sentenced to a course in gardening and to spending six months caring for the local town square greenery—as well as paying for fixing up the wrecked garden. Remedial punishment is not "doing something good because you did something bad" (you hit that kid, so now go and pick up all the papers in the patio), but rather "doing right what you did wrong before."

So we are talking about remedial punishment, always.

Formative

To be formative, the punishment must be in the same area as the fault. If, for example, a kid's fault is in the field of charity (example 2, page 181) where the kid hits another kid over the head with a tennis racket, our punishment must be geared at boosting the kid's charity levels. Ten laps around the college campus will do little to help the kid's charity. Just as the kid who has just insulted us will gain little by writing out, "I will respect my educator" four thousand times.

So we must know what area the kid has erred in and then pick an appropriate antidote. Sometimes our very punishment will teach the kid a lot about the connection between things.

For example, a kid is late for an outing. As a result, his bus leaves half an hour late, and all the kids in his group miss thirty minutes of fun in the theme park. Not good. So as a punishment he is told to prepare, serve, and tidy up after the evening snack. (As a practical consequence, he will have no time for snack himself.)

What has this got to do with being late? By being late, he showed that he didn't care for his group. Preparing the snack—and doing it well—and serving it shows that he does care. (And by the way, make sure the kid doesn't go to bed hungry. Give him a quick and silent minute or two to have a glass of milk and a cookie.)

> **Weak and worthless the educator who shuns punishment. Useless and destructive he who uses it alone.**
> GAELIC BOOK OF WISDOM

However, sometimes a kid's lateness can be the educator's fault. Maybe he wasn't clear in his orders, or maybe his word isn't respected—seeing that it's always changing—or maybe the schedule is too tight. But whatever the cause, it should be addressed. This formative aspect will put the educator himself to the test, as it entails much more than just dishing out laps or push-ups.

Being formative also means that our punishments must not deform other aspects of the kid. Two wrongs never make a right. If a kid has been disrespectful, making others lose their respect for him will be in no way formative. Push-ups in public view, as a punishment for a lack of respect, or for anything else for that matter, will only make the others lose their respect for that kid. Putting a kid in a classroom corner with a donkey's hat on for being lazy in his class work will be just as nonformative. We must never, ever, humiliate a kid in public. Even if we should deem fit to humiliate a kid in private, we must be aware that humiliation is a treacherous weapon and, more often than not, will in the end go against us.

Being formative means that our punishment must not be stupid.

Sending a kid out to do ten laps around the patio in the pouring rain isn't just stupid and totally unjustified, but also grounds for a legal case.

Denying a kid a meal is as anti-gospel as it is ridiculous.

Having a kid kneel in public is an outright abuse of an educator's authority.

Having kids write out "I must be good" one hundred times speaks wonders for the educator's creativity and grasp of his mission.

Having a kid do jumping jacks or run around on bended knees is not just laughable, it's criminal.

Keep in mind, maybe when we were kids we received such punishments, and maybe these punishments helped us. But these punishments are not the right way of doing things.

Effective

To be effective, a punishment must "hurt." By this we mean that it will push a kid to do something (good) that he would not do spontaneously. Any wrongdoing has two consequences: the visible and the invisible. The punishments we set, if they are to be effective, must address both consequences.

When a kid steals something, the visible consequence is that something is missing. The invisible consequence is that the kid has shown a lack of respect for another person's property. When a kid punches someone in the nose, the visible consequence is the bloody nose, the invisible—a lack of charity resulting (possibly) from overheated passion. It is this "invisible" consequence that will give us the key to effectiveness. Any punishment—or education—that aims at addressing only the visible consequences will fall way short of the mark. That is why writing lines and push-ups should hardly ever be considered.

As we have said, our punishments should be remedial (see page 181) and limited to the external forum (see page 180). But our education must be aimed at the internal forum, to forming the kid's heart. The more formative and effective the punishment, the more we will be able to use the external forum as a way of getting into a kid's heart.

The guy who punches the other in the nose will be punished (external forum, visible consequence) by being asked to do something that would normally be an expression of charity (the opposite of what he did)—maybe he could forego eating candy for a day and give any candy he buys on that day to the injured guy. But unless we address and try to educate (not punish) the invisible consequence (the lack of charity), our punishment will not be effective. Usually, the best way to address this aspect is to have the wrongdoer admit his error in private and then aologize to whoever suffered. It is this heartfelt apology that must animate the accomplishment of the punishment; otherwise the punishment will be hollow and ineffective. Sometimes this apology may not be totally wholehearted. Not to worry... it's a start.

To be effective, we must know when to implement the punishment. Usually we should not dish out a punishment there and then. If a kid is angry, or upset, or embarrassed because he has been caught in the act, he will not get the benefit of the punishment and will see it as punitive and not in any way remedial. A good course to follow is, "Jimmy, be in my office before supper." But never say, "Jimmy, we'll talk about this next week in dialogue." Don't let the sun go down without setting the record straight.

There are two other qualities that our punishments should have: *justice* and *celerity*.

Justice

Kids have a distinct sense of justice. Whereas adults may accept injustice out of weariness or because doing something about it may upset the way they themselves behave, kids are sharp about justice issues. And this is not a bad thing. In fact, this was one of the childlike attributes that Christ referred to when he said that only those who become like a child will enter into heaven.

We have to educate a kid's sense of justice, not ignore it. The guy who gets a tennis racket over his head will want his assailant to receive equal in return. He wants to see the other guy pay as much as he has—and maybe more—"to teach him a lesson." Justice must be forthcoming. We must address the situation. We are not taking vengeance here, but implementing justice. A wrong has been committed and must be righted. By giving the aggressor a suitable punishment (see Evaluation, page 179), we not only are forming the kid we punish, but also the kid who got the racket over the head.

Justice must also be visible to be considered accomplished. Saying something like, "Ah, forget it! The kid's having a rough time" is bad news for an educator. Punishment for the aggressor may simply be a matter of lowering his conduct grade. I am in no way advocating physical punishment as a just retribution for physical damage done. What I am saying is that justice must be done and visibly seen to be done.

Celerity

Celerity, not haste, is another quality of punishment. We have already said that we should be careful to evaluate the appropriate punishment, but now I also say that punishment must not be too long in coming.

An educator came to me one Friday and told me of a ten-year-old boy who had drawn an obscene design on the blackboard and asked me what he should do about it.

"Clean the blackboard and punish him immediately."

"Yes, I think I have to. What should the punishment be?"

As I knew the boy in question, a lively kid, very unsure of himself and desperately looking to be accepted by his peers, I suggested something that would show him that what he did was out of order and in no way helped him make friends.

"Have him write out ten qualities he thinks anybody wishing to be his best friend should have." "But that will take him ten minutes! I don't think that is really addressing the question."

"It is if you have him do it on Saturday morning when the others are at the mall. And have him scrub down all the blackboards in the school as well."

The educator hemmed and hawed.

"And don't forget to call his parents. Tell them what the kid has done, and what we are doing about it."

"I think this kid is precocious. I think he is a dangerous element for the others. I am worried about him, about what he could do to the others."

The educator was expressing a legitimate concern in a delicate area. I asked him what then he wanted to do.

"I think we should expel the kid."

"If you really think the kid is as dangerous as you say he is, then you must send him home immediately. Call his parents and say he's on the next flight home and explain to them exactly what has happened. I know the parents. I'll back you up."

The educator was hesitant. And he was right to be so. This kid was as hyperactive as they come. He wanted to grab his classmates' attention, and so what better way than by doing something totally stupid? Or maybe he was dared to do it. Maybe all the kids would love to do it, just to see what would happen, but no one dared, so he dared. After all, he was only ten, but you never can be too careful.

"Maybe I'll cut him off from the others for a week." "But if he's dangerous to the moral fiber of the school," I said, "he will be no better after a week of being by himself. And if he is a danger to the school, he must be sent home immediately. Personally I do not think he is, but we do need to be watchful. Another episode vaguely resembling this and I'll bring him to the airport myself."

But the educator wasn't convinced one way or the other. Was this the end of the story? He spent a week thinking about what to do and finally decided that he had overreacted and that the kid wasn't a danger after all—or maybe he was. In the meantime, justice was not served and the kid never knew why he was not punished for having done such a stupid thing. And the other kids thought it was quite all right to make obscene drawings on the blackboards.

Before punishing, check it out, and then do it.

A Note for Schools—A Good Beginning

In our work with kids, a good start is essential. Everything and everybody must be ready before the kids arrive. Improvisation wrecks education. But let us suppose that everything is in perfect order, the staff has been well trained, and the new kids arrive. It is obvious that the kids will come face to face with a whole load of rules and regulations that will be new to them. What to do when the kids do not follow the new rules?

The good running of the academy or school, external discipline in other words, must take precedence in the beginning. Kids must learn the rules about silence, about respect, about punctuality, about order. We will not have worked with them sufficiently in the first two weeks to allow us to deal individually with each kid. They will be treated, in the beginning I repeat, as a group. But individuals will break the rules. So they will have to be punished.

Now, if on day two a kid starts a fight and you get the two kids together and say, "Guys, I am really disappointed with you," more than likely they will not give a darn. A more effective punishment will be needed. And, at the beginning of the year, "effectiveness" is allowed to take on a different meaning.

We all agree that the kid's education is the goal. The academy or school is the means, the way, to attain that goal. Now, if the means does not work correctly, we will never attain our goal. So the immediate and urgent priority at the beginning of the year is to get the academy working well. At this stage, it would be erroneous to say that the kids' "education" takes second place. Our priority is to have the rules and spirit known and obeyed. The kids must realize that we take the academy or school seriously, even if at present they do not. And we must show them that we mean business. If they step out of line, there is a price to pay—and to pay immediately. No messing around allowed. The beginning of the year can be likened to the Old Testament—an eye for an eye. After all, these kids may well have "hardened hearts."

Before I go into some examples, let me immediately dispel the "grandfather approach."

The grandfather will say that what his grandson needs is attention, love, and care. The grandfather will say, "If the kid doesn't want to finish his dinner, just give him his dessert." "If the kid doesn't want to sleep, go and talk to him, tell him a story, see why he cannot sleep, be with him, and love him."

All fine and well, and being almost that age myself I empathize. But oftentimes grandfathers are a little out of touch with the real world. That is why God gives moms and dads—not grandparents—the responsibility of bringing up kids! In the examples that follow, please keep in mind that we are talking about the start of a new environment for the kids. The examples are inspired by what a mother or father would do—or would like to have done—in the same circumstances.

Here are some examples:

It's nighttime and the kids are in bed. It is a novelty for them to be in a dorm. Some will be whispering. Others will might be making funny noises. Even at this early stage, the educator's silent presence should be sufficient to quiet them down, but you will always have the little rebel. Go over to him, tell him quietly to put his slippers and robe on and bring him out into the corridor. Have him stand in the middle. "You don't want to go to sleep? Fine." Have him stand there an hour or so (that is sixty minutes, not a figure of speech). Don't go overboard. Don't send him outside. Let him see the others blissfully asleep.

In the dining room, three kids are really acting up. Have them leave the dining room and stand in the corridor away from each other. They'll miss whatever lunch they didn't finish, or if they missed lunch completely, give them ten minutes to eat once everyone has left—and have them eat in silence.

You call a kid and he ignores you. Have a kid nearer to you get the kid you called. When he gets to you say, "When I call you, you come." Tell him what you originally wanted to say to him and then add, "And by the way, no recess or shop for you today." During shop time and recess be around and have him stand somewhere you can see him.

A kid is not paying attention in class and is disrupting the others. Pull him out (not physically, of course!) and have him stand outside the classroom for the duration of the class. Say to him, "During recess you will copy the lesson you have just missed." You give him a place to do this, and you keep your eye on him. If he doesn't finish, or does it badly, say, "That's not good enough. Do it properly during next recess (or non-class activity)."

At the beginning of the year, it is important that the kids realize that you will not accept any messing around. This "Old Testament" period, however, should not last more than three weeks.

This will give you ample time to start a dialogue with each kid and to map out a personal program for him to start working on.

Having said this about the need for punishment, I must insist, for fear of being misunderstood, that the need for punishment is directly proportional to the educator's expertise and to his ability to form hearts. In other words, should an educator feel the need to punish, he would do well to first ask himself whether or not it is he, as the educator, who is at fault.

Things were running wild in a particular school. The place was constantly in a mess and the respect for youth leaders was nonexistent. Kids would skip class. The following year, I had occasion to visit the same school again. This time what I saw was the complete opposite. The place was in perfect order, the kids respectful and even happy, and the classes were full. Bewildered by such a turnaround, I asked one of the students how things had changed so much.

"Last year, we ran the place," he said, smiling, and then his face turned serious. "But this year, from the moment we arrived on day one, we knew who the boss was ... and it wasn't us!"

I spoke with the educator and asked him how he managed it. Did he inflict cleverly conceived punishment in bulk or what? "No, not at all," he replied. "We just went in real strict at the beginning, picking up on little things, not letting the kids in with untidy hair, little things like that. I think it's important for the kids to know who's in charge."[15]

No Place for Punishment

Some will say that if our families, schools, or clubs were working well, there would be no need for punishment. But this is a misconception. Wherever we have people, we will have errors and wrongdoing that need to be addressed and punished. The difference is that as time goes on, our punishments will change. Whereas at the beginning, the punishments may involve a lot of external elements, with time—if the educator works correctly-- the need for acts of drastic punishment will be replaced by more subtle and much more effective strategies: the way an educator looks at a kid, not choosing a kid for a particular task, or a simple word or two from his educator.

Here are a few examples of these finer, and more effective, punishments:

A kid, who is working on being punctual, is messing around and arrives late. The educator just glances at him and then at his watch and proceeds to act as if nothing happened. If the kid has been working on punctuality, it means that for him the educator's actions means something. And it means that he knows he has let the educator (and himself) down by being late. The realization of this, made evident by the educator's glance at his watch, will be punishment enough for the kid. No need to say, or do, any more.

A kid gets annoyed with another kid and starts a fight. You stop it. Later when you speak to the kid, you do not go into detail, but simply say, "That's not the way we do things here. Now, go and apologize." No threats. No apparent punishment. And yet the educator's words are punishment supreme.

The worst punishment for any kid will often be his educator's loss of faith in him. This loss of faith, of course, will be a put on, but the kid doesn't know that. It's the somber use-once-in-a-lifetime line, "Jimmy, I am very disappointed in you." Used at the right moment, this line can pierce a kid deeper and more sharply than the finest saber. Use this line with extreme caution; use it only once and never in anger. In fact, it is recommended that you make a visit to the Blessed Sacrament and check with the Lord before using this tool.

The above examples are for when you know the kid, when the kid knows the ropes, and when things are under control.

"This Hurts Me More than It Hurts You."

This famous and well-worn parental phrase is very true too for an educator, but in a different light. Usually a punishment will require extra work for the educator. If the punishment is of a solitary kind, that is to say, a punishment that the kid must carry out alone (picking up the papers on the grounds because he threw trash on the floor, staying in to makeup a lesson he missed because he was sent out of class, not watch television), the educator must be around. The educator must be supervising the kid. This supervision will pull the educator off his normal duties so arrangements have to be made. It might even mean a change of routine, so maybe we will have to get our hair cut or our car washed some other time.

I remember all too well a zealous educator who had a group of his kids do six miles around the gym one afternoon after school because they had insulted a teacher. The kids finished up around seven-thirty in the evening. The educator's wife was having a fit, because she had planned to go out with her friends for an early dinner. Tough going, but what's an educator to do? (Be a little more clever.)

Corporal Punishment

By "corporal punishment," we mean any physical contact with a kid that is designed to hurt him: slapping, hair or ear pulling, arm twisting, (use of whips…only joking!), etc.

Five good reasons for using corporal punishment:

1. It teaches the kid a lesson.
2. It gives an immediate solution to an immediate problem.
3. It is easy to administer.
4. Sometimes it's the only thing a kid will understand.
5. It is a good deterrent.

Five *better* reasons for not using corporal punishment

1. One lesson corporal punishment teaches the kid is that violence is acceptable. Another lesson is that adults can get away with losing their tempers. Another lesson it teaches is "tit-for-tat," the old "eye for an eye" line where "You hit me, I hit you" reigns. None of these lessons is correct.
2. Corporal punishment is like putting a band-aid on a skin tumor. Sure, with the band-aid in place you don't see the ugly spot, but you have done nothing but fool yourself into believing that you have done something to cure the illness.
3. Being easy to administer doesn't mean it's good. Sniffing cocaine isn't hard to do.[16]
4. Corporal punishment will be the only thing a kid understands if his value system is so screwed up that brute force takes precedence over human values. Fix his value system.
5. Corporal punishment is a good deterrent, but it is also an easy way out. If misbehaving can be equated with a

slap, then let me misbehave and I'll take the slap. It's worth it. It is a quick payoff. The kid will end up living on a physical level, where values and ideals have no place.

Noncorporal Punishment

You might say that any noncorporal punishment could be labeled "child abuse" or "violence." You may not be hurting the kid physically, but you are doing worse—you are hurting his spirit or his feelings. Let's say a kid steals another guy's roller blades. He does need to be punished, but you know you cannot hit him. So you say, "OK, Johnny, you will miss out on the outing this week because you behaved badly." Is this not hurting the kid?

It's a good question. If you cannot give yourself a satisfying answer right now as to why it is sometimes right—and indeed even our duty—to punish, read over this chapter again with this question in mind.

A Page of Sorrows

The basic rule is that a punishment should redress the wrong done by getting the kid to right his wrong. Punishments should be a token sign. The real punishment is not what the kid has to do (a minute's silence), but the very fact that he has to do something he would rather not do. The art of punishment must go hand in hand with the even more difficult art of encouragement.

To give a simple idea of practical punishments, here you will find a short list. I am not saying, "You did this, now the punishment for that is this!" A lot will depend on the kid and on the moment. I am simply giving a few examples of "acceptable" punishments that meet all the requirements.

Punishable deed	Punishment
Running indoors	Have the kid walk the distance once
Speaking in time of silence	One minute's silence during recess
Late (for something good like a movie or an outing) Access denied	Limited access (wait outside until halfway through the movie, only half a day skiing)
Late for class or other unattractive events	Double recuperation (one minute late, the kid will have to miss two minutes of break)
Bad table manners	Eat at a special "good manners table" (The educator will teach the kid the right way of doing things.)
Pushing	Last out (The kid who pushed must wait until all others have left the room before he leaves.)
Bad temper during games	Time out: withdraw the kid for five or ten minutes (never for the whole game)
Distracting companions in class	Immediate removal and later recuperation of the lost activity
Throwing papers on the ground	Double recuperation (pick up double the amount)
Kid doesn't finish his dinnerDon't leave the table until you have finished.	(Parents: if you know the kid doesn't like something, serve him just a tiny bit.)

Punishable deed	Punishment
Kid kicks his brotherConfine the kid to his room until he can say to his brother, "I am sorry and I will try not to do it again."	(Parent: Make sure there is no computer or TV in the kid's room!)

Using the Positive to Combat the Negative

This requires knowing the kid, not just his failings but above all his strengths.

A kid might be a good athlete but careless with his things. Neither sports nor tidiness have any particular value of themselves in the global picture. A guy who is tidy, or one who can dunk a basket may not be a better person for it. But we can use sports and tidiness as a training ground for inner strength (virtue) that really does have something to do with the person.

But here we hope to show how to use the positive to combat the negative. There are various ways of doing this.

1. By applauding the good, we predispose the kid to be better. He gets hungry for applause, if you will.
   A superior: "You've done a great job on getting to school this week on time and I will, as a result, unlock the gate. Now let's see if we can work on wearing our ties correctly."
2. Show how things are interwoven.
   Your star athlete may not be able to find his sneakers (maybe you've moved them just a tad).
3. Use the good as a goal, without overdoing it.
   "Once your room is fixed, you can go to the track." Do this in such a

way that the kid doesn't have to spend an hour tidying up his room. In the beginning, have him tidy up one or two things. Next time, add a few more.

All three ways are valid for us and can be effective as well as formative. However, one of the three ways is less in keeping with what we are pursuing. Which one? The third way: we are treating the kid here as more of an animal than a human. "Do a trick and you get your biscuit!" This way however can be useful, especially when working with a new group.

Home and Family

Before God creates a child, he makes sure that there is a mom and a dad. In fact, in God's book there cannot be a child if there is no mom and no dad. Clever, ambitious, and industrious as we are, man has found many a way around this. We have single parent families, and we can even have a child who comes into the world without a real mother or father. But these are breakdowns in the ways things should be. Often these breakdowns are portrayed as perfectly all right. But God thinks differently.

Put simply, a kid needs a mom and a dad—and a few brothers and sisters too, if you ask me. But the mom and dad are essential. And here we are not talking survival. We have cases of Tarzan-type kids who have grown up without the aid of humans and orphanages to prove that kids can grow up without a mom and dad. (Well, they grow. I'm not too sure whether they grow up, though.) When we say that "family is essential," we are referring to a child's development as a person, not just his physical growth or survival on the planet.

The family a child needs is a real family, not just a "man and a woman in his life." I will not go into the many types of pseudo-families that exist today, but suffice it to say that not all families today are the havens of serenity and love they should be, and not all families give priority to the positive development of a child as a person.

The fact is that not all kids have been afforded the benefits of a true family. I am not blaming anyone; I'm just stating a simple fact. In the same way I am not praising anyone when I state that, even in such a whirlwind world, we have many kids who have been gifted with dedicated and responsible parents.

For educators working in schools, these kids, both the lucky ones and the not-so-lucky ones, are the ones that we will be dealing with. In our dealings with kids we must never try to replace the family. Our aim is to help the parents—or even the parent. It is--and you will forgive my crudeness—Hitler-like to suppose that we can take over the role of the family in a kid's life. Sometimes we may be able to offer a less fortunate kid the serenity, motivation, guidance, and correction that he never gets at home, but this does not mean that we are taking the family's place. A kid needs a home. And none of our work must be construed as a "home" for kids. In a worst-case scenario, our efforts are but a supplement, never a substitute.

Schools and youth groups will try to create a friendly, challenging, and optimistic environment. These are elements that should also be present in family life. But there are aspects that schools and youth groups can never hope to—or even try to—emulate. The sentimental ties, the primary responsibility, the legal issues of parenthood—these belong to the family. Everything we do is to help the parents achieve a child's development.

In Genesis we speak of the duty, the mission, to form kids, but it must be clear that this duty, mission, and commitment have been delegated to out-of-family educators and that all such educators must work hand-in-hand with the parents. This does not mean that such educators should allow the parents to run our school or youth group by saying what should be done, where, and when. Out-of-family facilities will have their way of doing things, and while they may always be open to becoming more effective and to bettering themselves as educational institutions, parents are expected to respect their competence, just as they respect that of the parents'.

Put simply, out-of-family educators cannot compete with the family. They should aim to support and, when necessary, build up the family. And just as parents err if they consider their children as solely their own—and thus leaving God out of the equation—so too would educational groups err were they to leave the parents out of their equation. God, parents, educators, the family, and the kid himself—this is the team.

4

The Educator Qualities

The Qualities of an Educator

Whether it be a family, school, or youth group, the educator is key. In this section we will deal with some aspects of an educator's mission and some of the qualities I feel are essential. All of these qualities have to do with the educator's dealing with the kids. We will speak of confidence, leadership, "omnipresence," joy, demandingness, accessibility, and respect. In no way do I intend a complete treatise. For the moment, I will be happy just to offer some practical reflections on the human aspect of the educator. Some of these reflections are more relevant to some educators more than others, but the ideas hold.

It's difficult to put a finger on the basic quality of an educator. His mission is so extensive in range, so global, that each aspect would merit its own basic quality. However, there is one quality that does soar above the others because of its importance: confidence. This core quality is an animating certitude that gives solidity and value to the other qualities.

Confidence

Confidence has two main aspects. One is personal, or inward, and is comprised of skills and attitudes. The other is extra-self, or outward, and is manifested in our faith, or belief, in others.

Personal confidence[17] is the firm belief that we are doing what is right and that we can do it well. At the root of this belief, or attitude, is skill.

An airline pilot is confident that he can raise his 870,000 pound 747 jet off the ground once he reaches what is called "rotation" speed, which is 180 miles per hour. He has done all his preflight checks. He has positioned his craft on the runway and he is now easing the power into each of the four Rolls Royce engines. He knows that he has done everything right and that within ninety seconds he will be airborne. He also has been trained in detail as to what he should do should anything go wrong.

This example dispels a widespread conception that confidence is a kind of mystical inborn quality.

We all admire the at-ease style of some American presidents, although we may not agree with their policies. Maybe in the same situation we would fumble our words, say the wrong thing, wave to the wrong people, and trip over the carpet edge. "That man is so confident!" you will hear people admit. And maybe he is, at least as far as his outward appearance goes. But in actual fact he is doing no more than following all the briefings and tips that he has been given. He knows exactly where he's going, how he's to get there, exactly what he's going to say. As soon as the chopper door is opened, and the gangway secured, he will stand in the doorway for just enough time for him to smooth down an already smooth tie. He will start down the steps, lift his left hand no higher than his shoulder in a general wave at no one in particular (but he will have targeted a cameraman for his focus). He has practiced this a hundred times. He knows how many steps there are; he knows where the cameras are. (Some people have been known to bang their head on the way into the chopper, but that is a different matter.)

As he reaches the end of the steps, he will casually put his left hand out behind him. He knows that his wife will take it immediately. He will turn to her, and say, "Well, here we are, dear.

Home again." (That's what he always says. The mikes won't pick it up, because the engines are still dying down.) She will smile and give his hand a little squeeze. He will continue walking at a brisk pace, heading straight for the door that is just 180 yards away. Halfway there he will pretend to recognize one of the press agents, give a wave, flash a smile, and say something to his wife.

But today is the anniversary of the Denver drownings when forty-three people lost their lives, so he cannot appear too cheerful. His walk today must show strength, determination, and resolution. That's why today he will not stop and speak to the press, nor will his little dog be brought out for him to bend down and cuddle.

He is a model of self-confidence and purpose. But really all we are seeing is a guy who has read the book and rehearsed getting off a helicopter and walking across a lawn.

In both cases, the pilot and the president, we are talking about confident people, but not of some inborn or gods-infused aurora. We are talking implemented skill. And skill is learned.

When we talk of self-confidence, we are not talking about the simple skill of appearing confident. Skills are mechanical. Proper confidence is an attitude, a conviction, a "feeling." Confidence comes from knowing that we are able to put our skills to good use.

A person is not born confident. A person becomes or learns to be confident. The relation between skills (knowing how to do things) and attitude (I know I am good at it) is an interesting one. If I am good at a lot of things, will I be a more confident person?

We might know how to cook well. This is a skill. And we will be confident as cooks. But will this confidence filter down into our attitude? In other words, if we are confident in one area (cooking) will we be confident in others (personal relations, money matters)? Not really. And yet, we see people who have mastered just one skill, let's say public relations, and appear to be very confident people indeed, no matter what they do.

But this is somewhat false. If we analyze the case, we will see that some skills have more applications than others. A cook, after all, can only exercise his skill with pots and pans, usually in a kitchen, whereas a person who is good at dealing with people will have the chance to exercise his skill nearly every hour of the day, no matter where he is.

So the theory remains—self-confidence is born of skills. Knowing that we can do something well will give us confidence in ourselves. The opposite, of course, is the unsure or insecure person. He basically doesn't believe he can do anything, let alone do it well. As educators, we must be skillful people and we must also be able to instill this self-confidence in those we work with.

And on we go.

> **"Confidence" is basically two Latin words: "Con" (with) and "fides" (faith). Being confident means "having faith, or trust, in someone."**

The 747 jet pilot may be a confident pilot, but he may not be a confident mechanic. Our confident lawn stroller may not be a confident speechwriter. But they don't have to be. However, an educator's role cannot be reduced or limited to one single set of skills. He must know, on the one hand, how to get to know kids. Then he must know how to organize entertaining and educative games. He must know how to be an example of good manners. He must know how to motivate and guide...and so to be truly confident, an educator must know these skills and master them—and many more.

Before we say any more about confidence, we must make a distinction. Confidence is not bravado.

A drunk may be "confident" that he can drive home. He is convinced that he knows what to do and how to do it. But he has left something out of the equation. He hasn't factored in his alcohol levels.

This can happen too with an educator. Not that he gets drunk, but that he may have bravado rather than confidence. A new guy on the job may feel that he knows how to control kids. Maybe he believes that shouting is the way to grab attention, or that constant treats are the way to a child's heart. Maybe he has mastered these primitive skills and worked them to perfection. This would be our typical confident boot camp sergeant. His shouting skill leads him to be confident. He knows how to shout and he can shout well. But this "confidence" is pseudo-confidence. He hasn't factored in the point that he is dealing with men and not dogs. It's not real confidence; it's bravado.

So how can we determine whether our "confidence" is true confidence or just bravado? We have suggested that "personal confidence is the firm belief that we are doing what is right and that we can do it well." This "firm belief" in what is right must be an educated, or informed, belief. It is not what I think is right, but what I know to be right. And to know what is right, I must investigate, study, discern, and decide. It is not the first thing that comes into my head, nor is it what appears to be a good idea at the time. And thank goodness, there are people who can tell us what is right. The pilot will study his manual and have training flights with a qualified instructor. The president-to-be will have long sessions with public relations experts. And the educator can read his manuals, ask advice, and speak with his directors.

So a confident educator will be the person who knows that he can do well that which is expected of him as an educator. And in a nutshell, what is expected of an educator?

The answer comes in a seemingly contradictory line from Father Marcial Maciel's 1940s pen: an educator should be a "private soldier and leader of men." The "private soldier" part refers to the educator's role as a team member. He is not alone on the job. He must work with others. The "leader of men," or "of souls" to be more faithful to the Spanish original, gives us the ultimate finality, the ultimate goal of an educator's mission: to educate, to bring men—young or old—forward.

This military type nutshell might appear to be at odds with our personal approach. After all, nothing seems more impersonal than the military. But the phrase is an obvious simile that serves to show up the vastness of an educator's mission: he is a simple, honest-to-goodness hard worker at the service of his students, and he is also the one who must take the personal responsibility to stand up, inspire, and lead those he works with. Interpreting the simile to show the educator as a uniformed and unwitting member of an armed group would be to get the wrong idea of the simile.

The skills, therefore, that will lead to an educator's confidence are those skills required for his mission as a team member and also as a leader, as an educator. The book that you have in your hands contains ideas about many such skills. Knowing what these skills are and mastering them will help you to become a confident educator. And, as we have seen, "confident" means knowing that you can do the job well.

Up to now we have been speaking of confidence in its inward or personal aspect (personal skills that foster attitude). But now it's time to share a few secrets, or tips of the trade. The point is this—when you begin to be an educator, you are lacking experience. There's nothing wrong with this at all. After all, the very fact that you are beginning means that you have no experience in the field. Experience is what you get as you go along. (A sugar envelope in a Rhode Island restaurant suggests that "experience is what you have when you don't need it anymore," and while amusing, it is not exact and intended only as a joke.) So, we have the new educator dealing with kids, but he has had no opportunity to master the skills necessary for personal educator confidence. And the kids will simply walk all over the poor novice. When the educator eventually has mastered the skills, it will be too late, as least for the first set of kids. The kids will have no confidence in him.

So, as the new educator is gaining practical skills, even though he might not have the necessary skills, there are a few things he can do right from active day one that will give the appearance of self-confidence. Put simply, the novice educator can pretend to be confident. These tips are not intended to fool or "trick" the kids. Much less should they make us think that our mission is just a series of little tips or a wrong way of doing things that eventually, and mysteriously, turn out right—far from it. These "tips of the trade" are born out of experience. These "tips" are akin to the studio manager getting the television anchorman to sit on the tail of his jacket so that it will not ride up his back as he speaks. The anchorman never would have thought about it until he saw replays of his program and would start wondering what could be done to stop his jacket sticking out from behind his neck. The studio manager simply gives him a "tip of the trade" from day one.

Tips of the Trade

1. Walk to where you're going.
2. If you start a sentence, finish it.
3. Speak only when you know you're being listened to.
4. Wear clean, comfortable clothes.
5. Rest well.
6. Practice memory powers.
7. Know what you're going to do if something goes wrong.
8. Keep your problems to yourself.
9. See what skills work for others and personalize them.
10. Act professionally.
11. Keep an alert mind.
12. Check personal quirks.
13. Be a "yes or no" person.
14. Keep your distance.
15. Be your own authority.

1. Walk to where you're going.

Don't start out somewhere and then turn around halfway and head somewhere else. Give every movement a definite purpose.

Never go halfway into a room and then leave without showing that you have gone in to do something, or to get someone.

If you are going to take your place at a table and you are just about to sit down, and then realize that you forgot to put the salt on the table, just sit down.

If you go into the wrong room, go over to the window and look out, or pick something up off the floor...anything to show that you went in with a definite idea in mind and that you are not just lost in your own place.

If you are getting into a car and a kid starts calling you from the house, get into the car and wait for the kid to reach you. Don't stop as you begin to sit and stand again.

The main idea here is to show that you know where you're going.

2. *If you start a sentence, finish it.*

This means that you have to know what you're going to say before you start speaking. Seems obvious, but it is worth mentioning.

It's time for the kids to go to bed. Don't say, "OK, kids…." Kids grumble and interrupt, "Just another ten minutes!" "No, kids, it's…." You see then that the kids are glued to the computer screen and are pretending not to hear you. "Now, come on, boys, it's…. Boys! Turn that off."

Do not let the kids interrupt you. When you decide to speak, whatever you have to say is far more important than anything a kid can come up with. This may not always be true, of course, but we are talking tips of the trade here.

In the case above: "OK, kids. Time to go to bed. Please turn off the computer now, and get your pajamas on. I want to see you in bed in three minutes." End of story. Don't argue. Don't even let the kids think they can interrupt you.

3. Speak only when you know you're being listened to.

The class is without a teacher. You hear the noise and you reach the door.

Wrong: You barge in, point to the noisemakers, tell them to leave the classroom, and wait for you outside.

Wrong: You walk in and say "Silence! Quiet!"

Right: You simply stand at the door and look stern. (To look stern, put on a face with absolutely no expression. Don't move your head, or your hands, or your stance. With your eyes, scan the individuals slowly. Let them know that you see exactly who they are.) And wait. The kids will calm down. And when they do, speak to them in a soft, clear voice.

(School setting)

The dining room is abuzz. The meal is finished and the kids are getting restless. And you need now to speak to them. If you start saying, "OK, quiet...sit down and listen up…." you can be sure that most of the kids will not hear you. So what do you do?

I was visiting a boarding school, and during lunch the director wanted to say something. The dining room was humming with enthusiastic voices and the subdued noise of cutlery and plates. It wasn't very noisy, but it wasn't quiet either. The director put down his knife and fork, touched his mouth with his napkin, put his wrists on the table, and slowly looked up out across the dining room to one of the farthest tables. Silence spread out from the main table where we were sitting and within seconds should a pin drop we all would have heard it bounce. "Today, is a special day for Harry. He scored his highest mark for conduct this year. Well done, Harry!" He smiled and the kids applauded, but did not speak. The director turned to me as he picked up his knife and fork. "He scored ten out of ten." The kids began speaking again and within seconds the dining room, which a moment ago was silent, was again bubbling with happy noise.

"How did you get all the kids to be quiet?" I asked, totally baffled. "Simple," replied the rector. "The students know that when I put down my knife and fork, wipe my mouth, and look up and wait, I want to say something. Someone will always see it, and the kids will fall silent. And the silence spreads real fast. Neat, isn't it?" And it certainly was. The wisdom of signs!

So back to our noisy dining room. We should have a sign for the kids to be quiet. If you are using a microphone, a gentle tap should do. Or use a discreet table bell, or just one solid handclap. Use something simple. Just do it once. Don't bang away on the microphone, or jangle the bells, or clap your hands as if you were trying to draw the attention of a herd of cows. Make sure your kids know what the signal means.

And once you have given the signal, give a good example. If you want the kids to listen up, listen up yourself. Don't speak to anyone. If a kid comes up to you and asks permission to finish his apple, put your finger to your mouth, and ignore him and point to his place. (Of course he will be allowed to finish his apple, and you will tell him that later, but right now it's quiet down time. One thing at a time.)

4. *Wear clean, comfortable clothes.*

As well as having to give a good example in our attire, clothes can help our self-confidence. Wear clothes that fit the purpose and make sure they are comfortable. In a school setting, avoid using new shoes on the job, as they can hurt your feet. If you're a man, make sure your collar fits and that your jacket doesn't hamper your movements. If your collar is too tight, you will want to open it, and if your jacket is tight, the same can be said.

Make sure your clothes suit you, your age, and your position. If you are used to wearing collar and tie, make sure that your casual gear is also elegant and well matched. If you are used to wearing casual, make sure your suits suit you and that your tie matches.

Make sure that your clothes are in good repair. Don't use anything that has a hole in it or that is frayed. This applies to undergarments as well. If you are a woman, make sure your stockings are not torn and that the hem of your slip doesn't show.

Ensure that your clothes and footwear are suited to what you are doing.

When you get the chance try out this experiment:

Put on normal, casual clothes, but make sure something is wrong. For this experiment, use an old shirt or an old pair of trousers with an evident tear. Pour some cold soup on the front of the shirt. Make sure your shoes are dirty. Go to the nearest mall, go inside and walk the length of it, stopping to go into a shop or two. Go back home.

Put on your very best clothes, the very best you have (but avoid the very glamorous). Choose a nice well-pressed suit, a crisp shirt, and if possible, new shoes. Go to the same mall, go in, and walk the length of it.

Now examine your walk. You will find that when you were well dressed you behaved differently. Your stride was more confident, your back was straighter, and your head was higher. The explanation for this is that we tend to live in the clothes we wear. Dress messy, we act messy. Dress casual, we act casual. Dress formal, we act formal. The habit may not make the monk, but it sure helps him to behave like one.

5. Rest well.

There is no substitute for food, exercise, and rest. When we miss out on sleep, little things can go wrong and lead to bigger things. When we lose sleep, we are not "all there" and our powers are not what they should be. A priest friend of mine, weathered in youth work, said that, "working with kids demands that you be in tip-top shape all the time." And he knew what he was talking about.

If you feel the need for extra sleep, get it. Don't sneak it. And much less, do not try and go without it. Many simple everyday problems can be traced to a lack of sleep. And many cases of clinical depression can also be traced to initial unovercome difficulties resulting from a lack of sleep.

6. Develop memory powers.

This may seem like a weird and unnecessary tip of the trade, but it is neither weird nor unnecessary. We use about ten percent of our lungs. We use less of our onboard memory. Memory can make a big difference.

Out-of-family educators not only have to remember a kid's name, but also his birthday, the names of his brothers and sisters, his dog, cat, and horse, what he's good at, and what he is working on at present.

Parents have to remember the names of the kid's friends, their birthdays, their kid's after-school activity program, the times his favorites shows are on, and the names of his teachers.

We have to remember the kids' short-term goals that are constantly changing. The more we can remember the better. All this will not only help the confidence we have in ourselves, but will greatly enhance the confidence the kids have in us as well.

If you don't have a good memory, try getting one. (See page 150 on active study for yourself.)

7. Know what you're going to do if something goes wrong.

This is a Boy Scout principle. It has nothing to do with making our life complicated trying to answer an infinite number of "What will I do if...?" scenarios. But knowing what to do when something goes wrong is a lesson learned from experience, not the dictate of a weak mind. "That never happens here," or worse, "God will provide," are born of compliance and only go to show a total in-depth ignorance of what can happen when kids are around. (Something that may not have happened here yet, something might happen soon, and God has provided the world with you to foresee problems.) We can work on the assumption that, where kids are involved, the worst will eventually happen.

While seldom, an educator will sometimes be called upon to give guidance when something serious happens. But here are some of those things that you should be practically prepared for always:

A kid drowning

This can happen because of a bang on the head from the wall of the pool, or a kid slipping and falling into the pool, from cramps, or simply from a kid not knowing how to swim. This is not a first aid manual, but next time you're at the pool, just check and see if there is a long pole with a person-hook on it. This will be the first thing you will use should the need arise.

A kid choking

This is not restricted to the dining room. It can happen anywhere.

Finding a kid unconscious

Do you gently try to wake him and then pick him up? Do you cradle his head and wave air at him? Do you start giving him artificial respiration?

A fire

Fires happen.

Here we are talking "tips of the trade" that help us be confident, but I am not saying that we should know what to do in the above cases in order to feel confident. That is putting the cart before the camel, or whatever you tie your cart to. All personnel working with kids must know basic first aid and lifesaving skills. Know them and practice them in real and professionally monitored situations. Such training is a basic requirement for all educators. It is a requirement, not a plus. It is obligatory, not an option. Having said this, and rather firmly if you'll forgive me, there is no doubt that knowing what to do when such things happen gives the educator no small degree of self-confidence.

Other little things can go wrong too. Knowing what to do in these cases can be very helpful. Experience will tell you what they are and what you should, or could, have done. Here are some school examples and things you could do (and things you shouldn't do):

The bus for the outing has not arrived on time

Have the kids go to the recess area. Don't have them hanging around.

You arrive for lunch and find that the staff is off for the day.

Contact your director and ask for instructions. Don't send three kids into the kitchen to see what they can rustle up.

The electricity goes out

Keep on doing whatever you and the kids are doing. If the emergency lighting doesn't come on, full power will be restored soon. Don't start switching on and off the lights and certainly don't start telling the kids anything negative, such as "Don't move!" If needed, say something positive like, "Please carry on with what you're doing."

You are with your kids, and you hear someone falling down the stairs

Bring two kids with you and go investigate. Don't go alone. If there has been an accident, you will need to send someone to get extra help. Don't ignore it.

Your wake-up alarm goes off, and you don't feel well at all

Call another educator and tell him. Make sure you have someone look after your kids. Get back to bed. Don't just turn the alarm off and let them find you.

A complete list of things, big and small, that can go wrong, would be quite impossible to draw up. Kids can be very inventive! But knowing what to do in serious situations will certainly be good for you as well as being beneficial for the kids.

8. *Keep your problems to yourself.*

We all know the scenario—things have gone bad at home, and the boss comes in to work annoyed with the world and its inhabitants. Or things have gone bad in the office and at home, the family and even the dog suffer. An educator, whether he is live-in or not, will also have his ups and down. Knowing how to keep your problems to yourself and not take them out on the kids, or worse, blame the kids for your problems, will boost your self-confidence greatly. This is a tip that comes with time and effort, though. Here are some ideas that might help you:

Fix yourself a "hello routine" and stick to it.

First impressions, even on a daily basis, are important. Get into the habit of saying "hello" to fellow workers, staff, and students in a certain way. It might simply be by saying "good morning" to everyone. Sometimes you won't feel like saying it, but stick to your routine.

Take a breather.

Remember that whatever—and I mean whatever—the situation, you are really doing God's work and ask him to give you a hand. This is another little habit you might like to get into.

Have a detailed daily schedule and stick to it.

Whatever your personal problem, laziness is the front door to total misery.

Wear something you particularly like or that really suits you.

When you're feeling bad, take extra care to look good. This is gospel. When you fast, use your favorite cologne.

If you find the kids start getting to you, be extra careful with what you say and keep orders to a minimum.

If symptoms persist, consult your doctor. Keeping problems to yourself does not mean keeping them totally to yourself. We are fortunate enough to work with people who care about and for us. Let them know, and together work on it.

You know something has gone very wrong if you, in search of comfort or advice, share a personal problem you have with a kid. The reasons for such behavior may be varied, but the end result is the same—the compass has lost its magnetic tip.

9. See what skills work for others and personalize them.

An educator had problems controlling the kids, especially at night. They just would not keep quiet, no matter how much he exhorted them. This went on for a week and the educator knew that if he didn't get a handle on it soon, he would be unable to get his kids into shape during the year. He had noticed that another educator had a wonderful group of kids that bedded down in silence every night. Our educator was clever enough to investigate.

The fellow educator was a stern guy, although he had a heart of gold. After saying "Goodnight!" he would just stand there and silence would fall. If a kid came up to him to ask him something, he would look at him with a face as cold as stone and simply point to the kid's bed without saying a word.

Our educator, being among the most expressive and happy-hearted educators to hit an academy, felt unable to be so harsh. "What happens if a kid wants to tell you something important or isn't feeling well?" he asked. The other educator replied, "Once everybody is in bed, I point to the kid and call him over."

Our educator realized that harshness was not the secret, but the absolute "no talking" after the educator had said "Goodnight!" was. So he thought that he would do the same. But he concluded that he was unable to put on the stern face that his fellow educator used so convincingly, so he would keep his smile but do everything else the same.

It worked.

Being an educator does not mean that we have to get into a cast iron suit everyday and coldly recite a part. We do certainly have a role to play, an example to set, but we must give this role our own interpretation. Al Pacino could play Indiana Jones, but his portrayal would be different from the one Harrison Ford gave it. Better or worse, who knows, but certainly different. The script would be the same, but the "feel" of the movie would be different.

A little trick here is for us to be clever enough to believe that we do not know everything there is to know and that others may very well have a better way of doing what we are trying to do.

Deep down, this is humility. Far from inert passivity, this humility leads to personal betterment and professional advancement.

So analyze what works for others. Get the key concept out of it. In the example above, there were two concepts: the apparent harshness and the clear "no talking" mandate after the "goodnight." The key concept was not the apparent harshness. But don't go overboard either. If something works well for you, don't worry about changing it.

> **Whatever goes wrong, pretend it is normal procedure and take it in your stride. Have you ever noticed how airline cabin staff will always be talking among themselves on takeoff and landing? They know full well that these two moments are among the most dangerous of flight. Or have you noticed how, on a bumpy ride, they keep on serving coffee or, if it really gets bumpy, efficiently store everything, sit down, and start chatting among themselves about lipstick or a recent game of golf? They are talking for our sake.**

10. Act professionally.

As we came out of the tunnel, we saw that the road ahead was covered in ice. Our speed and the bend in the road ahead spelt out one word—crash. I invoked my Maker and looked over at my dad. "Tighten your belt," he said calmly, without taking his eyes off the road and without changing his grip. The back of the car swung around and we were traveling sideways. Then backwards. Then straight again. I preferred backwards because I couldn't see the rock face that we were sliding towards. "Tighten your belt?" Yes, I had tightened my belt. "This will be bumpy, but we'll be fine." Call it trust, call it wishful thinking, but for some reason I knew that we would be alright, although I didn't know how. I looked from my dad to the fast approaching wall and back to my dad. His hands had changed grip to take up a "ten minutes to two position."

With the wall just thirty yards away and with two seconds of skid left before the impending impact, my dad pulled the wheel fully counterclockwise and the car swung awkwardly to the right. We smashed into the wall broadside. The car lifted off its left tires and bumped down again. A hubcap ran away on its own. Not a window broke. My dad turned off the engine and for the first time looked over at me. "That was rough, wasn't it?"

And it certainly had been. Had it not been for my dad's great skill and knowing exactly what to do, I could see us splattered across the wall. As we clambered out of my side of the car, I asked my dad when he had learned how to skid drive.

"Never did." I remembered then—and to this day—his steady look, his serene hands, and his automatic command, "Tighten your belt." He obviously knew what he was doing, he obviously knew what was going to happen, and he knew that we would be alright. "But you knew exactly what to do."

"Just acting professional." "You mean you didn't really know what to do?" "Hadn't a clue. But the last thing I wanted was you going all hysterical on me. I didn't want you to be more worried than you had to be. Just acting professional."'

Most of us will come across situations that we are not really prepared for. Hopefully they will never be as dangerous as the skid on the Wicklow mountains cited above. Hopefully they will be far from life threatening. It might simply be a matter of the car not starting. Act professionally.

11. Keep an alert mind.

There is nothing as bad as having nothing to say and having to say something. If you have something to say, say it. In other words, if you have nothing to say, say nothing. But an educator will often be called upon to speak when he might have nothing to say. Here are some examples:

You're on a trip. You're tired and would be quite content to gaze out the window and watch the world go by. But Tony needs a little pepping up. His parents have just been to see him, and he's feeling homesick. So you feel it your duty to go and cheer him up. But you've got nothing to say. But you go up to him anyway. "How are you?" (Not too original, but it gets worse.) A grunt. "Looking forward to seeing the museum?" Another grunt. "Looks like rain." You just can't think of anything good to say, and the poor kid knows it. He turns to the window. You've made him feel worse. His folks have just gone home, and now he's stuck and disappointed with the only person he had hopes would be able to cheer him up.

Always have something up your sleeve. Sports are good. First because kids, be they boys or girls, will have a sports hero and second because a lot happens in sports, things are always changing.

You know Tony is sold on the Giraffes. So you go up to him.

"How's it going, Tony?" (This isn't a question. It's a "Hello.") "What happened to the poor Giraffes yesterday? That last inning was something. What do you think about this new Mendez guy?

Any good?" "Not really. Higgins is way better." "Maybe, but Mendez was good yesterday all the same. I don't think it was his fault the team lost." "Well, if he hadn't thrown the ball at the umpire." "He did no such thing, come on!"

Whether you like sports or not, it can be very helpful to know what's going on. It can make you confident that you can talk to a kid about something he likes and knows about.

Here's an example from a boarding school setting:

A visitor came. After we showed him around and had a pleasant supper, we asked him if he would be kind enough to address the students who were waiting for him in the auditorium. All of a sudden he got nervous and said he hadn't anything prepared. We said it didn't matter (little did we know!) and that "anything" would do. He could tell them what it was like to be a famous musician. He insisted that he'd rather not, but taking his refusal for shyness and not nerves, we insisted further. And he reluctantly agreed to grace his hosts.

He stood in front of the boys speechless. He rubbed his hands and looked around nervously. Maybe had there been a piano he would have gone over and played something, but in those days we were lucky to have what we called an "auditorium." So there he stood. It only lasted less than a minute, but it seemed an hour. One boy raised his hand and stood up.

"Sir, why did you decide to play the piano and not the guitar?"

"Well, now, son. The answer to that is easy: we had a piano at home. We didn't have a guitar." He smiled nervously, and everybody laughed good-naturedly. Another hand went up and then another and then another. The session went on for about half an hour, and when it was over our visitor had lost all his nervousness and could only say what a great group of boys we had. But I will never forget his nervousness. After that, we never insisted that a visitor address the boys if we detected that he preferred not to.

As educators, we may often be called upon to give an impromptu talk. It won't be an invitation. We should always have something up our sleeve to say. A general, all-purpose one is fine. Knowing that you are ready for such occasions will help you to be confident. You won't have to run or stand there and look stupid.

12. *Check personal quirks.*

We all have them—little things we do without really knowing we do them. It might be rubbing our hand over our chin. It might be punching one fist into the other hand. It might be flattening down our hair. It might be a way we purse our lips.

I remember one guy who, when he was asked something and was unsure of the answer, would rub the back of his neck. We used to have great fun asking him his opinion on difficult things just to see him do it. We told him about it, and he assured us that he had never realized it. And as he said this, up went his hand to his neck! We laughed so much and he along with us. Bringing it to his attention helped him get rid of it.

Quirks will usually have their root in a lack of confidence. And this is certainly the impression they give—a lack of personal confidence. Apart from the humorous side, such quirks can damage our effectiveness as educators, because they portray us as an unsure person.

The problem is that we aren't aware of it, and so we must be told. So ask a personal friend for help on this one. After all, we are not talking character defects here. Ask every now and again.

13. Be a "yes or no" man.

Nothing could be more gospel than this. Put simply, it means saying "yes" when you mean "yes" and saying "no" when you mean "no." We can find surprising practical examples in our everyday life as educators. Come with me.

We're in a supermarket. We all know the scene. A kid will see something he wants. He picks it up and puts it in the shopping cart. The mother sees this and takes it out and puts it back on the shelf. The kid goes, "Ah, Mom!" The mother says, "Not today!" But the kid insists. He picks it up again and holds it. The mother tells him to put it back. The kid tries another tactic—he makes noise to attract attention to his mother's cruelness. The mother will insist that he put it back; she might even move away. But the kid insists. He carries the item with him. The mother notices and says, "Put that back! Right now!" The kid decides it's time to make more noise. He throws a little fit. People walking by eye the mother ,wondering why she is being so mean to the adorable kid. (Or at least that's what she thinks they are thinking. Actually, they are wondering how come this mother has never trained her kid to accept a "no.")

The fight goes on. The mother pretends nothing is happening, pulling stuff off the shelf that she never intended to buy and reading the labels intently. The mother might even try to take the thing out of the kid's hand with a pull. But the kid doesn't let go, and his little fit is going rather well. He's red in the face and tears are coming. Looking good, he thinks. At this point the kid decides an extra push is needed and so launches into, "You always buy stuff for my brothers and you never buy anything for me! I hate you!" The mother is fighting on many fronts right now. She has a hostile kid and a hostile audience. (Oh yes, the audience is hostile all right—the audience is hating that kid.)

For the sake of peace, and throwing all her resolutions out the window, she grabs the item and places it none too softly into the shopping cart and moves off. The kid smiles to himself, for he knew it would end this way. It always does. He always wins.

Let us follow that kid home. And sure enough, when told to do his homework, he will make a fuss and the mother will say, "Alright. Another ten minutes and then it's homework time." He's watching a television program and won't come to the table. The mother will turn off the set and he will turn it back on again.

Let us rewind. We're in a supermarket. A kid picks up something off the shelf and plops it into the cart. The mother sees it, and simply says, "John, put that back, please." No big deal. The kid puts it back and carries on as if nothing has happened. After all he knows that when his mom says, "Put it back!" she means, "Put it back!" It's a lesson he learned years ago. One day out shopping, he did try to get the better of his mother. He had taken something off the shelf and put it into the cart. His mother said, "We're not buying that." He threw one heck of a tantrum. He even got down on the floor and kicked and kicked. He remembers how his mother ignored him. When they got to the checkout, the mother simply took the item out and put it aside. He did stamp his feet in a final effort, and he remembers well how the girl at the desk just looked at him and said, "Now who is being a naughty boy?" and put the item out of sight behind her. He didn't like that at all. He had tried it once or twice again, but always met with the same result.

There was another supermarket example—the cereal case. While shopping, the kid asks his mother if he could take a certain box of cereal home. He had seen the ads. The mother said that the cereal wasn't any good, but the kid asked if he could try it anyway. "It's not that good, but if you want it, you can have it." They took the cereal home. No big deal. The following week, out shopping again, the kid asked if he could get some pancake mix. "They say it's great, Mom!" The mother's answer? "When you finish all that horrible cereal that we brought home last week." "But, Mom, it's awful!" "What did I tell you last week?"

And another:

The girl was only six, but she helped her mother to do the shopping. The mother would say, "You're in charge of getting the soap powder for the dishwasher, and I want you to find a nice dessert for Saturday's lunch." It usually turned out that kid got the same washing powder as they used at home, but the little girl always enjoyed searching out something special. If there was a new dessert product, for example, the mother would make a big thing out of it and would discuss it with her daughter. The mother would read the label out loud in search of traces of peanuts, because one of the kids was allergic to peanuts. When they hit upon the "May contain peanuts," the girl would say, "We can't have that!" and would go off looking for something else.

Such a team approach to shopping was not only fun for both mother and daughter, but it also helped the kid learn about shopping.

Now, let us leave the supermarkets and head back to class as we continue our tip about being a "yes or no" person.

The kids are in class but there is no teacher yet. A kid sees an educator outside the classroom and comes to the door. The educator, without knowing what the kid wants, says, "Go back to your desk." And the conversation goes something like this:

"But, sir..."

"Go back to your desk right now."

"We have no teacher and I was wondering if...."

"Tim, I have already told you to go back into your classroom."

"I was wondering if I could do my math homework now."

"I said, back to your desk."

"Please, sir. Let me do my math homework now."

"OK, you can do your homework until the teacher comes; now please go back to your desk."

"My books are in my outside locker. May I go and get them please?"

"No."

"Please!"

"No."

"Oh please, sir. I cannot do my homework without my books."

"All right, but be quick."

So, who is running things here? Obviously the kid. He has the educator wrapped around his little finger. Here's how things would have worked out better:

The kid comes to the door. Your main concern right now is to quiet the class down. So any individual consideration may be left aside for the moment.

"Go back to your desk, please."

"But, sir...."

You have said all you want to say to this kid, he has heard you, so say no more. Ignore him. This in itself is a sign of confidence in the kid, confidence that he will do exactly as you have asked. Look past him into the classroom. Should the kid insist, look him straight in the eyes and point to his desk. But do not say any more to him. Not a single peep. If things are really bad, you may want to stand at the doorway so that everyone can see you. The insistent kid might still be begging for your attention. Turn to him as if you hadn't previously noticed him. You can say either, "Are you still here?" or "I will see you in my office at break." (And when you see him at break, have him stand at attention for two recesses to learn a little respect for authority.) In either case, point to the kid's desk.

And what if the kid in question was feeling a heart attack—or something less serious—coming on? Do you just ignore him? Shouldn't we be like the Good Shepherd of the Gospel who forgets about the ninety-nine and goes off after the one? You can be sure that the Good Shepherd made sure the ninety-nine were perfectly all right and well cared for before he went running off in search of the one. And in the example above where I suggest you "ignore the kid," I do not mean that you ignore him all together. Once all the kids are quietly sitting down, you could call that kid over and speak to him at the door, or you could go into the classroom and say, "Any questions?"

Kids will push us just to see how far they can go. Kids are pretty good at this. They'll push and push until they hit the line that they cannot cross. Kids are good too at finding our weaknesses.

I remember the case of a kid who didn't get on too well with his science teacher. Rather than cause problems in class, problems he knew would result in his being punished, the kid would look for excuses to miss the class. He had found that his educator was not sympathetic to medical urgencies, so he gave up his pleas of stomachaches and headaches. But he did hit upon the educator's love of spiritual direction and regularly asked to speak with his educator. The educator was happy to help the kid through a particularly difficult time, without knowing that the kid's problems were just make-believe, and were always solved just before recess began.

Having said this, we must not confuse the "yes or no" principle with "let me think about it," a response that can often be necessary and formative. If a kid asks permission to go off on a weekend with his friends, rather than snap out a "Yes, of course" or a "No. Not this time," you could say, "Let me think about it."

And sometimes an "I'm not sure" is called for. A kid might ask, "Where are we going Sunday?" (The kid is hoping that the answer will be "McDonalds"). "Could we go to McDonalds?" "I don't know. We'll see." This can be acceptable, but only if we really do not know. If we already have our mind made up, better say so from the beginning. Otherwise we are only trying to fool the kids and this is not good. And when you do decide to go, or not to go, it is good for the kid to know why you decided that way. He may not agree with your reasons, but at least he sees that you did consider it.

14. Keep your distance.

In many schools in Latin America, there is the practice for kids to line up and "take distance." They do this by holding their right arm out in front of them at shoulder height until they touch the back of the shoulder on the kid in front of them. As educators, we do well to do basically the same thing—take and keep our distance.

This in itself is a difficult art, especially for out-of-family educators. Educators must be warm-blooded people, people with heart. It will be this heart that motivates our concern and care for the kids. Far from us the coldhearted educator who looks upon his charge as just a job he has to do. I would even go as far as to say that an educator must love his kids. He must be careful not to confuse infatuation with love. Let the educator leave any infatuation he might wish to have for his girlfriend!

In another part of Genesis we will talk about the relationship of the educator-kid. Parents must never become their kid's "friend," because they are parents. More about that later; right now I want to touch on how an out-of-family educator should love his kids.

The love an educator should have for his kids must be modeled on the love Christ had—and has—for those he came to save--a love based on each person's worth as a son of the Almighty, a love that is lived out in the daily concern for the kid's well-being and formation, and ultimately for his eternal salvation. This love will urge us to know the kid as he is in order to help him become what he is called by God to become. This love will put us on the same wavelength as the kid. Only in this way will he receive our message. This love will urge us to go step-by-step with each kid as he struggles to live up to God's call. This love will open our eyes to the misery and greatness embedded in each soul. It is this love that will be our secret power as we live out our day-to-day life. It will give meaning to dryness and fatigue, light to darkness, and strength to weakness.

True love, applied to this educator-kid bond, is nothing more than the educator doing all that has to be done, so that his kid is able to become a better person.

But this love can all too easily turn sour. When we start "loving something about the kid" rather than "loving the kid," alarm bells should start clanging loudly. Love can all too readily be diluted into human empathy or horizontal sympathy. It can, if we are not careful, slip into mere affection and get bogged down in the mire of self-gratification, the very antithesis of love.

In practical terms, keeping your distance means not getting emotionally involved with your kids. This also applies to parents, strangely enough. How many times have some parents thrown their parental responsibility out the window because they get emotional! Losing your temper with kids is emotional. Spoiling a kid is emotional. Letting a kid get away with things is emotional. Not drawing the line for fear of hurting the kid is emotional.

To do this, keep prayer and confidence levels high. Ask God to help you keep your love lead-crystal Christlike. And be open with your personal spiritual director about this aspect of your work. It will be natural that you will enjoy some kids more than others, but be ready to stop yourself if you find yourself slipping. Here are some signs that may indicate your love is becoming tainted:

- You use one of your kids as a measuring stick for other kids, or use him as an example for others to follow.
- During recess, you look for a particular kid.
- You give a particular kid chores that require him to be near you or to have extra contact with you (in charge of your office, a team captain, the guy in charge of bringing the first aid kit along, or even worse, your personal secretary or your own waiter).

- You spend more time with a particular kid than you do with most others.
- You find yourself praying a little more for one kid—by name—than others.
- You consider that a particular kid needs special attention because of some difficulty he may have.

While the above behavior may be explained by other motives (a kid is low in self-esteem, so you give him a special job to do, or you pray a little more for him), we do need to be careful.

For out-of-family educators, a good practical rule of thumb is to run things by your boss. If you feel that a particular kid would benefit by being a team captain, check it out with your director. If you find yourself being a little overly concerned, then you know you are slipping. If you feel a kid has need of special attention, run it by your director. The problem may not be as serious as you would want to believe. This confidence in your director will help you. Parents, a good idea is to sound out what your friends have to say. I refer obviously to those friends who know and spend time with your family. I am not saying that you have to do whatever they tell you to do, or suggest you do, but it will give you an outside look. This can be quite valuable.

15. Be your own authority.

We have all heard it again and again--the mother who says, "Wait until I tell your father!" The teacher who says, "Go and see the principal!" And we have people who might say, "Don't let your parents catch you doing that!"

As educators we are, so to speak, the bottom line. Teachers in their classrooms and mothers with their kids are the bottom line. By this I mean that we must not pass the buck. We must not pass on our responsibility. Put another way, we could say that it doesn't matter what "your father" thinks, or what "your educator" says. What matters is what I think, what I say.

Only in limited instances is it appropriate for an educator to say, "I'm going to see what the director says about this."[18] The word of an educator, even though he is a trainee, should be final, and the kid should see the whole family or school represented in his educator.

This is not to say that we must be closed and not allow the kid access to higher authority. By no means—a kid has the right to go to a higher authority whenever he sees fit to do so and, as educators, we should facilitate this channel should the kid wish to use it. Of course, this applies basically to schools, as a kid should see his father as a higher authority than his mother.

And when I say that an educator should be his own authority, I do not mean that he should be an authoritarian, barking out orders as a sergeant major might. Nor do I mean that the educator is an authority accountable only to his own conscience. Parents are responsible before God. Out-of-family educators are responsible before the school authorities and the parents from whom he has received his authority.

And speaking of this "authority" aspect, there are one or two other things that come to mind:

It is very nice to say that an educator should gain his authority (moral command, if you will) over the kids by showing an attitude of service, of charity, and the like. Put another way, the kids will do exactly as the educator says simply because they know he has their good at heart and that he really only wants to serve them. And we would not be far off were we to tend to this. However, in the real world quite often we do not have time for the kids to get to know us that well. If you are dealing with kids in a youth club, or if you are in school, you will have new kids every year, and you cannot let things run aground until they finally realize that it is love and service that motivates you. Leave the grandfather approach (see page 190) for later. Your job as an educator is not to get the kids to see what a wonderful joe you are. Your job as an educator is to help the kids form themselves. So don't be afraid of appearing "tough"—not rough, but "tough." Be kind too.

The other point, and one that is behind **genesis**, is the following case:

An educator was new. The kids after the first week were walking over him, running rings around him ... cracking open jokes about him. The educator goes along and asks for advice. "Have them respect you," was the wisdom dealt out. "Sounds good," said the educator. "But how do I have them respect me?" "By making yourself respected." While this is good advice in itself, it only contributed to making the poor educator feel more confused than ever and less adequate than before. The "how to" was totally missing.

The point here is that in the real world we need the theory, but we also need to know exactly how to implement the theory. Genesis hopes to show, among other things, how you can get kids to see that you are motivated by love and service, and what you can do to have kids respect you. We want to be practical. What good mother will avoid reprimanding her child because she loves him? What good father will shy away from "laying down the law" because he respects his son? In a weird way, it is by "imposing" authority that we gain authority. It all has to do with the way we impose authority ... and with kids, sometimes we do have to impose authority.

After these few tips, let us see some other educator qualities related to confidence.

Believe in What You Are Doing

Up to now we have spoken of the skills that lead to a personal attitude of confidence. But there remains one aspect that is essential if we want our self-confidence to be solid, one aspect that will give cohesion to our acquired attitude—confidence that what we are doing is worthwhile. Believe in what you are doing.

In this money-marked world, where cost is so often confused with worth, it can sometimes be difficult to evaluate an educator's role. It is impossible to put a price tag on something that goes beyond value. In essential terms, an educator's mission has nothing to do with money. We may speak of "formation" as our "product" and of "selling our product." People pay the tuition fees and "buy" formation for their children. But this is not exactly the case. It is like a travel agent selling "peace of mind" by advertising a week in a remote log cabin on a restful lakeside. At best, the agent can sell you a week "away from noise," and in doing so might help create the circumstances that favor peace of mind, but he cannot sell you peace of mind.

To be more precise, our "product" is not formation, but the setting, or custom-built opportunity for formation. The family, school, or youth venture will offer the kid what he needs for his formation. Obviously a school will offer more means than a weekend club, and a boarding school more than a day school, and a family more than all of them put together, but in the end what we are "selling" is not formation, but the means with which a kid can form himself. And these means are not merely the material elements (good facilities), nor are they simply good teachers, enthusiastic instructors, and interesting activities. Nor are these means just an expert body of people who will know, motivate, and guide the kid towards formation. Nor is it just a healthy atmosphere that favors positive growth. It is all of these coordinated amongst themselves and orientated towards a kid's formation. There are costs involved. Light, laundry, food, books, footballs... and even salaries. And when parents pay, these are the costs they are paying for. The costs they pay lay the groundwork for formation, but they do not buy formation, no more than your five hundred dollars a week by the lakeside will buy you peace of mind.

An educator will receive a salary, although some are volunteers (parents, for example!) But even when an educator receives a financial reward, it is more a "thank you" than a material equivalent for the work done—much in the same way a kid will pick a flower and give it to his mother. He is not paying his mother, but simply saying "thank you." Or when you put a few dollars in the Sunday collection, you are not trying to pay for confession or Mass, but simply expressing your thanks by helping to pay the parish bills.

So an educator's job, like a mother's, a priest's, or a doctor's, really has no price tag. It doesn't belong to the world of money. We cannot express the worth of an educator in financial terms. It's a different ball game.

Now, an educator will rarely get the chance to save a kid's life by fishing him out of the pool. An educator is not a modern day Indiana Jones who soars through his every day snatching the lives of men, women, and children from the clutches of death. Nor is he the brain surgeon who will perform an almost miracle operation and save the life of the patient. The time a kid spends with an educator, when compared to a kid's life span, is almost nothing. Timewise, it's almost insignificant. And yet, an educator's input can make, should make, must make, a difference to the kid's life. A difference flavored by eternity.

Extra Self-Confidence or Outward Confidence

Here's a strange aspect of the skills based self-confidence we have been speaking of up to now: one of the most important skills to be mastered is that of confiding in others.

To be a good pilot, you must know how to fly an airplane, but you must also have confidence in others. You have to trust the air traffic controller who tells you to take such and such a vector. You have to trust the runway maintenance crew. You have to trust the mechanics who checked your plane. You can sure fly the plane, but there's more to flight than flying. And this trust a pilot has in others isn't born out of his not being able to do everything himself and having to leave it up to others in the hope that they will do it as well as he would. No. He is not "leaving" anything up to others. The pilot has his job to do and the air traffic controller has his and the mechanic has his. The pilot will work with others. In fact, to be a good pilot, he has to work with others. This doesn't take away from his skill as a pilot, not does it diminish his self-confidence. This is rather obvious, but when we apply the concept to an educator's mission, we begin to discover new and practical aspects that we may not have thought about in depth.

There are four "people" the educator must have confidence in:

- Those who work with him
- The family, school, or center where he works
- The kids he is educating
- The Man behind it all

Confidence in Those Who Work with You

Here we refer to those who work directly with us, or to those who have a direct influence on the kid under our care. For an educator these people include one's spouse, fellow educators, teachers, sports instructors, and the chaplain.

Having confidence in our fellow educators means quite simply that we respect their ability to do the job right. In practical terms, this means that we will not overestimate our own skills to the extent that we consider ourselves to be the only ones capable of guiding the kids in our care. And in even more practical terms this plays out in:

- Asking our coworkers (spouse, teachers) for their observations on the kids. (Keep others updated on your work. Avoid mapping out little fortresses where only you have access. Be discreet when you have to be discreet, but don't let pseudo-discretion cloak your every move.)
- Sharing with them any communicable information and ideas you might have on a kid. (You cannot discuss matters that have come out of personal dialogue, but you can certainly share impressions and together collaborate your efforts regarding the personal formation of the kids.)

- Delegating as much as possible to them should you be in a position of command. (If you are a dean in a school, you can delegate to your educators, if you are an educator you can delegate to your assistants or to the teachers or coaches, and if you are an assistant you can delegate to certain kids.)

A word or two on delegating:

If we look at the Latin word, we can get an erroneous meaning for "delegate." In the Roman language it means to "untie." It means that we cut ourselves off from the responsibility and hand the ties—the controls—to another. But for us this meaning is not altogether correct. An example will show what we really intend:

You are riding a chariot with another person. You have the reins. You decide to delegate. You "untie" the reins from your hands and give them to the person riding with you. But you stay riding in the chariot. You will let your fellow rider guide the horses and maybe you will dedicate yourself to studying the map or to enjoying the scenery. You will not be a "back seat driver" telling the person with the reins what to do in every moment. This then is what we mean when we say "delegate." We do not mean that we pull over, hand over the reins, and wish the other well as he hurtles off into the sunset

Now in order to delegate there are one or two things we have to check:

First, we must be sure that the person we are going to delegate something to is capable of fulfilling the task. Now, here we must be careful. There is an innate tendency to feel that deep down we are really the best. In spiritual terms this is called "pride." And so we must be attentive. Sometimes there is the temptation to feel that the other person isn't quite up to doing what we would like to delegate. So a good rule of thumb here is to check with your director, and if he agrees with your delegating a certain responsibility to a certain person or not. As educators, we must be predisposed to delegate.

Secondly, there are certain tasks or areas that we just cannot delegate. Our responsibility is one of these. An educator (and here we refer specifically to the educator and not to an assistant) is ultimately responsible for his kids. He cannot delegate this responsibility. He cannot, for example, leave the whole area of human formation up to others and dedicate himself to video making, sports, or any other activity. He can share the tasks that derive from this responsibility (like delegating supervision duties or human formation dialogue), but the ultimate responsibility is his and this he cannot delegate.

An educator's *constant presence* is another aspect he cannot delegate. An essential characteristic of an educator is precisely this—his constant presence. It can happen that an educator will find excuses to be away from his kids. If these are legitimate, that's fine. But sometimes we find that an educator will offer to go shopping, or that he will tend to spend a little too much time editing a video, doing paperwork.... We cannot delegate this constant presence.

And when we delegate, we must also *verify*. This does not mean that we might as well do the job ourselves, but we must check and see that whatever we delegated is on course.

If, for example, your ask your older son to look after the young ones while you go out shopping, call and see if everything is all right. This is not so much as to "spy" on him, but just to make sure that he is doing well and to see if he needs any help. If you delegate the laundry service to a kid, check with him to see how things are going and ask if he needs help or has any ideas that would improve the service. Or if you ask someone to draw up a project, program a competition, or do a poster, do not wait until the agreed delivery date to make sure the thing is done. Check beforehand so that if things are not going according to plan, you can do something about it.

Delegating is an essential skill of any effective person. It is part of the strategic principle—***work, get others to work, and let others work.***[19]

Confidence in What You Work for

Working as an educator, you will be working within a structure that is, hopefully, inspired by the gospel. Catholic families are certainly God-inspired, and our schools should be too. Not only should the goals be rooted in Christ's teachings, but also the methods. And this can be something of an eye-opener. Any decent educational environment will in fact strive to recreate, or live out, the gospel—another Bethlehem, another Nazareth, another Capernaum, another Jerusalem.

A neat insight of the gospel (if we can put it that way) is that its message is not entirely focused on the future. While eternal salvation might well be the bottom line, Christ's teachings are clearly focused on the present too. He tells us where to head, but also how to get there. And in a weird twist, he also says that for us eternal life, our final goal, has already begun right here and now. Our present is part of our future.

The gospel goal, in essence, is not personal salvation. It is community salvation. Christ never said, "Save thyself." He said, "Go unto all nations and spread the Good News." By doing this, by helping others to get to heaven, we can get there. We cannot do it alone. Not only do we need the help of others, but we need to help others too. And it is this need to help others that is at the core of family and is the essence of any educational institution.

The goal of our efforts then is to prepare kids to be apostles (effective Christians) and in this way, to "apply" or to "be in the running" for personal salvation. This puts everything in a definite light. Competitions, discipline, good manners, studies, everything is done with an eye to preparing the kids to help others—not just to their being "complete" or "self-contained" people.

If, for example, we insist on a kid getting the best possible grades, it is not because we want to be able to say that our schools achieve great academic results—although this may be a good promotional line. We do it because a kid who does his best to be a good student is learning the secrets of self-betterment, effort, and duty. These qualities are essential if he is to be of any help to others. And being a good student will put him in a future position that will enable him to help others.

So this "nonpersonal" aspect of the goal, this "concern for others" that we learn from the gospel, must be important for us. But Christ also gives us the method, the way, to attain this goal. Down to the smallest detail, the gospel shows us how to live, think, and even sleep. If earlier on we have spoken about the qualities we seek to instill in our kids, it is because we find these qualities in Christ. Here are a few examples:

Awareness of Being a Son of God

"Our Father, who art in Heaven..."

"My Father will send the Holy Spirit..."

Generosity

Christ's whole life was a giving of self—we can think of his relentless preaching of the Good News and his death on the cross.

Willpower

Duty before pleasure can be seen throughout his life:

"Let us move on, for this is why I have come..."

"Let not my will but yours be done."

Responsibility

St. Paul tells us how Christ took upon himself the sins of the world to save us and in Christ's life we see that he was willing to suffer even death to accomplish his mission.

Discipline

When he was a kid, he was subject to his parents. And he also said that we should, "Pay unto Caesar what belongs to Caesar."

Hard Worker

St. John tells us that there would not be room in the world for the books, were they to be written that could contain all that Christ had done. And St. Mark gives us an almost hour-by-hour account of a normal day in the life of Christ.[20]

Constant

From the very beginning (Christ's birth), we see Christ preaching the very same message he would preach throughout his life, a message resumed in the Sermon on the Mount.

Initiative

Christ came to earth, became man, of his own free will. We can see this in Isaiah. But a point of Christ's initiative that I find particularly interesting is the way he detects the need of people to understand his message and his inventiveness in the use of the spoken word through his parables.

Self-sacrificing

Christ had nothing to gain from coming to live among us. And the crucifixion is the ultimate act of self-giving.

Internal Discipline

Again and again we see Christ driven by his perfectly focused understanding of what he had to do.

Well-Mannered

Christ cared for the next guy. He treated everybody with respect (even those peddlers in the temple, but that's another story). Even when he invited himself to Zacchaeus' house for supper, he was being well-mannered. In fact, even though it might appear to show Jesus as being most unmannerly (you just don't invite yourself over to someone's house for supper)—this case shows that he understood the essence of good manners to perfection. Think about it. Perfect manners are nothing more than putting the other person first and having regard for his feelings. Jesus knew that the guy wanted to invite him and he knew too that he would never muster up the courage to do so. So he did exactly what the guy wanted. Good manners are being a step ahead of the other guy—in a good sense.

Another episode of good manners is when Christ didn't sit down to lunch until he saw that all four thousand that were with him had something to eat too. He had to do a miracle on this one, but the lesson remains.

We also spoke of our prototype kid being full of joy, serenity, drive, and optimism, just as Christ was. And here we have a little lesson—joy doesn't mean laughing your heart out. Joy is something else. Joy is that inner and overriding warmth that comes from knowing that you are loved. It is stronger than anything that tries to get in its way. The Gospel according to St. John goes out of its way to show us that Christ was full of this joy, aware of this great love his Father had for him.

But Christ had a sense of humor as well, which was quite refined and quite sharp. The most volatile of the Twelve was Simon. We see him flare up on numerous occasions in the Gospel. A passionate man was Simon. When Christ announced that he was going up to Jerusalem to die, Simon said he'd go and die as well. When Christ told him that he would deny him, he was indignant and said "No way, Lord!" When the Risen Lord appeared, Simon jumped into the water—he had also nearly drowned in a previous episode—instead of waiting for the Lord to arrive. And yet Christ called this guy Peter, which means, "Rock." I guess it was a private little joke among them. A joke, but also a mission statement that was certainly no joke. Christ sure knew how to treat people right and get them to give their best.

There is no denying Christ's drive. He knew where he was going and didn't let anyone get in his way. The devil tried in the desert. Simon Peter tried to dissuade him from going up to Jerusalem. But he just kept on going. And Christ had optimism. More than looking on the bright side and ignoring the dark side, optimism comes from weighing the situation on hand, weighing the positive elements with which the situation can be dealt with, and from knowing that we have Someone all-powerful giving us a hand. Christ, who knows what's at stake, who comprehends what's in a man's heart, knows that his Father will not abandon anyone who makes a sincere effort. "Seek first the Kingdom of God." "There are many mansions in my Father's house."

Of course, these qualities can all be seen too in the Blessed Mother in the Gospel. But as radiant as her example may be and is, she is not the prototype. Christ is. And the Gospel gives us the how and the why we should do things.

Christ has been called a revolutionary. We tend to imagine a guy with a beret and a gun, with his fists in the air and giving passionate speeches when we say revolutionary, but a true revolutionary is one who "turns things around," he "revolves" something. And Christ, in this sense was a true revolutionary. He turned the way people thought around. The Pharisees set everything on the actual doing of things, but Christ taught that it was how you do things that mattered. God looks to the heart. He didn't say that we should not do things, (He did get baptized, he did say "Give unto Caesar…") But he emphasized that it was the how and why we did things that was important. (However, the term "revolutionary," because of the many bad overtones it contains in our language today, is not a term I like to use when referring to our Lord.)

A key insight into turning things around was when he said, "Man was not made for the Sabbath, but Sabbath for the man." And, "Love your neighbor" instead of "An eye for an eye." This certainly turned things around.

In practical terms, when applied to our mission, this means that our focus must not be the mere exterior accomplishment of a set of rules ("Walk, don't run," "Respect your elders," "Do as you are told," "Keep quiet at night") but the accomplishment of these rules based on internal, or personal, motivation. In essence, it's the difference between what we call external and internal discipline.

Christ also shows us how we, as educators, should work. We must be knowledgeable. He knew Scriptures when he was twelve. When he was grown up, he taught in the synagogues and left people agog with his insights. He knew where he was going with each person he met. He was trying to save them and get them to save others. He was inventive (think of his parables). And perhaps the biggest lesson he gave us what that of his selflessness. He was a man totally given over to his mission without seeking a reward other than that of doing his Father's will; that of a man practicing what he preached even unto death.

An extremely useful exercise is to take any aspect of our methods you care to mention and trace them to the gospel. You will find that there is a definite and unpretentious link to the person of Christ. This direct link with the gospel should give us confidence in our organization. And more—it should give us an overwhelming sense of joy and satisfaction that we are involved in something so directly Christ-related.

Another element to consider that should lead to confidence in what we work for is the quality of the people who work within it. Any teacher worth his salt will live for teaching, as any coach will live for his sport. Both mother and father will be totally dedicated to their kids. Experience will show that people who work with us on kid formation will have their work as a priority. It will be something that permeates their everyday lives. Knowing that we work alongside people committed to the same goals will stimulate us, and as well as giving us an example to follow, it will lead to confidence in the organization that we work for. And we're not talking workaholics here. We are talking simple, qualified, and dedicated people.

Confidence in the Kid We Are Educating

This means that we should believe that our kids are capable not only of perceiving the goals we set out for them but that they can also attain them. As a rule, we should have complete confidence in our kids from day one. Let's not work backwards. "I will not have confidence in this kid until he proves himself to be worthy" is both a smug and deformative approach in personal relationships. A priest I had the honor of working with once said to me, "I have complete confidence in you. But if you make me lose this confidence I have in you, it will be a hard job for me to regain it."[21]

Here are some examples:

It's time to tidy lockers. Once we are sure the kids know what to do, let them do it. Avoid being like a brooding hen that puts her beak into everything that is going on. You can go around, encouraging, even saying things like, "Something missing there, Tommy," without actually pointing out what is exactly wrong. Once time is up, then you can review what the kids have done. Verify.

It's time to go to bed. Once you give the "silence signal" (see page 140), let them do it. Be present, walk up and down quietly, but avoid saying things like, "Into bed now, guys, in silence" or "Hurry up! Keep quiet!" You have told them what to do and now have sufficient confidence in them to believe that they will do it. Verify.

It's time for sports. You give the kids four minutes—or whatever—to get ready. Once again, avoid dressing them yourself. I have seen well-intentioned people help kids tie their shoelaces. (We're talking ten-year-olds here!) Let them do it. Let's not be like the overbearing mother who feels that her twelve-year-old is incapable of combing his hair or of putting on his sweater correctly. Let us be content to verify.

Having confidence in kids goes way beyond the practical "getting-things-done" arena. When speaking with kids, they must sense that we believe in them. Dictating short-term goals without taking the kid himself and his opinions into account will go against us.[22] On the contrary, treating the kid as a thinking person will greatly enhance your success and the kid's betterment.

Compare:

"Now, for this week, I want you to pay special attention to your math class, even though you don't like the teacher."

with

"O.K., Henry. How do you think you can be more open to others? Let's focus on being open to teachers. Pick one that you find it hard to get along with. ("The math teacher.") Good. Now, how do you think you can be more open?"

Have confidence too (believe) that the kids can always be better. Never accept a plateau situation where you believe that the kid is about as good as he can ever get. Keep leading them further.

You can start on the basics (punctuality, tidiness) and go from there. Sometimes, however, an educator may think that well-made beds and straight lines are about as much as he can ask for. "You can only be so punctual. You cannot have the place any tidier. You cannot have the kids dress any better. They're just about perfect," might be the line of an educator. "How can I get them to be any more punctual? How can I get them tidier than tidy?" But even in the "perfect" school there is always room for improvement. Where?

On the inside. Take punctuality: OK, so the kids are punctual, always on time. But why?

The perfect kid will be punctual because he sees it as a loving response to what God's will is for him. And not simply that God wants him to be on time, for the sake of being on time, but as a concrete way of accomplishing his mission.

While a kid might say that this is really why he does things, we would do well to ask ourselves how deep this conviction goes. In all too many cases, it turns out to be nothing more than a reflex response as meaningful as the "Have a nice day" you get at the checkout in your local store.

So, you start by getting the kids to be punctual because "that's the way we do things" (external discipline). Then you move up and say it's because "it's you're duty as a person" (the beginning of internal discipline). Then you move up and show how being punctual is a way of doing what God wants you to do (here we are getting into the higher spheres). Next you can move up and show how punctuality can be an expression of love for God (almost there). Then you try and get the kid to do it as an expression of his love for God. And finally you try and get the kid to do it as an expression of his willingness to respond lovingly and effectively to the mission that God is calling him to do in life (now we're really flying!)

And if the kid's punctuality is perfect, as just described, how about their concern for others (love or charity, rather than just simple peaceful coexistence)? How about being tidy?

When you think things have plateaued, go to the chapel and ask the Lord if there is anything more you can do for him. Expect a "Yes!"

Confidence in the Man Above

If we were to limit ourselves to believing in ourselves and in others on a human plane, we would certainly achieve much. We would have men of character and of human virtue. Students would become good students, boys would become well-mannered young men, and sons would be obedient and responsible--up to a point. When life comes to the crunch, these kids would crumble. For human virtue, based on human faith, can only go so far. Human virtue gives little or no answers to life's bigger questions such as death, suffering and, more importantly, even life itself. And just as our mission must have a strong element of human confidence (in ourselves, in others), it must also be soaked in confidence in God.

We are not alone on this mission of kid formation. We didn't start it and we will certainly not be there at the end of it. We are, even as parents, simply helpers along the way. When we work as educators, we are like people whose paths cross with the kids and run parallel with them for a while. If our time is well spent as we walk with them, our contribution will be invaluable to them, but really it's not our show. We just have a part to play.

In our work, we are trying to get the kids to become what Christ wants them to be. We must believe that if we do our best, God will bless our efforts and it will be him, not us, who will see to it that fruit comes forth. He will not only give the kid the graces (the help, the strength) to do what is expected of him, but he will also ensure our strength and courage, patience and constancy (see Help from the Wings, page 107). "Doesn't God your Father know what you need?"

Confidence then is key. Believing in ourselves, in those who work with us, in what we work for, in the kids we are trying to help, and in the Man above are all essential.

Leadership

Confidence is a tool. We now need to put this tool to work. And an educator puts it to work by giving his kids a direction in life. An educator leads. He's a leader. There are some fundamental errors floating around about the type of leadership we want to talk about. Let's straighten them out immediately.

First, being a leader does not mean you are a better person than those who are not leaders. It might mean that you are faster, but it doesn't mean you're better. You might have a better vision of the global goal, but this does not make you better than those who might follow. So being a leader is more about position than about privilege.

You see, in our Christian perspective, we do not have better people or worse people. We have people. They might appear good or bad. Only God knows. And while some people may be better at certain things, they are not necessarily better people for it. The only time we can use the term "better person" is when applied to one person. We could say that, "I am a better man today than I was last year when I spent all my money on bets and booze," or "Johnny is certainly better this year—he is more concerned about the others and he does more for them than last year."

Another misconception regarding leadership is that it is great to be a leader. Well, according to leaders I know personally, it is not so great at all. It's windy and lonely up there. And it's not easy to lead. Much more comfortable to let someone else open the way and for you just to follow through.

Another misconception is that on a team not everybody can be a leader. Wrong again. A team does not exist for the benefit of the team. It exists for the benefit of those for whom, or with whom, it works. And for these people, each team member must be a leader.

And my favorite misconception is the one that says a leader must have fair hair, blue eyes, and be great fun at parties.

And now, after getting those ugly misconceptions out of the way, let's see what a leader is.

Vision

In its most essential meaning, a leader is someone who has something others want. You cannot be a leader if no one follows. You simply cannot lead nobody. But if you do have someone who follows you, it is because you have something that attracts him. It may be money, and so we have the money leader. People follow them either in the hope of getting money or just because they like the money atmosphere and want to be close to it. It may be a social fame that people hang around you for, either because they want fame or at least want to be part of it. It might be athletic ability, and people follow either to enjoy what they see or because they want to imitate it. People will follow political leaders because they believe that the guy in the nice suit will come true with his promises and make things better for them.

But our mission as leaders does not fit into any of the above categories—not because the ones I have just mentioned are bad, but simply because they are not good enough. What should be our "attraction" as leaders? Why should people follow us? Because we have a vision, and we know how to get there. That's why.

As leaders we must—and this is imperative--must have a clear and detailed vision. This vision is not of our own making. It is from God, and it is based on what man is and what he is called to become. Hazy religious leaders abound today. "Be-good" preachers and their followers usually end up down in the middle of some jungle drinking Kool-Aid.

The first and most important quality of us as leaders must be our vision, the goal to which we have been called to lead people. So if we are working in academies, or in schools, or on retreats we must see our vision clearly. When we say we want to help people become saints, we must know exactly what a saint is and how he behaves. We don't have to invent things here, but we do have to do our research.

In the academies, we have it neatly laid out in front of us: academic excellence, comprehensive human development, and solid spiritual formation. But what does all this mean—in detail? This we must know if we are to be the true—and effective—leaders we have been called to be.

Knowing How to Get There

Vision isn't everything. It's where things start and where things end. But as leaders, the second quality we must have is knowing how to get there, and this includes knowing how to get other people there. It is not enough to say that a saint is a sincere, responsible, honest person. We need to know exactly what being responsible means and how to get people to be responsible.

Let's talk briefly about something we sometimes get wrong. In part it is due to a linguistic mishap. We are talking leadership. We are talking direction. In Spanish, "dirección" can mean "address," but it can also mean "administration" or "management," and here we have our linguistic hiccup. Management deals with the day-to-day running of a company, of a school, or of a country. In the United States, management is often referred to as "administration." ("Administración" in Spanish usually just refers to "money management.") So when someone from Central or South America says "direction," they often understand "dirección," that is management, as the day-to-day business of getting things done. But in English, "direction" (leadership) does not mean the day-to-day running of things. Direction—leadership—means the giving of orientation, or to point in a certain "direction." Quite often we can find "leaders" so involved with "management" that they fail to give direction. The day-to-day bustle distracts them from leading. They get tied down with the urgent and forget the important. Direction and management are two different skills and two different jobs. To be a good leader (director), you must know what goes into management and how things are done, but a good director leaves this management up to the managers.

But now, back to where we left off:

Inspiration

A leader must inspire. Here we might get a bit heavy, so we might need to slow down a bit.

Our type of leadership must inspire. This touches the essence of our role as educators. We know that "e-ducator" comes from Latin and among its meanings is to "lead out from." A teacher will lead students out of their ignorance into the light of knowledge, for example. But we will carry this a bit further.

Before we lead a person, we delve deep down into a their inner self. We dive deeper than emotions. We dive deeper than thought. We dive until we arrive at that innermost God-made sanctuary where the vision we propose will find an immediate, thirsting, and enthusiastic echo. It is from this deepest depth that we lead the person towards that vision. In fact, our dream will not find a true echo in a person unless we manage to get down to, and touch, that innermost chord; and our real vision, friendship with, and dedication to God, will not materialize.

If we want a girl to dress nicely, we can appeal to her vanity. If we want her to treat others correctly, we could appeal to her sense of compassion. If we want her to be faithful to God, appealing to vanity or to human compassion will not get us anywhere. She might dress well so God might think well of her, or because she wants to treat God nicely especially because others treated him so badly, but in itself this is not what we are leading her towards. It may well be a fine start—and oftentimes it is—but it is not what we are really leading her towards.

And so for this "e-ducation" to be successful, we need to get right down into the heart of a person. We must make real contact. This is what we call I call "inspiration." When that innermost chord is touched, when the door to that deepest sanctuary is opened—we have contact, we have inspiration. A leader must inspire.

Care

A leader cares.

An employee accepted a new job. He was given a simple little place in which to live out in the country. The cottage had not been lived in for some time, and there was no electricity and no water. Within a week, the employee, in his spare time, had cleaned the place up and had managed to get electricity connected, but he didn't have the time to get new pipes and hook up the water supply. Showering with cold mineral water would have to do for a while. Nuestro Padre paid a short, unexpected and informal visit... "Just passing through." At eight-fifteen the next morning, the little house had running water.

A leader must not only have vision, know how to get there, and know how to inspire, he must care for those he leads. Practical-honest-to-goodness running-water care. Far from the "How are you today?", this caring spirit makes the leader go out of his way to ensure that those he leads are well looked after. A leader must care in detail for those he leads.

Aspects of caring

A checklist (out-of-family educators):

- During breaks, do all your kids have something to eat?
- (boys) Do their pants have holes in them?
- (boys) Are their pants the right size (not too tight or too long)?
- Are there mirrors available so that kids can check their personal appearance?
- (girls) Are their skirts the right length? Maybe they're a little too long in the hope that they will soon grow into them!
- (girls) Are skirt hems well stitched?
- Are sweaters well fitting and full bodied (as opposed to the "sack-of-potatoes" that adorn many a student)?
- Is there a qualified person readily available to attend to upset stomachs, cuts, and scrapes?
- (academies or retreat centers) Is each single bed comfortable with strong springs?
- At any moment of the day, does a kid have to spend more than three minutes to find you?
- If your kids have to play a game against a visiting or outside team, are their sports uniforms crisp and clean?

The simple rule of thumb is this:

Do unto others before they do unto you...sorry, that's not the one I was looking for. Rather, do for others what you would like them to do for you. Pretend for a moment that you are every kid in your charge. Now ask yourself, "What would I like the educator to do for me?" Then, as educator, if the desire is within your ability, do it.

Faith

A fifth quality will spring quite naturally from the four we have just mentioned. When we have a clear vision, when we know how we can get there and how we can lead others there, when we know how to inspire, and when we really care about those we are leading, a tremendous faith in our mission will blossom—faith that we can really do it. In its turn, this faith will quicken the fire within us to lead courageously. It will nourish our down moments and spur us on.

Leading from the Front

Now, the best way to lead, the only way to really lead, is from the front—otherwise we are not leading, we are pushing. You lead from the front.

Hopeless is the coach who expects his players to chest manage a ball, if they have never seen him do it. Remember how you felt when the gym teacher would tell you to do five laps of the field or of the gym, and he just stood there?

Once I was involved in putting on a play in school. We had one every year; it was a tradition. We had all been given our lines and did our best to learn them and come in on cue. It was exciting. We were passionate fifteen-year-olds, and we all discussed the roles we were to play, and we each gave them our personal input. During a rehearsal, the director got rather annoyed.

"No! No! No!" he wailed from below. "This is the climax. We need more...." He clenched his fists and searched for a word he never found. "Try it again, and this time with more...." (And the fists again.) Nobody really knew what he meant, and we never did get it right. After numerous attempts, the director gave up and as if to justify the failure blurted out, "You will never become professional actors." And none of us ever did.

The following year, another class was chosen to put on the Christmas play. And another director had been chosen. Since my brother was in the cast, I waited for him one afternoon after school while they were rehearsing. I entered when some poor kid couldn't give the director what she wanted.

"This is the climax," the director was saying. (I had a certain déjà vu feeling.) "We need more emotion here." (At least she had found the word.) "I want your voice to wobble with emotion and I want to see tears coming down your cheeks." (Tall order.) The poor kid was at a total loss. He just stood there, embarrassed by being asked to do something he could never do. And annoyed too, because he was in front of his friends.

The director came up onto the stage.

"Look," she said as she crossed over to where he helplessly stood. "Here are some tricks." She stopped in front of him. "To... to get... to get your voice to... to wobble... just... keep... just keep taking in... little sharp gasps of... air. And then let the air out again in little gasps as well." She had the kid's attention. We all thought she was going to break down. Then she did.

"And, to get tears into... into your eyes... just think of something... of something real sad.... Your dog has just been squashed, your mother has just died after a long illness...think! Concentrate. Don't concentrate on crying, that will come. Just think of your poor little crumbled-up dog as he lies in the mud after so many years of true... and loyal... friendship." She stopped, unable to say anymore. She fumbled for a handkerchief and dabbed her wet cheeks.

Forget about being able to get our voices to wobble—and my brother and I could never really get the tears to flow either—but the kid in the play certainly managed to get it right for the three performances. It was quite something to see. And many moms cried.

So this is what I mean by leading from the front. If we want a kid to do something, show him how it's done. Let him follow. Our job is not to show kids how to slam-dunk or how to act out a drama role. For that, we have good coaches and able instructors. Our mission is to teach our kids how to practice virtue.

Leading from the front has another point I'd like to clear up.

Did you ever have a teacher who really knew his stuff? Well, basically, to be a teacher you need to know your stuff, otherwise you don't get qualified. But here I mean that kind of teacher that lets you know that he knows everything and that you are pretty dumb not to grasp his teachings? Chemistry teachers are pretty good at this. Some math guys really excel. We could say that they are leading from the front, but really they are not. They are like the enthusiastic mountain hiker who goes out with a bunch of unfit guys. He streaks out ahead of them, calling back every now and again, "Come on!"—his voice getting fainter each time. He will of course stop and wait for his buddies. But he will stop and wait just enough time for them to catch up with him, and then off he goes again! He's had a chance to rest up (as if he ever needed it), but affords no such luxury to those windless unfortunates who have just caught up with him. They just get more and more tired. This enthusiastic mountain hiker is in front, and you could say he is leading, but this is not the kind of leader we need to be.

We must be out front, of course, but not too far out in front. We can keep moving forward, but we must adjust our pace to those we are leading.

This leading from the front has many practical applications (and the situations may vary):

When it's time to clean up the dining room after a meal, dig in yourself—not barking orders, but almost as one of the kids.

When it's time to go out and enjoy the snow, get excited, and play. Even adults can have fun in the snow.

If you watch a movie with a touching ending, don't be afraid to cry.

If you expect the kids to be on time, be on time yourself...always. Don't use your authority as a shield for being late.

If you're particularly tired, don't be afraid to show it, but use it to show how you are able to continue doing your duty, and to do it well, in spite of your tiredness.

Sing in the chapel when you're supposed to. So what if you're not a Pavarotti![23]

Let us not be afraid of kids catching us making a sneak visit to the Blessed Sacrament or to a statue of the Blessed Virgin Mary.

Leave the door to your room ajar so kids can see how tidy it is (and tidy it better be). If you have valuables and fear they will be stolen, have administration look after them for you. And speak to the director about the guy you believe is a thief!

Be wide-awake and totally alert at all times, especially first thing in the morning and last thing at night. Half of this is easy for everybody. Morning people will be bright in the morning but dull at night. Night people will be dull in the morning and bright at night. An educator has to be both. A shower and coffee in the morning helps if you're a night person. A five o'clock shower and coffee can help if you're a morning person.

Eat with the kids and show them, without always telling them, how's it's done properly.

Pick up that piece of paper you see (even if you might feel it degrading to do so—but I don't see why it should...after all, it's your place as much as it is the kids').

Say "thank you!" when a kid does something for you.

Use "please" not as a plea but as a mark of respect.

The above, however, must never go against our being an educator. If you play with the kids in the snow or on the field, remember that we do have some rules governing certain aspects. We, as educators, cannot play in any serious game with the students. By serious games, I mean matches or tournament games. We can kick a football around, shoot a few baskets, throw a Frisbee, skate around... but as educators, we can never participate in any game where we could be seen as an adversary, or in any game that could excite us so much that we momentarily could lose control of ourselves. We must always give absolute priority to our being educators. If playing with the kids means we lose sight of some of the kids we are supposed to be supervising, we cannot continue playing.

Omnipresent

This is a divine quality that we do well to master, or at least to simulate. A kid, in any of our apostolates, should always see two things: a trash can and an educator. We can talk about the trash can some other time. Suffice it to say that no qualitative relation is inferred.

Omnipresent means being everywhere always. A good educator will be everywhere and always. Of course, he doesn't need to be. The kids will work, study, play, go to bed...all by themselves. After all, we are educating them in conviction and responsibility, aren't we? But nonetheless, an educator will always be there. And not "just in case" something goes wrong. We are not firemen ("just a call away"), nor are we policemen patrolling the streets or the corridors. We are educators. Here is why we should be everywhere always:

First, because when we are dealing with kids anything can happen. Anything. Usually our very presence will be enough to ensure against any avoidable mishap (fights, bad language, indecent behavior) but even when an accident does happen, when a fight does break out, by being there we can act immediately and stop it from getting worse.

Secondly, being there gives us the opportunity to observe how our kids act and react. Oftentimes we can see if they are living up to their personal development program. From their interaction, we can also find many examples that will help us, either in dialogue or in night talks, to get our message across with concrete illustrations and examples.

Thirdly, being there gives the kids a sense of security. Not the security that comes from armed guards walking about, but the peace of mind that a kid has when he knows his dad is there with him. An educator is not the kid's dad, but the sense of security is of this order.

Fourth, being there lets us offer a suggestion ("Why not let Graham have a turn?"), give a word of encouragement ("Come on, my granny plays better than that!"), or recognize something well done ("Good one, Bill!") The situations create themselves—and by being there we have the chance to make the most of them.

This omnipresence does however tend to become burdensome by virtue of the fact that it must be constant. We cannot "be there always" just some of the time. We must be there always. This reason alone would validate our working as a team, but when "you're on" you're on.

Now let me suggest some hows.

Tips on omnipresence for a dean of students:

1. Be unpredictable in your daily movements. Apart from designated times for dialogue, your daily movements must appear to be "erratic." We cannot be like the nighttime watchman whose every move can be foreseen.
2. Wear shoes and clothing that make no noise.
3. Have keys that will allow you access to routes not traveled by the kids, and use these routes.
4. Emerge from rooms that you have no obvious reason for being in. If the kids are expected to walk down a corridor, let's say to go to the auditorium, casually step out of a classroom that they will be passing.
5. Occasionally be just a little away from the place you're expected to be. When the kids go to the dorm, for example, be just slightly out of sight. You can be looking out a window.
6. Don't spring traps. Just be there. By this we mean avoid jumping out at the kids. And don't be anywhere that leads to suspicion or ridicule. Don't be waiting for the

kids out in the woods. Don't hide behind doors, or if you do, pretend you are putting up a notice on the door.

7. Never be in your office for more than thirty minutes, unless you are following an approved dialogue schedule.
8. Work as a team with other educators. Mention to them any kid you may have seen away from the group (even if the kid was just going to the bathroom or going to answer a phone call).
9. Ensure respect for the rules of the academy or school even if the offender is not one of your kids.
10. Establish a quick walking route that will encompass kid areas, and non-kid areas, and do the route at least twice a day.
11. Be off-the-cuff about your "divine" attribute. Don't go running from A to B. Breeze in and out as if being there was the most natural thing in the world for you.

Joy

There is no substitute for joy, nor can it be splashed on like aftershave every morning. Confidence, leadership, and all other educator qualities wither and are useless if we do not have joy. And joy is not something we go out and conquer, such as the virtue of obedience or of self-discipline. Joy is the fruit that springs spontaneously from a clear conscience.

When we speak of joy being an essential quality of an educator, we are referring to that inner joy that can only come from knowing that one is doing one's duty. We are not talking about "feeling good" here. We are talking about joy.

Being with kids and feeling their happiness and enthusiasm can be contagious—and sinister. It can all too often make us feel that it is our happiness we feel, when really all we are experiencing is their enthusiasm.

A trainee/educator spent a good part of his every morning visiting the primary school, especially during recess. He obviously enjoyed the antics and happy spirit of the kids. Over lunch he would talk, radiant, of what he had seen. His enthusiasm was evident. And he was much liked by the kids, always having a new trick to show them and always teasing them with his clever riddles. It was only halfway through his first term as trainee that this particular educator realized that he was beginning to hate his job. It was taking him away from the enthusiasm of the primary school. He was, after all, educator of studies.

But he was a dedicated young man, so he shouldered the burden with a spirit of sacrifice and got down to what he was supposed to be doing—looking after the academics in the school. He enjoyed this work much less than roaming around the primary school, but he realized that he was now happier. He was doing what he was supposed to be doing. And although his visits to the bubbling primary school were fewer, they were much more enjoyed by both himself and by the kids.

So we need to be careful not to get distracted and mistake a certain superficial enthusiasm for joy. The more we understand our role as educators, the better equipped we are, and the more we try our best to give our best, the more joy will spring up from within us.

This joy is an essential quality for an educator. Kids sense joy. And the deeper our joy, the deeper our success will be as educators. There is no faking joy. Kids can see through falseness and farce much quicker than we sometimes might like to think. It is joy that will give you long-standing credibility.

So, in practical terms, where is this joy to be seen? Here are a few questions that will point you in the right direction:

Joy: A little checklist:

1. Do you enjoy your work?
2. Would you do this work even if you were not paid for it?
3. Do you welcome the challenge a kid with a difficulty provides you with?
4. Have you spoken to every kid in your group (or section) at least once these past two weeks on a person-to-person basis in formal dialogue?
5. Do you enjoy being with the kids in your group or section?
6. Have you prayed by name for each member of your group or section within the past twenty-four hours?
7. Do you try to look your best for your kids?
8. In the past twenty-four hours, have you exchanged at least one form of greeting with each kid in your group or section?
9. Have you corrected at least five kids in the past twenty-four hours?
10. Would you volunteer to spend your next day off in the hospital with one of your kids who is sick?
11. Are you qualified in CPR?
12. Do you pray for yourself?

The answer to all the above should obviously be "yes," even the last one (for he who thinks that he can be an educator without asking continually for strength from above may not have understood yet what being an educator is all about). The questions, in fact, point to just some aspects of your competence as an educator. And the more competent you are, the more you are suited to the work, and the more you give yourself to those under your charge, the more joyful you will be.

When Fr. Flanagan was setting up the first Boys' Town in Nebraska in the 1920s, one evening he saw a teenager slowly approaching the main building with a load upon his shoulders. Realizing that the teenager was actually carrying another boy, and that the state of his clothes indicated many miles of dusty and tiresome travel on foot, Fr. Flanagan asked, "How did you manage to carry that kid for so long?" "He ain't heavy, Father. He's my brother."

Ode to the Educator

An educator may get tuckered out, but never tires.
An educator may hate getting out of bed, but loves what he gets up for.
An educator may get discouraged, but never loses heart.
An educator may long for a day off, but doesn't want to miss a beat.
An educator may get annoyed, but never angers.
An educator may be good, but is forever getting better.
An educator may stumble, but never loses his way.
An educator may fall, but never stays down.
An educator may be proud of his kids, but never satisfied.
He may have, but never hold.

Demanding

A good educator will be demanding of his kids. At the same time, he won't be gruff, but kind. He must never accept the state of things today as final. Kids, adults too, change daily. In the chapter on positive motivation we have talked about how an educator should be demanding with the kids. Here I just want to emphasis this aspect as an essential quality of the educator.

As a general rule of thumb, this "demandingness" is based not on a perpetual and insatiable discontent, but rather on our view of things as they should be. Put another way, we should not be demanding that the kids be continually more punctual or tidier. After all, you can only be so punctual. Either you're punctual or you're not. Our demands must be a result of us having compared the present state of a kid with the expectations we have for that kid in particular. It's like this:

We are on the top of a hill looking down. We see the kid coming up towards us from below. We see how much more the kid has to go before he reaches where he has to get to. We can also see what stands in his way, and indeed we can see ways he can circumvent such obstacles. So we shout down to him, encouraging him to go on and telling him which way to go.

This is a far cry from another illustration: we are hacking our way through thick, unending undergrowth, barely able to see ten feet in front of us. And we shout out to the kid, presumably lost somewhere in the bush, "Come on! Keep going!" Maybe the kid has already gotten to where he's supposed to be!

Our demandingness must be based on our knowledge of what this kid has yet to attain. It's hopeless, if not indeed ridiculous, to demand of a kid that he get straight As in math when he is only capable of a B. "High ideals" are well and good, but they must be attainable.

I remember a competition we ran many years ago. The idea was basically a good one, but we didn't think things out well enough. Faced with the problem of campus litter, the competition awarded one point for every piece of paper deposited in one of various bins. There was a prize for the kid who reached a certain amount of points. But the competition flopped. In fact, it never really got off the ground. With experience the reason was plain. It wasn't that kids minded picking up pieces of paper. It was in the fact that to attain the prize the number of points required was one thousand. While greeted with initial enthusiasm, the kids soon realized that it would take forever to clock up such a number (the campus was not that bad!), and so all interest was lost.

Another example that I well remember and that serves to illustrate this topic dates back to when the academies were just beginning. Wanting to make a kid more responsible, I designated him my personal coffee maker. He was delighted and boasted of his appointment. But during my first lunch after the appointment, no coffee was forthcoming. In the afternoon, I asked the kid what had happened. "Why?" he asked. "What's wrong?" "What happened to my coffee at lunchtime?" "Oh," was the reply. "I didn't know you wanted coffee at lunchtime." And indeed it had certainly been my fault. I had to be more precise in my demands. So I said, "George, may I please have some coffee during supper."

Suppertime came and I was duly presented with a cup containing what George referred to as "coffee." It had a pale, cold look to it. I sipped it. My first thought was to give it to the kid for bringing me such bilge water full of grains, but then I thought a little. Maybe the kid didn't know how to make coffee. I asked him to show me how he used the coffee machine.

He slid open the compartment where the filter would usually go and poured in two teaspoons of coffee grains. Then he got some cold water from the tap and poured it over the grains. He closed the compartment and the water piddled down into the coffee carafe. He hadn't used a filter, hadn't put the water where it was supposed to go, and hadn't even turned on the machine. That is when I learned the importance of making sure that a kid knows exactly what and when to do what we demand of him. Sometimes we can take just a little too much for granted.

We can apply exactly the same principle to the demand we make of a kid to "be good." We have to be sure that he knows how to get the job done.

Another point to consider here, a point that sets an educator's "job" apart from most others, is that our demandingness of the kids must be a reflection of our demandingness of ourselves. In fact, if one of our roles is that of setting a good example, and it is, then we should not be demanding of our kids if we are not demanding of ourselves. And given that we must be demanding of our kids, we must be demanding of ourselves. We are not selling shoes. A shoe salesman does not have to buy, much less wear, what he sells. We are not shoe salesmen. We must wear what we sell, and sell what we wear.

Accessibility

Julius Caesar had it right. He said that one of a leader's qualities should be his accessibility. In an educator's life, this means that a kid should always be able to speak to him. Here we have two key words: "always" and "speak."

Always means always. An educator's time is not his own. Even at night, an educator must not close his door. It must be left slightly ajar. This for supervision (you hear things better with an open door, no matter how big a window you might have), but it is also a sign that you, like your door, are open. In "Tips of the Trade" (see page 216) we mentioned the need to keep your personal difficulties or problems off campus, and here we find another reason for doing so. Rarely will a kid approach an educator who appears grumpy, irate, or flustered. Always also means that those working with you know always exactly where you are. An educator who cannot be found within ten minutes is a poor educator.

Speak means that a kid must be able to approach a person who he knows will listen. This is why an educator must show that he welcomes kids coming to speak with him. Gruff phrases such as "What's wrong with you?" and "What else?" should be replaced by Christian courtesy lines such as "How can I help you?" and "Is there anything else on your mind?"

Of course, we must train kids too so that they don't come expecting a royal ear when you are up to your eyes getting the section ready for class or trying to get a class into order. But should a kid express a desire to speak with us, and if we are unable to speak to him immediately, then we must give him a definite time in the very near future. Use "right after supper in my office" rather than the generic "later."

Respect, an Educator's Hallmark

"When I turned fourteen, I was given a room of my own. A day or two after I moved in, someone knocked on my door. It wasn't locked. In fact, it was even ajar. Who could this be? I wondered. I had never said, "Come in!" in all my life, and I felt awkward. So I got up and went to see who was there. It was my dad. "May I come in?" I was taken totally aback. Since when did my father have to have permission to roam his house as he pleased? It might have been my room, but it was his house. I smiled, stood aside and said, "My room is your room!"

As with many things, we all agree with respect in principle, but sometimes it somehow slips our mind in practice. We will define respect and then go on to see how an educator can put into practice this quality.

Respect is giving a person his due place and acting accordingly. As Christians, we are convinced that Christ may be seen in every child, woman and man and as such we should treat them as we would treat the very Christ. But as well as this overriding respect, there are certain "areas of competence" that I would like to point out.

Before getting into practical examples, I think it convenient to dispel conflicting concepts regarding "respect and authority." Some will say that authority determines the amount of respect that should be shown. (In a business, the CEO will command more respect than the security guard.) Others will say that respect has nothing whatsoever to do with authority. (We should respect the beggar at the door as much as we respect the nation's president.) If we combine these two we get an "Animal Farm"-type conclusion that states, "All people should be respected, but some should be more respected than others!" So perhaps we should define the relationship between respect and authority.

Put simply, we can say that we must respect the person, and

we must also respect their competence.

For example, we will respect a doctor as a person (because he is a son of God) and we will respect his competence, or authority, as a doctor (because he has studied the subject for many years and knows what he is talking about). Two people, a college dropout and a medical physician, come to dinner. We will treat both exactly with the same respect. We will look after each one with the same degree of concern. But should a discussion evolve around medical matters, we will take the doctor's view or comments more into consideration than those of the college dropout. Not because one is a better person than the other, but because one is more competent as a doctor than the other.

What sometimes goes wrong is that people will often tend to give "competence respect" where no "competence respect" is due. An actress, who considered herself to be more famous than she actually was, appeared on an evening television talk show. The host (more hairspray than brains) also had a scientist on the show who had just published a book on world poverty. After asking the actress about her life as a movie star, the brainless host then asked her what she thought a viable solution to solve world hunger might be. She proclaimed that the only answer was to bring down the birthrate by whatever means were available. The scientist was given a few moments to have his say. He wasn't a particularly attractive man. He was bald, had a pronounced chin, and was obviously nervous. But he said that data showed that there is more than enough food and water in the world for three times the present day population, and that the real problem was in distribution. As the scientist began giving some specifics, the bored host interrupted him and asked the actress what means in particular would she consider useful to bring down the birthrate. Any witless person following the program would have been led to believe that the actress—and not the scientist—was the expert on the topic. The program was a clear example of attributing "competence respect" where there was absolutely no competence.

The word "respect" comes from Latin and originally meant "to look upon," or "to take into consideration."[24] If you are ever at a restaurant and notice a group of businessmen having lunch, you can see who is the most respected by the way the others keep looking to him. "Do unto others as you would have them do unto you" is Christ's basic rule for the respect we should have for the person, while his "Give unto Caesar what belongs to Caesar" is his rule concerning the person's competence. They are two concepts that run together in the same direction, not two charging lance bearers in a medieval tournament.

It was necessary to go into this in some detail, as it can happen that all too easily we too can get things a little confused. Having clear ideas will help us respect each other and each other's areas of competence.

Respect for Those "Above" Us

An educator will always be working under somebody. Usually he will have an educator general and a director over him. It goes without saying that in private and in public, an educator owes his superiors deference. Here are some areas that sometimes we might not pay much attention to, but that are an integral part of this area of respect:

When in the presence of a superior, you should not sit down until you are invited to.

If you are waiting in a superior's office, keep your eyes to yourself and avoid scanning whatever papers may be on the desk.

Stand up when a superior comes into the room, unless there is a senior superior already in the room.

If the superior leaves the room, stand. If he comes back in again, stand. Try and avoid taking the "slow-stand-up-mode," that consists in slightly moving in your chair and pretending to get up, as it only points to a certain trace of laziness.

Let a superior speak as much as he wants to and avoid trying to run the conversation. Let him lead, or at least, should he wish to follow, give him ample opportunity of taking up the lead whenever he may want.

Respect for Those Alongside Us

An educator works alongside many people: his assistants, the teachers, the sports people, and even, strange as it may seem, alongside gardeners, cooks, and dishwashers.

An educator will never disagree with one of his assistants in front of the kids. If it came to the crunch, he could. He has the authority to do it, but here we are not talking authority. We are talking respect.

An educator will knock on a classroom door, or attract the teacher's attention some other way, and be invited in before he enters the classroom. Once again, we are not dealing with authority, but with respect. The teacher is in charge of the class, and an educator will respect his position.

In like manner, an educator will respect a sport instructor's competence and avoid giving orders to the kids while they are under another's care. For example:

An educator is an avid tennis player. He watches a coach lead a class. But he sees that the coach is not showing the kids what the educator considers to be the right technique for the forearm smash. So the educator steps on to the court, takes the racket from a kid and says, "Look, Willis, watch carefully. You pull your right arm back over your shoulder and behind your head. You almost touch your left shoulder with the racket before you start the forward movement, that's the secret..."

The same example, which can only be interpreted as interference, can be applied to singing class, to the making of posters, to classroom situations...anywhere where the educator is not the person directly in charge of that activity. A different matter, of course, is encouragement.

Our avid tennis educator is welcome to shout out his encouragement to the kids on the court, "Come on, George! You can do better than that!" But he must always be careful not to give instruction, even if this is merely repeating what the coach has said. If the coach thinks it necessary to repeat a command, let the coach repeat it. That's his job.

If you do find that a teacher or instructor is not doing the job as you would like him do it, speak with your director. It would be optimal if the educator had a good working relationship with the teacher or coach that would allow frank interchanges in private. ("Coach, I always find that if I do it this way it works out much easier for me.") But all too often such comments may be taken as interference. The best judge of this will be your director. He may well suggest that you yourself mention the point to the coach. If this is the case, remember that, at least officially, the coach is the expert and be prudent (don't push, in other words) when you mention your concerns to him and avoid, at all costs, telling him what to do.

Following the same lines, we could mention other examples:

You arrive at dinner to find that the food that should be hot is cold. We do not want our kids eating cold stuff that should be hot. The wrong way to handle this would be to send the food back with the waiters (who will usually be the kids themselves) and have the cook heat it up. The right way would be for you to excuse yourself from the kids for a moment, go into the kitchen, and mention to the cook that for some reason the food seems to be a little on the cold side and would there be any possibility of just heating it up for the kids. Normally, the cook will say, "Sure, no problem!" and the situation is settled.

But in this example, the educator will have other things to consider. Maybe the cook is in a really bad mood. Maybe the time for supper does not permit a ten-minute break as the food is heated. In such cases, the educator may prefer not to cause waves and might decide to go ahead with the cold food. However, should this happen, he should inform the director within the hour of what has happened so that such service is not repeated. The worst thing an educator could do would be to let the whole thing go without doing anything about it.

Respect for those who work alongside us has myriad other applications as well. Here are a few:

You will not allow kids to leave a patio or recess area dirty (out of respect for the hard work of whoever cleans the place).

You will ask the bus driver to advise you if the kids are doing anything out of order so that you can tell the kids. Or you might like to tell the bus driver that he should not hesitate in telling the kids about the rules on his bus. The same can be said for waitresses in a restaurant.

You will say hello to the shop assistants if you bring a group of kids into their shop, and you will thank them as you leave.

If a teacher is lining up his kids before they go into class, you will not try and distract him, nor much less will you start barking orders over the teacher's head.

Having respect for those who work alongside us will in turn lead to a healthy and enthusiastic working environment. Overflow applications, such as congratulating a coach for a good training session, or complementing a teacher on the quality of the kids' work, will enhance this greatly. The educator should make a personal note of saying at least ten positive things a day to those who work beside him.

Respect for Those "Under" Us

Here we are referring to the kids under our care. Should you care to check the index, you will find various references to the respect we should have for the kids. Here I just wanted to call to mind the fact that it is impossible to respect a kid too much, and it's all too easy to be disrespectful.

An educator who doesn't acknowledge a greeting, an educator who caresses a kid, even in a well-intentioned manner, an educator who doesn't attend immediately and effectively to a kid's complaint of "not feeling too well," is showing a grave lack of respect. An educator who is gruff, who omits the use of "please" and "thank you" with the kids, an educator who opts for punishment instead of prevention, an educator who shouts down the kids in an effort to be heard, would do well to reconsider his calling and contemplate removing himself to some military establishment.

Respect for kids has nothing to do with "being soft" with them.

The kids were slouched in their chairs as they relished the movie. They reminded me of transatlantic travelers stretched out precariously on their seats doing their best to convince themselves that they are in a bed. I mentioned the fact to the trainee. "Let's leave them alone. It's only a movie. Let them relax." Detecting softness in the trainee that would greatly hamper his work in the future, and having counted at least fourteen boys asleep, I asked him to have the kids use the chairs as they should be used. "Very well," was his reply and he got to work.

He stopped the movie, turned on the lights, and gave the semiconscious kids a stern lecture on the formation of character and the way chairs were to be used. Far from being proud of the trainee, I was cringing. He had passed from being too soft to being too hard. He came up to me, rubbing his hands. "How was that, eh?"

"Next time," I said to him as the movie started up again, "just walk over to one guy and motion him to sit up. And then motion to him to pass the word down his row. If you start at the front you will only have to tell one or two kids and all the others will follow."

We must be firm but kind. We must respect the kid, not his failings. This calls for no little effort on our behalf. As I have mentioned, it is all too easy to be lacking in respect for kids. Usually such lack of respect will be totally unintentional, and herein lies the difficulty. With so much to do, and with overload and personal exhaustion sometimes a factor, an educator's handle on respect is an easy grasp to let slip. In this area, an educator will do well to keep an eye on himself as well as on his kids, and he would do even better if he also remained actively open to any observations or comments his fellow educators might have to make.

Sense of Humor

If an educator had all the above qualities except this one, he would be a wonderful person—and extremely boring. As a result, he would have few friends, be they kids or otherwise. People would respect the poor educator and, on his passing to that great school in the sky, people would reflect upon his dedication, his sense of responsibility, and his wisdom. But few, very few, would mourn his friendship. It may seem strange that a sense of humor should be so key in human relations. However, if you think about your friends, you will discover that humor indeed is an essential element in friendship.

To define "sense of humor" is beyond me, but I can describe it. It is being able to stand back and smile at ourselves. It is being able to go beyond the here-and-now-nitty-gritty of things and see the "bigger picture." It means being able to grasp the very moment as it passes and enjoy it for what it is. It means being able to make other people smile with you. A sense of humor must not be confused with being able to tell a joke, or with being the "life and soul" of a party. Nor is it to be equated with a "devil-may-care" attitude. Nor should it be confused with wit, as sharp as it may be. A true sense of humor is born of the knowledge that God is our loving father, and that not only does he care for us, but he also enjoys us and enjoys the good we do. It is born of inner peace. And it is born of suffering, for only he who has suffered and suffered well, can smile and smile well.

In our dealing with kids, we must be prompt to let our sense of humor shine through. Be demanding and everything else we must be, but we do well not to spare our good humor. A tip here is to know what the kid likes and like it too. Or, if you cannot like it, hate it, but let the kid know by your attitude that you hate it, not him. And if you can get the kid to smile as you hate whatever it is you hate, then you have him. In some instances we can equate a sense of humor with a sense of fun. If, for example, the kids are all excited at a sports competition, get all excited and worked up yourself. And let the kids see this.

This sense of humor we must have should not make kids of us—it should not deprive us of our adulthood. But we can appreciate and enjoy many kid things that are good and wholesome. We will not pretend to enjoy them as if we were a kid. We enjoy them as an adult, but we will enjoy them. Or if we cannot enjoy them, let us enjoy the kids enjoying them. That will do just fine for starters.

I recall arriving late to school one day. (Well, to be honest, I can recall arriving on time one day, too.) As I expected to see the principal standing at the gate waiting to catch latecomers, I got off my bike and wiped my hands on the chain. As I rounded the final corner into the schoolyard, there he was.

"Terribly sorry I'm late, Brother...my bike... the chain..."

I showed him my greased hands and wore a suitably glum look.

The principal stood motionless, rattled his keys as was his custom and stared straight at me. I blinked hard a few times for effect, and I did my best to give him an innocent and yet repentant stare back. But I knew he saw through my little ploy, and I prepared for the worst. (And the worst in those days was pretty bad…very sore on the hands and sometimes on the ears.)

"Mr. Murray," he said, hardly moving his lips. I took a deep breath as his arm began to move. I closed my eyes. As it was thought cowardly to duck, I stood my ground. When nothing happened, I opened my eyes and saw that he was pointing to my classroom. "Off with ye!" was all he said. I knew my chain story hadn't held, but I didn't know what had saved me. He was still looking at me sternly, but as I left he started to shake his head. And I saw he was beginning to smile.

Of course, that didn't really stop me from being late again, although I did make a real effort. But punctuality to one side, from that day on I saw that man in a completely different light. Apparently he was human. And with time I discovered him to be a knowledgeable, dedicated, and enjoyable human as well.

Another Look at Vision

Global Detailed Vision[25]

As with any leader, vision is key. A leader without vision is blind. This vision an educator must have for his kids must be both global and, at the same time, detailed.

By *global*, I mean that global understanding of what we are really looking for with our kids. Basically we want them to be faithful, enthusiastic, capable, and dedicated followers of Christ, and we want them to live out this in whatever forms of life they choose. It is, if you like, a general view.

This general view or global vision may tend to be rather vague and unattainable unless it is detailed. As educators, we must know what goes into the makings of a faithful, enthusiastic, capable, and dedicated follower of Christ. It is this detailed global vision that will give balance to our efforts. In fact, what we call "integral formation" is not attainable if we do not have this detailed global view.

An enthusiastic trainee/educator was excellent at controlling the kids. He could get them to do anything he chose. His main concern was to have things running well, in shipshape order. A walk through his section's dorm at any time of the day was proof of his effectiveness. And his kids stood out as being the most sharply dressed and well groomed of the academy. He had his "secret weapons" to attain this: competitions, personal contact with the kids, and good sports results were his specialties.

As the months went on, however, it was observed that his focus on externals was becoming somewhat of an obsession for his boys. One afternoon a fight broke out as the boys were getting ready for a presentation. Finding himself without polish, one student had borrowed a companion's shoeshine kit. This led to the fight, as sharing was not the order of the day. The educator barred the two from taking part in the presentation as punishment for having fought.

Not long after, voices were raised in the dining hall as a group sat at their empty table. An argument was going on as to who the designated waiter was for that meal. Nobody moved to stand up and serve. Hearing the uproar, the educator decided that such shouting in the dining hall should be punished. The students at that table had to sit through the meal in silence and forego lunch.

Such examples—small, normal, and insignificant as they might seem—were however, indicative of a malfunction within the section. It was not the fighting or shouting that was indicative, but the reason the educator attached to his punishment. In the fight over the polish incident, he addressed the fight, not the lack of generosity. In the shouting in the dining room, it was the lack of decorum he attacked, and not the fact that nobody was willing to follow the example of Christ who came to serve. The trainee had a good detailed vision of what went into the makings of external discipline, but beyond this he was blind—blind to the details of Christian virtue and blind to the global vision.

If the previous case shows a lack of global vision, the following case (invented as an illustration, although based on individual instances) denotes a lack of detailed vision.

The academy's interim director was at pains to secure the global vision: "The kids come here to be formed. And they can only be formed if they feel happy and at home. We must be demanding and firm with them." His theory was right on. As in any summer course, time is short and so the director decided to focus his team's attention on spiritual things. His experienced educators were to dedicate themselves to giving spiritual direction, and a four-week campaign was designed to get the kids to live the virtue of sincerity—"the basis for sanctity"—according to the interim director. Confession and Holy Communion were high on the agenda, as was the effort to create a comfortable family atmosphere.

Sincerity posters adorned the walls and a points system awarded those who went to confession and Holy Communion. Night talks were mystical and vague—"Be good as your heavenly Father is good." The schedule was full of activities and outings that guaranteed that practically all the students had a great summer.

As the course was ending, all kids made the promise of being good Christians from that day forth.

It was only months later that the real story began filtering out. Parents began complaining about how was it possible that their kids had received little or no English instruction. Others wondered at why kids had been allowed to smoke. Petitions came in for replacement of things "lost" or stolen. One parent wanted to sue the academy for having allowed bullying among the students to have gone unchecked. Some complained about the lack of sleep because the kids had been allowed to talk until they fell asleep. Other complaints ranged from the poor laundry service to the excess of "fast food" meals, from the lack of supervision to the excess of spiritual talks. While all complaints, resulting from what the kids told their parents and friends, were all of a somewhat innocent nature, one cannot help but wonder about the effectiveness of such a "global" strategy.

It is detailed vision that will enable the due importance of punctuality as well as the due importance of personal effort, and the due importance of attention in class as well as the due importance of generosity. No aspect of formation should suffer because of another. Each aspect should benefit. Our demands for punctuality, for example, should be geared to a desire for greater self-betterment, and this in turn to being better prepared to serve others. Sincerity must be focused not only on telling the truth and making "a good confession," but also on a kid's conscientious dedication to being every day a truly better person. Academic achievement must be seen not solely as an entrance tool to further education, but as an expression of hard work, constancy and responsibility. Making sure a kid gets into the habit of making his bed correctly every morning goes way beyond keeping the place tidy—it trains the kid in personal discipline, in the art of being independent, in respect for others, in constancy, in perfection, and in time management.

An educator must know where he is leading his kids, and he must know exactly how to get there. He must know every single step of the way. Would you board a plane if you knew the pilot didn't know where he was going and didn't even know how to get the plane off the ground? Of course not. But....

But look at all those wonderful mothers who have brought their children up well. Now, please do not tell me that from the outset they knew exactly how their children were to be and knew exactly how to handle every situation (possessing a global and detailed vision). These mothers took no courses on how to bring up kids, and yet they have succeeded admirably. So, are we to take the need for global and detailed vision as a "good idea" and nothing more? Have you just wasted twenty minutes in reading about it? No.

Give me a wonderful mother and I will give you a wonderful heart and a wonderful mind—and a lot of hard work. We cannot simply put good motherhood down to "animal instinct" (the mother knows how to look after her chicks, so to speak). Mothers do not automatically bring up children successfully. Good mothers take years getting ready. All right, no special classes in any school, but their whole life is a preparation. A mother is a fountain of life, a miracle all on its own. (We men are left way behind when it come to miracles.) A good mother's psychology, her mindset, her personality, her very being is geared towards this great miracle of life and its "afterwards." And were you to take a good mother aside and ask her what she wants for her newborn child, you would soon see that she does have a very clear picture in her mind. Of course, in the day-to-day business of childrearing, she may make a mistake or two, but on the whole you will discover that a good mother knows exactly what to do. Just because she hasn't written a book on it, doesn't mean she doesn't know. All educators have a lot to learn from these wonderful mothers.

Professional educators, as we strive to be, are not mothers however, or at least not of all the kids we are called to educate. And as professional educators, our mission is somewhat different. While we must have a predisposition to education (a wanting to help others), we must also master the tools we need to ensure our success, morally at least,[26] according to the goals set out for us by the institution we work with. Global and detailed vision is essential for us.

Effective Roles

"You're just like my father" is something an educator will hear now and again. It may be said as a compliment, as a rebuke, or as an affective hook.

As a compliment:

On a weekend retreat, the kids were settling down for the night. A kid comes up to his educator and says quietly, "That was a great story. You're just like my dad—he always makes sure we go to bed feeling good."

The remark was taken as a compliment. "I only wish I were half as good as your father. Good night and sleep tight."

As a rebuke:

"You're not going out to play soccer dressed like that. Please pull your socks up and stick in your shirt," said the educator.

The kid grumbled under his breath. "You're just like my father... nothing's ever right."

As an affective hook:

The glum kid slides up to the educator. "What's the matter with you, little man?" asks the educator. "Can I talk to you, please? You're like my dad, and I feel I can talk to you."

Looking at the simple phrase: We should take compliments in our stride and accept them humbly. But the other two instances cited above are danger warnings.

A kid who answers back needs to embark, or to be embarked, on a course of immediate rectification. The fact that he tags the rebuke with "You're just like my father" could mean that he sees you as just an authority, and maybe an unjust, figure. But it could also mean that he sees you as his father. And this is dangerous. It's dangerous for your mission with the kid because he doesn't see you for what you are: an educator, his educator. In this case an educator would do well to say something like, "You haven't seen anything yet!" and then seriously revise the approach he has to the kid in question. An experienced person will always put himself into the equation when analyzing a fault he has discovered.

Whereas case one (compliment) could be put down to simple good manners, and case two (rebuke) to a simple lack of discipline, case three touches another area totally.

An educator must always keep his distance from the kids. This is to help the educator keep his mission in perspective and avoid any overconcern for a particular kid. However, sometimes in this area of natural—and even good—affections, it will be the kid who serves the ball. And the educator has to play well if he doesn't want to lose the match.

The Educator and the Father

Increasingly, we are finding kids who come from a weak family environment. This is no fault of the kid's, and we would be rash even to blame the parents, although they may apparently be at fault. Business pressures and a lack of knowing what goes into the makings of a father, on the father's part, or even marital breakdown, are quite often to blame. But the fact remains—some kids thirst for a father figure. And some think they have found one in their educator.

Initially, for the educator, feeling himself as a "father" may be quite satisfying. It shows total trust and indicates an affective bond that the kid wants to establish and foster with his newfound father. However, the experienced educator will immediately hear alarm bells ringing that indicate serious problems ahead. There are two main concerns here:

One, the educator cannot be a father figure forever…maybe for a year, maybe three. The kid needs a father figure, but the educator cannot spend the rest of his life caring for this kid. When the kid leaves the club, section, or school, he will end up feeling abandoned and in a worse state than before. So the first concern is for the kid himself whom the educator is called to educate and help.

The second concern is for the educator himself. Giving in to any father figure status, the educator is changing his relationship with the kid. This is a delicate point. An educator must consider the kids as "his kids." In effect, he must care for them as the best of fathers would, as the best of brothers would, as the best of mothers would. But his concern and care for "his kids" is not the same concern that a father, mother, or brother will have. We can look at it this way:

First, there is a legal relationship that ties the kid to his father. This relationship obliges the father to care for his kid in each and every aspect: his physical well-being, his psychological health, his education, his formation. This obligation lasts as long as the kid is alive and does not end with the father's death. A father must do his best to make provision for his children even should he himself die.

Secondly, there is a bond of affection that stems from the very fact that the kid is related so closely to his father—a bond that has grown over the years and hopefully will continue to grow well into adulthood and beyond.

The relationship an educator has with a kid is different in both of these areas. Firstly, there is no legal tie between educator and kid. There is a legal contract between the kid's parents and the school or academy, but not between the kid and his educator. Much less is there a direct blood bond between the two. And secondly, there is no comparison between the objective affective relationship that an educator might have with "his kids" and the affection that binds a kid to his parents.

An educator's responsibility is a delegated responsibility. The kid's parents delegate this responsibility to the school, youth group, or academy, and this responsibility is limited in time and in extent. An educator is not responsible for the kid when he is not in school, for example. Nor is an educator, even an academy educator, responsible for remedial psychiatric care that a kid may need.

Looking at it another way, in an attempt to clearly see the difference between being an educator and a father, we can use this example:

A busy man buys a car for his wife to help her get around. He would like to have been able to drive her around himself, but he is a busy man. She never complained about not having one, but the man saw that a car would help her not only to do the shopping, but it would also give her the chance to go out and meet up with friends. The woman was delighted with the car and was very grateful.

As time went on, however, the husband began realizing that the wife was spending more and more time away from the family and often found that the kids would come home to an empty house. The woman got so involved in so many things that she was rarely at home, and even when she was, she was in a hurry to go off to a meeting or an important appointment that she simply couldn't miss.

So the man decided that it was time to put a stop to this and to take the car away from his wife. But he never got the chance. Pushing the car to speeds it was never designed for, she crashed into a tree that jumped out in front of her. And that was the end of the wife and of the car.

The educator is the car. His aim is to get kids to where they are going. The educator, just as the car, should help people to be better, more efficient, and happier. And just as the car in the story was a substitute in a certain sense for the husband, an educator is a substitute, in the same sense, for the parents. But just as in the case of the car, the educator is not the husband, and if this means of transport is used in a way that it was not made for, disaster is a certainty.

So if an educator tries to become a father figure, or if a kid tries to make him become one, apply the brakes. You might just still be in time to get back on course and get the kid to where you're supposed to be getting him.

Well Said

"It takes a couple of decades to realize that you were well taught. All true education is a delayed action bomb assembled in the classroom for explosion at a later date. An educational fuse fifty-years-long is by no means unusual."

- Howard Hendricks

"Some people are like cats. They don't know what they want but they always want more of it. And there are people that are like dogs—no matter what they get, they are grateful."

- Celtic Book of Wisdom

"We have two regulatory systems: legal and etiquette. The legal system prevents us from killing each other. The etiquette system prevents us from driving each other crazy."

- Judith Martin

"If the road is easy, you're going the wrong way."

-on a sugar envelope at a restaurant in Nevada

"A pat on the back moves people more than a kick in the pants."

- Celtic Book of Wisdom

"When we don't know what to do, we usually do what we know we can do."

-BBC analyst's answer to why Yeltsin fired his complete cabinet in 1998

"If an educator really enjoys his work, there is an excellent chance that he is doing a great job."

-Celtic Book of Wisdom

A Few Thoughts on Burdens

The burden of example

An educator carries a heavy burden. And sometimes it can easily slip off and hurt—and even crush—those whom he has been called to educate. Here's the situation:

Any educator who is on the job has certain human qualities. Otherwise he just wouldn't be there. But, like it or not, kids do look up to their educators. And kids look up to their educators not just as authority figures (someone who tells them what to do), but as persons. In fact, kids, in their simple way of looking at things, will look to the educator as the incarnation of all the values and virtues that the educator tries to instill in them. This may seem rather unfair of the kids. After all, nobody's perfect, and the kids should realize that not even his educator is a perfect person.

Now, I'm not saying that an educator sets himself up as an example of perfection. "Do everything and behave always just like I do and you'll be perfect" is not an educator's line. In fact, any mature educator is all too aware of the gulf that exists between what he really is and what he is trying to get his kids to become. But what I am saying is that, because of an educator's position and given his role in the student's life, a kid will tend to look for perfection in his educator. This is the burden an educator carries.

Faced with his mission, the educator can do one of three things: he can hide his negative areas (for instance, an educator isn't tidy so he keeps his door locked). Or he can be honest and say, "Hey, this is what I am. I don't want you to be like this. But this is me. I'm not hiding anything here. I'm untidy in my personal things; it's not great, but that's me. Accept me as I am." Or he can take a leaf from the book "he reads" his kids and constantly make an effort to be a better person.

What is the greatest thing an educator can do for his kids? Give them a solid formation? And what does this mean? And anyway, we do not form kids, we simply offer them the means with which they can form themselves. Let's be as concrete as we can be with this. I think that the greatest thing an educator can do for a kid is set a good example—in everything.

An educator who offers compartmentalized examples is ineffective. This educator is great at telling stories, but, hey, those suits he wears are way off. This educator is great at supervision, but he gets so uptight. This educator is really kind to you when you have a problem, but he lets the group get away with murder. This educator invents great competitions but I never feel comfortable with him in dialogue. This educator... and so on.

What we are concerned about is setting an example of a well-educated and mature person who is capable of carrying out his mission in detail and in style: a man of culture, of wisdom, of experience, of fun--a man who has lived and who lives for others, and for others alone. So to be true to our mission as educators, we must know ourselves. And we must be constantly working on a definite program that will make better people of us. And at the same time, we must make sure we minimize our negative area contact with the kids.

Let's say you still haven't got to the point where you can give a decent night talk. Get someone else to give them until you learn.

But learn. You get uptight when you have to control your group by yourself. Then, don't do it all alone, get help. And learn how the others can do it. You're nervous in dialogue with the kids, and this makes them close up. Don't give dialogue. Get someone else to do it, and learn the "tricks of the trade." Fast. An educator is never asked to do anything a mature adult is incapable of doing. If you think you're not up to something, get help, and learn. And learn fast. After all, this is what we tell the kids, right?

And don't ever accept a negative area. If you smoke and believe smoking gives a bad example, quit smoking. Or if you're really hooked on nicotine, and Nicorette® doesn't work for you, don't smoke in front of the kids. This doesn't mean that you are hiding it from the kids. Smoke smells, and the kids will know you smoke, but at least keep from smoking in front of them. Up to now, smoking has not being labeled a sin, and so it is not the same as an educator getting stone drunk on his day off and hiding that from the kids.

When Christ said, "Be perfect," he wasn't making a suggestion. He was telling us what to do in no uncertain terms. And "being perfect" is a process. It's not something we attain. It's not the end of the road. It's the day-by-day, moment-by-moment effort to be just as God wants us to be. That's perfection for a human. Perfection for an angel is something else. Perfection for an angel means that he has no flaws. Perfection for us humans consists in doing our best to be exactly as God wants us to be.

So don't be ashamed to show kids that you too are getting better—but not at their expense.

This, then, is the burden an educator carries, a burden that puts the educator's mission alongside that of parenting and the priesthood. Like it or not, a lot is expected of you as an educator. Your kids will look to you not only now, but later on in life too when they have grown up and no longer have you beside them.

The power of burden

And there is another point to consider. As educators, we are always on the front line. But this very fact more often than not can be extremely beneficial for us as educators. Many have mentioned to me how being an educator has helped them themselves.

"I used to use a lot of course words," said one educator to me. "In the beginning, I used to keep them for my day off. But now I find that I am much better off without them!"

"Before becoming an educator, I was what you would call a 'practicing Catholic.' I went to Mass and did my best to stay in the state of grace. But when you teach, you also learn. Being with the kids, recognizing the responsibility I have towards them, has opened my eyes to all the great things a Catholic is supposed to be. Now I guess you could call me 'an enthusiastic—and practicing—Catholic.'"

> **There is more joy in giving than in receiving.**
> ATTRIBUTED TO JESUS CHRIST

"At the end of the year, most kids will come up to you and thank you sincerely. But ever since my first year as educator, I was convinced that it should have been me who went up to each kid to thank him for having done so much for me."

"I hate to say it, but I feel that if I were to stop being an educator, I would begin being a worse person. 'Situations don't make the man, but prove what he is worth,'—but I believe that there are some situations (and being an educator is one of them) that really can make you a better person."

"At the start I was told to act tough. Not harsh, but tough. So I acted tough. But it was an act. But I was never told to 'be sincere' or to 'be punctual' or to 'be a man of strong willpower and self-control.' But being with the kids, demanding punctuality and order, and demanding that they make a real effort makes you be more punctual, tidier, and more demanding with yourself."

"When you're in charge of kids, you feel you have a certain responsibility towards them to be as good as you can. I found deep fulfillment in this responsibility."

"A silly thing, but it just goes to show how much these kids have helped me. I nearly drowned in a pool as a kid, and ever since then I have been afraid of the water. It's a kind of phobia, I guess. But there was this kid under my care who had also nearly drowned when he was small. When he went to the pool for the first time in the academy, I told him that he didn't have to swim, but that he would have to stay with his class. He could read a book or whatever. 'I want to try,' he told me and jumped in. I admired the courage of that small kid so much. If he can do it, I said to myself, so can I. On my next day off, I went to the pool with a colleague, took courage, and dived in. When you see what kids are capable of doing—in the good sense—you apply it to yourself."

"OK, it's rough going. The hours are long and you are always on call. But I have never been so deeply happy in my life."

(All authentic educator statements, some examples changed.)

Keeping Kids Happy—A Poor Excuse

It is here I take to task an idea that I have heard expressed on (rare) occasions: "The important thing is to keep the kids happy." While having kids happy is important, it is not the important thing. Normally, kids will not be faced with life's great questions, although it must be admitted that even while young some are indeed exposed to some of the more dramatic and painful sides of life (a death in the family, parental breakup, personal complexities). But normally kids, because of their age are shielded, as they should be, from these sad but real chapters of life.

But this pseudo-philosophy that proposes that all is licit and good as long as "the kids are happy" is a betrayal of our mission as educators.

Happiness, joy, is the fruit, not the seed of formation. Promotion demands may be high, but only when we realize our task in life as educators will we be able to satisfy promotion with what it really wants—formation. Superficial butterfly happiness is but a cheap substitute for quality education. If people want the former, let them take their kids to the movies or to McDonald's. If they have come to us, it is for something else.

A Secret Deep Within

There's a secret deep within the heart of the great educators of our time. We see it in Don Bosco who entrusted the congregation he founded to the care of a young man. We see it in Fr. Flanagan who founded the first Boys Town in the world, a town where the boys themselves would be mayor, worker, reporter, and farmer.

For us, this secret boils down to a simple truth, or way of treating the kids, and it is this—treat them as capable adults. Believe in those you have been called upon to form. Make them see the importance of what they do, make them feel that what they do is important. Give them importance.

In Italy we have a case in point. Although a Catholic country, religion teaching is reduced to a one-period-a-week class that deals more with religion comparisons than it does with the teaching of the Catholic faith. Boys wanting to make their confirmation must attend special classes, organized by the parish, over a three-year period. Each week involves two forty-five-minute classes for the students.

"Luigi used to take his confirmation classes more seriously than school. He would really study for the exams that they ran in the parish," confirms the kid's mom years later. Given that Italian kids have to forego football and other national passions, the fact that a dry religion class could compete with such stamina is surprising. As I have the good luck of knowing the person who ran these classes, and upon seeing the faithful attendance every Wednesday afternoon and Sunday morning, I asked him, "What's the secret? How come these twenty-five kids come day in, day out, hail, rain, or shine?"

"Well," he answered. "One reason is pure truth, the other, show business. I firmly believe that the basic truths of the Catholic faith are important in the everyday lives of people: the Creed, the sacraments, and the Commandments. That's the pure truth. But how do you get kids to react with seriousness and responsibility? A little showbiz technique, that's how. Make it important. For example, don't let a kid into your classroom if he cannot answer two basic questions from your previous class. Get them to form a line outside the classroom before class and, as the bell rings, ask each kid a question to test his grasp of the previous lesson. No one gets into the class if he doesn't answer correctly. This way, the fact of even getting into class is a triumph for the kid. This way, they feel that class is important and not a free-for-all."

"And so you would deny Catholic teaching to a kid if he missed a class and did not know how to answer questions pertaining to the previous lesson?" I asked. He paused before answering, thought for a moment, and calmly said, "Definitely."

Being a little wet behind the ears, I ventured that we could not simply turn kids away just because they missed a lesson. "Freely we have learnt," I said quoting loosely from Scripture. "Freely should we teach."

"Indeed" was his reply. "But there's something there too about pearls and dogs.... Don't panic!" He reassured me. "I have turned many a kid away from class. But may I assure you that I have never turned them away. They will show up for the next class and will know the answers to the two lessons they have missed. How? By getting the notes from their companions. And they go the extra mile because they feel challenged. In school, a little note from their mom will get them off useless homework. But what I am teaching here is so important. Every class is so important that to miss it can be mildly catastrophic—or at least that's what I make the kids feel. And it works."

Of the twenty-eight kids initially enrolled with this teacher's class, twenty-five made their confirmation three years later with the group they had begun with. One flunked attendance throughout the three-year period, one made his confirmation one year later with his brother, and one moved. Sometimes "charism" can be reduced to simple show business...and heartfelt conviction.

Another example:

When visiting my hometown of Dalkey, in Ireland, I drove up to a youth center one evening. Although there was nothing going on, I was greeted at the door by an enthusiastic but very young teenager. He welcomed me and asked how he could assist me. Many years previous, I had helped set the center up, but now I just said that I was interested in having a look around. It was then I decided to try the kid out.

"Maybe my kids would like this place," I baited. "It certainly is something," he answered. "What age are your children?" I played along. "Well, one is just two and the other is nineteen." "Oh, this club is just for eleven-to-fourteen-year-olds," he apologized. "But let me show you around." And he did. He was attentive, well mannered, and polite in the extreme with no sugar.

After I had seen just about everything, I came clean and complimented him on his style and dedication. After all he was, at tops, thirteen-years-old and it was a lovely sunny May afternoon. And here he was in a big house all by himself, working.

"Well, I'm in charge of Public Relations every Wednesday afternoon, and I'm here from after school until teatime. I answer the phone and the door and get as much homework done as possible."

Treat a kid as a capable adult and he is capable of acting sometimes with more dedication than an adult. Treat kids as unthinking, incapable-of-thought babies, and you will end up having to change their diapers.

I cannot help but feel that this is a secret well worth learning.

SOMETHING ELSE IN OUR FAVOR

The à Kempis assertion, "What annoys us in other people is quite often our own biggest failing" is a keen insight. Not only does it help us understand the hidden workings of how we, as people, are made up, but it also gives us an extremely practical rule of thumb. Another similar assertion, this one not from Thomas à Kempis, can also be of benefit to us in our work with kids—a kid's biggest failing is what he really wants to put right.

On the face of it, this affirmation may seem a little too simplistic. Here's an example:

A kid has a nasty temper. He cannot control himself. At the slightest provocation he blows up, he won't listen to anybody and he just goes berserk. On the football field, he shows little patience with others and thinks that he is the only one that can play the game successfully. Now, please do not tell me that this kid is overly concerned about fixing this character error. It can be argued, in fact, that he sees such behavior as an essential part of himself and is quite happy to let it thrive within him. So how does this principle hold?

The problem with many simple ideas is that usually there is a missing link. And this missing link renders them unworkable. Leonardo daVinci was convinced that man could fly in a machine. The idea was simple, but the missing link (the concept of "lift") was unknown to him, and so his dream never really came true—for him. It took the Wright brothers to come up with the link.

In the late forties, the "fast food" concept was born, but the missing link (total and absolute uniformity) stopped the idea from getting off the ground. It was only when the McDonald brothers bought the few initial restaurants and added this element did the idea really blossom.

So too in this case—the idea that what a kid does wrong is really what he would like to correct, is valid. But there is a missing link. In fact, there are two missing links that we will now attempt to discover.

Think Twice

It may have happened to you, and it has certainly happened to me.

John was a fast driver. He considered himself a good and safe driver. But in fact, he was a reckless driver. He had never had an accident though and had never caused one. But one day, while stopped at a set of lights, he saw a car coming up behind him, weaving up neatly between the patient line of cars. Within a few seconds, this car had reached the stoplight. He simply ignored the red light and sped on. John was mesmerized at such reckless driving. Then, thanks to the à Kempis principle, he suddenly thought twice. "I've done that a hundred and one times!" He decided that he had better mend his ways.

So here we have the first link—awareness. We cannot fix something if we don't know it's busted. But note—our reckless John had often been told he was a reckless driver, but never paid any heed, or he took it as a compliment! People had mentioned it to him again and again. And he had even had a few near hits that scared him momentarily, but these never convinced him of the need to change his ways. It wasn't until he himself thought twice did he realize just how dangerous a driver he indeed was. The decision to mend his ways was his and his alone.

Applied to our work with kids, we must state that this "awareness" of failings is not the result of constant reminders. It is not the result of shouts or strict rules and regulations. A kid who is naturally untidy will always tend to be untidy no matter how many days you bark at him to clear up his room. The shouting, or asking, may get the room tidy for an hour or even a week, but the kid will always be untidy. It is not until the kid realizes that he is untidy, and that untidy is not good, that he will decide to do something about it.

So to achieve this state of awareness in a kid, we must be patient and demanding, kind but firm, constant, and positive. It will only be motivation, as described elsewhere in this book (see "Positive Motivation"), if we can get the kid to think twice.

Do-ability

This link, do-ability (pronounced "du-ability"), is as important as the awareness of which we have just spoken.

Sam knew that he really should show more affection towards his parents. He lived away from home, and months would slip by without him ever calling or writing. He was aware of this failing and detested it, but never got around to doing anything about it.

Deep down, we ourselves will have a fair awareness of our own failings, and yet all too often we sit and lament the little progress made. Or we accept the situation and resign ourselves to do nothing about it. Or we make a vague proposal to "do something." This is due, in most cases, to a lack of do-ability--either we think we cannot effectively do the thing right, or we fail to DO what is needed to right the wrong.

So a deep down conviction that the right way is do-able is essential. And this conviction must be practical in the extreme. It is hopeless for a kid to be aware of his bad temper and to think that by simply saying to himself, "I must control myself," he will master his ego. It is impossible for John to be a good driver unless he has a detailed "to do" list. He must resolve to obey speed limits, to yield at yield signs, and to stop at all stop signs. He must decide not to let other drivers annoy him. He must avoid flashing his lights.

As educators we must assist kids by giving them a step-by-step guide as to how the virtue they need is do-able. (See "100 Short Term Goals" and "Human Formation Dialogue.") But awareness of doing wrong and the knowledge of do-ability are not by themselves sufficient. To do the thing right, we have to do.

Now, doing the thing right can come about backwards, and this often happens. For example, without an awareness of his reckless driving and without a detailed "to do" list, John, our reckless driver, may on occasions drive superbly. Maybe there's a patrol car on his tail. Maybe he's taking the boss out to dinner. He'll drive well, but he will not be a good driver, if you get the difference. A kid may do all that is necessary to keep his room tidy without ever thinking that really he should keep it tidy. But he knows that there will be no television for him if his room is a mess. This is what I call the backwards approach. On the short-sighted side, agreed, but hardly formation.

The actual doing of the right thing must be a logical consequence of a kid's awareness of a failing and of his desire to improve. But there is no escaping the fact that he must do. He must follow his "to do" list. He must work. And here again, our role as educators is indispensable. The kid will need constant and positive encouragement and guidance, kind correction, and objective acknowledgment.

We can apply these principles to a lot of things, like the Commandments, for example. They are the "to do" list if we want to be followers of Christ. But by simply listing the Commandments, no one has ever won anyone over to Christ. First, we must want to be followers of Christ. Then we must realize that we can be. Then we ask for the "to do" list—never the other way around. (Please note that this is not an argument for not baptizing kids until they are old enough to decide for themselves. What good mother would let her baby suffer just because the baby was incapable of saying, "Would you ever be so kind, mom, as to give me some of that medicine for the pain I have in my tummy?" Nor would any good mother avoid giving her child all the protein, minerals, and vitamins he needed in order to be healthy and strong. I guess we could feed them bread and water until they are old enough to go to the store and get what they wanted themselves... yeah, sure.)

Festina Lente (Hurry Slowly)

In our work with kids, we must "hurry slowly." If we are good educators, we will be able to guide the kid to this "think twice" awareness of his failings. We will be able to demonstrate a virtue's do-ability, and we will be capable of accompanying him along the road to virtue.

The fact remains—when awareness clicks, there is no one more interested in a kid's formation than the kid himself.

5

Technical Support

A Quick Reference Section

Troubleshooters

The kid's room is a mess.

Preliminary checks

- Check and make sure each kid knows how to make his bed properly and how and where to store his clothes. It may be necessary for you to show each kid how to do things.
- Check and make sure the kids have sufficient time to keep their room tidy on a daily basis.

Solutions (home)

- Tidy the room up with the kid. Let him do most of the work, but you help too. Refrain from complaining.
- When things are all done say, "Now let's keep it that way, shall we?" (The "we" is actually "you," by the way. It's just a nice way of putting it.)
- Do not tidy up the kid's room when he's out of the house. It's his room. He must keep it tidy. And if he wants it untidy to "suit his creative temperament"? Sorry, it may be his room, but it's your house.

Hints

- Never tire of correcting the kids.
- Never allow a kid go to bed if any articles are on the floor.
- How's your room?

The kids are not going to Holy Communion.

Preliminary checks

- Check that the kids have access to more than one confessor on a regular basis and that they know what priest is hearing confessions and where.
- Check and see whether or not the kids are being offered spiritual direction and personal dialogue on a frequent basis.
- Check that the kids are not overstressed about examinations and make sure their schedule allows for demanding and exciting recreation (organized sports are by far preferable to movies and computer games).

Solutions (schools)

- Use talks to illustrate the difficulties involved in being a true Christian and the great rewards that are to be had (many stories from Don Bosco's writings can come in very handy here).
- Avoid referring to the phenomenon (of a low Communion rate) in public with your kids.
- Pray for the kid.

Hints

- Never let an educator be seen counting those who go, or who do not go, to Holy Communion. Rather than say to a kid, "I noticed you didn't go to Holy Communion today," try "And when was the last time you invited Christ into your heart?" Let the kid tell you.
- Kids who are not up to receiving Holy Communion (either because they have eaten candy or because they feel they may not be in the state of grace) are to be applauded for their respect of the sacrament rather than reprimanded. However, given the fact that only with Christ can man be truly happy, and recognizing that those who do go to Holy

Communion have made an effort to receive him, these kids should be applauded even more.

The kids get fidgety in lines (schools).

Preliminary checks

- Do you expect any kid to be in lines for more than two minutes? If so, you might like to consider another forum. Lines are for regrouping and possible uniform inspection.
- Do you allow talking in lines?

Solutions

- Insist on silence and speed in forming lines.
- Try a "pre-lines" call strategy. Give the kids a countdown to lines time. Or allow them to talk while waiting for you to give the definite signal for formal lines. But once this signal is given, you must instill silence and order.
- Let the kids know that if the line has not been "passed" (told to move on) within two minutes, those responsible will be retained and held accountable. In any event, let the line pass before two minutes is over.

Hints

- Avoid using lines as a punishment. Regrouping is an essential part of our way of supervising kids. Using lines as punishment will only get the kids to hate them.
- Praise lines well made, and praise kids whose uniforms are well presented.
- When you call formal lines, set an example of the order and silence that should reign. Don't talk to anyone and stand up straight in front of where the lines are to be formed. Act like a statue. Use hand signals if necessary.

Some of your kids shy away from dialogue and spiritual direction.

Preliminary check

- It could be that the kid is shying away from you. When you notice his reluctance, offer him another person with whom to have dialogue.
- Check to see if your dialogues are realistic, challenging, and positive.
- Do you schedule your dialogue for times that take kids way from what they like doing?
- Who does most of the speaking in a dialogue with you? If it is you, you need to reverse the proportion.
- Check the other qualities of your dialogue (constant, prudent, kind, objective, positive).

Solutions

- Keep your dialogues short as a rule, never longer than twenty minutes. If you find that you need more time, it will be because you are using dialogue time for other purposes (reviewing some of the kid's responsibilities that could and should be reviewed in another forum, or giving dialogue when you are walking around and continually getting distracted with other duties).
- Before each dialogue begins, be sure to have a concrete, short-term goal to propose to the kid in keeping with his personal program. It may well be that some other short-term goal may come out of the dialogue itself, but don't count on it. Improvisation gives the (correct) impression that dialogue (for you, and therefore for the kid) is unimportant.

- Take secondary measures to see to it that the kids like coming to dialogue (if necessary during a class they do not like, see to it that where you receive the kids is not stuffy and that it is pleasing to the eye, and have candy or sodas discreetly available)
- Let the kids know that you attach great importance to dialogue. When in dialogue, try not to allow yourself to be disturbed; program and publish your dialogue times with foresight and be faithful to these times.

Hints

- We do not oblige our kids to receive either spiritual direction or dialogue. While both are essential parts of our pedagogy, we cannot force them on anybody. We should motivate kids to use these means, and such motivation must be perfectly and totally positive and full of the utmost respect. Sometimes there is the temptation to shun kids who are reluctant. This is a negative response on our part and is easily detected by the kid, turning him against us.
- Just because a kid doesn't want to speak of himself, or doesn't want to open himself to you, does not mean that he has some secret and disturbing problem.
- Always have something new to say to the kid. If we keep repeating the same line, we will get boring. Constantly read material that will give you practical examples that you can use. Be able to quote examples from the kids' day-to-day lives.

The kids don't pay much attention in class.

Preliminary checks

- Have you prepared your class well?
- Did you leave something concrete for the kids to do last time and have you revised it now?
- Since your last class with this group, have you shown personal interest in the kids' progress?
- Do you treat your class subject matter as important or is it just a time filler?
- Do you walk into the classroom without having the kids stand up in silence by their desks?
- Have you ever walked into a classroom that had papers on the floor?

Solutions

- You might try making up a series of five to ten simple questions that capsulate the classes content. Quiz the kids on these before you begin your new class.
- You might begin to grade the kids' attention—not their lack of it.
- You might avoid sitting down. Keep moving around.
- You might pay attention to the way the kids are sitting. Discreetly signal them to sit up straight when you see them slump.

The kids are always running in the corridors.

Preliminary check

- Is there always an educator with the kids as they move from one place to another?
- Does the educator turn a blind eye to running?

- Do the kids have sufficient time to walk from A to B?
- Does the group move from A to B as a unit or as straggling bits of a disbanded army?

Solution

- Spill oil on the corners or put up trip wires. (Bad solution)
- When you see a kid running in the corridor, ask him to please walk.
- If running persists, have the kid retrace his steps and come back walking. Make sure you watch him. Do this as many times as you see him running indoors.

Hints

- Do "top and tail" group movements. Have one educator lead the group, with another taking up the rear. Do not allow kids to lag behind. Move the group as a unit. This does not mean that they have to walk in single file. Usually it is more human to have them walk along together as a group.

The kids don't like the hikes.

(By hikes, we understand those outings that imply contact with nature and usually will entail a good amount of walking.)

Preliminary check

- Do the kids go on hikes simply because someone thinks they are a good idea and a necessary tool to form manhood?
- Does each hike have a definite goal for the kids to attain?
- Do the kids enjoy the hikes?
- Do educators have to be continually pushing the kids to walk faster?

- Do the kids have comfortable shoes?

Solution

- There is no doubt as to the benefits of having kids come into direct contact with Mother Nature. Make a list of these benefits. You will almost immediately see that while a hike might seem a great idea to you, it often is a meaningless exercise for the kids. So, rather than hone in on the benefits, hone in on the mission.

  Here's an example: "Tomorrow we are going to do Lumpy Mountain." The kids groan. Another aimless trek through the hilly woods in the cold and mist! "It will make men out of you!"

  Now let's put it another way: The day before the hike, an educator goes off and lays down three different series of signs and hides a "treasure."[28] The day of the hike, the kids are divided into three teams and given clues as to where these signs are hidden. Once a team finds one sign it will lead—albeit cryptically—to another, and then another. These clues will lead the team to the treasure eventually and this treasure can then be exchanged for a prize back at the base (a special movie or a special supper).

  Baden-Powell knew this trick very well, and scouts will never just "go for a walk." In fact, in English, if you want a person to go away and do something totally useless, you will tell them to "Go take a hike!" So give each hike a goal, or as the Seekers put it, "a mission."

- You also might try to make the hikes special from other outings. Kids might be allowed to eat candy during the hike (they need the energy). They might have a barbeque lunch. They might be allowed time for special games that they enjoy after lunch. All these elements are not possible during some outings, but they can be a definite "plus" attached to hikes.

- If you see a small group of kids that doesn't particularly like the hike, walk with them at their pace and speak of interesting things. Avoid pushing and pushing and pushing. A push now and then is fair enough, but too much pushing can only set the kids against you and the hike. Later on, in dialogue, you can refer to the hikes as a way of helping the kids: the kids can help the others relax, they can do little things they don't really like and thus form their character, they can develop their stamina (necessary for whatever sport you choose to mention), they can try out their new boots, etc.

Hints

- Avoid the "I-like-it-therefore-you-like-it" line. The fact that I smoke doesn't mean that you will like it.

  I remember an educator who wanted his kids to rest up during exam time. Being sold on basketball, he had them play basketball everyday after lunch. Most of the kids really enjoyed the game, but there were two that hated it. They would do their best to play as well as they could (which was pretty pathetic at the best of times), but they never enjoyed the game. Apart from anything else, they felt humiliated. When their friends would pass them the ball, they would be quick to get rid of it, not knowing exactly what to do with it, or even how to handle it.

  The two kids did mention to the educator that they hated the game, but the educator, more interested in "forming" the kids than in giving them a chance to rest up and clear out the cobwebs—which was the original object of the exercise—simply said, "Oh, come on! You'll enjoy it."

Well, they never did enjoy it. They didn't do well in their exams either, and their previous trust in their educator as a capable person plummeted. In this example, the educator should have seen that two of his kids didn't enjoy the game and that basically this lack of enjoyment was due to their not grasping the basics of the game. He could have given them lessons during the recess period after lunch, and thus built up their confidence. Or he could have taught them the rules and asked them to be referees. But he didn't.

The same can happen with hikes. A walk through the hills might be an invigorating and restful activity for a thirty or forty-year-old man, but kids are different.

Some of the kids form impenetrable groups.

Preliminary checks

- Are the kids organized into teams that they enjoy being in? (If not, they will make their own "unofficial" ones.)
- Is the educator preferential in his treatment of the kids?

Solution (If you discover a closed group among your kids)

- Detect the leader of the group and "get to work" on him. In Spielberg's Schindler's List, Oscar Schindler met up with the cruel commander of a concentration camp who would shoot people at random from the balcony of his house. Becoming friends with the commander, by way of many gifts, Schindler finally got his opportunity.

One night after supper on the balcony, the commander was drunk and admired Schindler's control. "You never get drunk, even though you drink."

"That," replied Schindler, "is power." He continued, "A poor thief was dragged before the powerful emperor. The thief trembled, because he knew his life was in the emperor's hands. But instead of condemning the thief to death, the emperor said, "I forgive you. Go." That, my dear Amon, is power." Both the commander and Schindler laughed, but the next day, we see the cruel commander forgiving people instead of shooting them. Schindler had "gone to work" on the commander.

The leader of a closed group is what we refer to as a negative leader. This does not mean that the kid is himself bad. Oftentimes it is simply that he feels the need to lead and has found no better way of doing it than by exercising his leadership power in a negative fashion. "Getting to work" on such a person simply means giving him channels to exercise his leadership in a positive fashion. This must be done on a one-on-one basis. You speak with the kid, admire his qualities, and show him that the youth group, school, or academy could use a person with his talents.

Next, get him to do things for you. Take him under your wing, so to speak. Do not try to override whatever authority he may have, or thinks that he may have, over "his" kids. Get him over to your side, and "his" kids will follow. This way you can form the kid right, and more often than not you will end up with someone who is totally on the side of good and who will look to you for direction.

- Be extra vigilant with the group. Sometimes a negative leader may go beyond unchanneled leadership.

A boy managed to smuggle in pornographic magazines to school and secretly showed them to some of his companions. Bound by this secret, a closed group was formed.

One day, the educator, one with many years of experience, called for locker inspection and had each kid stand beside his locker. When he came to inspect the locker of the kid who had imported the magazines, he had the kid open his locker. When a corner of a glossy publication was uncovered, the educator said, "Close that locker and wait at the door until I have finished inspecting the others." (In this way, the educator avoided humiliating the kid before his friends, and the kid was grateful.)

Upon finishing locker inspection, the educator had all the other boys continue with the normal schedule. He then asked the kid who was waiting at the door to remove anything that he shouldn't have in his locker and hand it over. Strange as it may seem, the magazine had been a present from the kid's older brother. The kid was punished (I think the educator had him remove the lock to his locker for a month.) But that was the end of the closed group. With no binding motive, the group simply fell apart.

Hints

- The fact that kids group together spontaneously is perfectly normal. What the educator must watch out for is whether or not the groups are open or closed. An open group will be positive. It will get involved in the academy, school, or youth club activities and initiatives. It will be willing to take in new members. It will be enthusiastic. It will enjoy being a group with the educator present.

A closed group will keep very much to itself. It will shy away from getting involved in things it doesn't have to get involved in. It will not accept new members. It will be secretive and stifled giggles will abound. When the educator is present, members of the closed group will eye each other constantly.

An open group will strengthen the members of the group, while members of a closed group will have no individual personality, preferring to "follow the leader." An open group will bring out the best in each member, while a closed group will tend to bring out the worst.

My kids are getting low grades.

Preliminary checks

- Does the person who is in charge of their study periods organize "directed study," or does he simply have "study hall?"
- Are we dealing with a below average IQ group?
- Are these kids participating in challenging, nonacademic projects (sports, drama, apostolates)?
- If this is a group in primary school, with just one and the same teacher all day all week, is the teacher a good teacher or is he bored or frustrated with the group?
- Is the group looked upon by the teachers in general as being a "dumb group?"

Solution

- Make clear the unacceptability of such low grades.

- Analyze each case and discover the root cause and fix it.
- If kids are slow at academics, they may well be fast at other things (sports). Use this positive quality to encourage them to do better in studies.
- Ensure that study time is a challenging experience and not a chore. (See the "In Italy" example on page 311.)
- Set small attainable goals for the group—as a group—and reward progress. If the group's monthly average is 6.5, offer a special movie if they manage to get it up to 6.7.

Hints

- Individual personal tutoring is hardly ever the answer. It might be a good money waster, but it does little to help the kid. In fact, it will usually leave him worse off. If a kid is doing badly in school, it is often traceable to laziness or to a lack of interest. Having private lessons only serves to make life even easier for him. With individual tutoring, we attack the symptom and not the cause.[28]
- Sometimes kids have academic problems because they feel they have fallen behind. In many cases, it will turn out that it is a single point that they have not mastered, and when this single point has not been grasped everything that follows is pure confusion. If the kids are doing calculus and don't know how to use a slide rule, they will be lost. Not because they are stupid, but because the teacher has not detected that they do not know how to use the slide rule (maybe someone else deserves the label). Or if a kid hasn't grasped the basics of algebra, trigonometry will be doubly difficult for him. Or if a kid learning English as a second language has never grasped the fact that English

has "auxiliaries" that are not present in other languages, he will be forever making huge mistakes in grammar and syntax. In such cases, the teachers should trace the kid's basic cause deficiency and settle that.

100 Short-Term Goals

We have seen that it is usually a kid's behavior that will dictate the short-term goals we offer him (see page 68), but sometimes we might find that a kid is almost perfect and his outward behavior doesn't suggest any short-term goals. In such cases, you might like to run through the following. Feel free to add your own.

A short-term goal must have the following qualities if it is to be effective:

1. They must be in keeping with the kid's personal formation program.
2. They must be attainable within a ten-to-fourteen-day period.
3. They must be measurable.
4. They must be challenging.
5. They must be useful.

Notes:

1. Each of the following short-term goals should be accomplished at least once a day for the duration.
2. Many of these goals are interconnected. Many of the short-term goals listed for generosity are applicable to willpower and good manners.
3. To evaluate accomplishment, sometimes it will be necessary for the kid to say exactly what he did to reach the goal. For example, to cultivate generosity, a kid might be

asked to lend something. The kid will be asked to remember what he lent. This is just to ensure that the goal has effectively been reached. The educator, when suggesting the goal, must tell the kid that he will be asked about its detailed accomplishment.

4. A general, acceptable, and extremely beneficial short-term goal is that of making a visit to the Blessed Sacrament to ask for help in acquiring the virtue the kid is seeking. However, the educator will be careful not to make this his number one choice for every kid every time. If not managed correctly, or if abused, it is inclined to shift the burden of virtue acquisition unto God rather than unto the kid.
5. These short-term goals are intended for use within dialogue.

To cultivate generosity:

1. Share your recess candy.
2. Offer to let the other guy go first through a doorway.
3. Offer your seat, when allowed, to another guy.
4. If you're picking kids for a team, pick one that you know the other guy will not pick.
5. Lend something that you know another kid admires (a pen, your skateboard, your rollerblades, or a CD).
6. When you lend something, don't ask for it back. Let the other guy offer to give it back to you and then take it.
7. If a classmate asks you for a piece of candy, give him two.
8. Offer to help someone carry whatever he's carrying, no matter how small.
9. Pick up anything that another person might drop (pencil,

book).

10. If another kid gets a chore (that involves missing out on something good like a movie, sleep, or recess) ask permission to help him.
11. Do a hidden act of service.
12. Dedicate one recess per day to making the others happy.

To cultivate responsibility:

1. Arrive thirty seconds early to some activity you are usually late for.
2. You are in charge of the tidiness of your classroom. Between classes, quickly pick up any papers that may have fallen to the ground.
3. You are in charge of the area immediately outside your classroom. Keep it totally litter free.
4. Ask for a chore.
5. Make a special effort to keep your class notes tidy, and ask for extra time (during recess) to redo anything that may need redoing.
6. Make a special effort to keep your locker extra tidy, and ask for extra time if you need it.
7. If you are in charge of clearing the table, finish it well, before the other guys have finished clearing theirs.
8. Do not speak in class when you are not supposed to, and dedicate yourself to doing what you should be doing.
9. Finish your homework, allowing yourself enough time for your educator to quiz you on what you have studied.
10. Before you start your day's activities, ask the educator if

your uniform is acceptable.

11. Come up with one idea every two days to make your group better and suggest this idea to your educator (for example: an idea for a poster, a competition, a movie worth seeing, a game, to way to keep the dorm tidy).
12. Make a special effort to do well what you are supposed to be doing especially when nobody is watching (studying, keeping silence, showering, showering well, not messing with others when doing a special chore like laundry, preparing an activity, or cleaning up).
13. Pick some aspect of your duty that you find hard to accomplish because you are worried about what the others will think of you, and make a special effort to do it regardless (silence in the changing room, making the sign of the cross before meals, standing up straight when with your friends, paying attention in class).
14. Keep your personal things in perfect order (classroom locker, clothes locker, sports locker, dorm room).
15. If you lose something, find it. (The educator may wish to "help" the kid lose something.)

To cultivate obedience:

1. When you are told to do something, do it immediately without hesitation or question.
2. If you see that you are going to be asked to do something, (pick up a piece of paper, be quiet, stand or sit straight) do it before you are asked.
3. When you are told to do something, report back once you have finished and ask it there is anything further to be done.

4. Look for something that needs doing and offer to do it (clean the blackboard, get chalk for the teacher before the class begins, hand out music sheets)
5. When told to do something, make a special effort to do it well.

To cultivate willpower:

(Take special care here to ensure that short-term goals are indeed useful in themselves. Not eating dessert for a week may form the will, but it goes against a child's nutritional requirements. Having cold showers all the time might make your will stronger, but they certainly don't get you clean, and for people over fifty, cold showers can even be dangerous.)

1. Be willingly do something you do not like doing. During the morning recess, drink water instead of soda.
2. During the morning recess, eat fruit instead of candy.
3. Get up the instant you are called.
4. Take care to shower well and leave yourself enough time to give yourself a blast of cold water before leaving.
5. Keep your shoes perfectly polished throughout the whole day, buffing them as often as necessary.
6. Keep your shirt tucked in at all times (even on the sports field).
7. Keep your hair tidy, combing it in the bathroom, as often as may be necessary.
8. Never be the first one at your table to start eating.
9. Before you eat anything, make sure the guy beside you has something. If you are at recess, and the kid beside you has nothing, offer him the first bite of your bar, or the first piece of candy.

10. Always offer your last piece of candy, but don't leave the other guy to dispose of the empty wrapper.
11. Never pass a piece of paper on the ground without picking it up.
12. Make time to stop in to make a personal visit to the Blessed Sacrament just to say hello.
13. Keep your feet together while at table.
14. Keep your hands out of your pockets.
15. Avoid stretching the arms of your sweater over your hands.
16. Avoid leaning up against the walls.
17. Sweat on the playing field.
18. Stop what you are doing as soon as you are told. Don't continue for an instant. When you're called to leave the pool, go to the nearest wall.
19. At the end of recess, stop playing immediately.
20. Stop eating when your group stands up to pray (ask permission to finish if necessary).
21. Sing as best you can in the chapel (during the hymns, obviously).
22. Pick the class you least like and at the end of the class, present your copybook to the teacher and ask politely for it to be checked.
23. Lift your feet. Don't shuffle.

To cultivate external discipline:

1. Observe attentive silence in lines.
2. Stand up straight when you are standing.
3. Sit up straight when you are seated.
4. Raise your hand and wait to be called upon before speak-

ing (in class, in lines)

5. Be among the first to be on time for every activity.
6. Greet your educators and teachers politely everyday.
7. Use "please," "excuse me," and "thank you" even with your friends.
8. If you get annoyed, take a deep breath, ask Christ to help you over the moment, and count to ten.
9. Always wear the appropriate and complete uniform. Check the day before to ensure you have everything you need, and if you don't, get it.

To cultivate constancy:

1. Pick a chore or activity that requires extra effort and do it for the duration. Report to your educator at a certain time every day to see if there is anything that needs doing (before morning lines, in recess, after meals)
2. Apply any short-term goal for an extended period.
3. Pick the school subject you are doing the worst in and aim for a higher grade in the next assessment. (The educator will ask the kid his permission to tell the teacher so that the teacher can monitor the kid's progress with special care for the duration.)

To cultivate sincerity:

1. Make a real effort to be punctual.
2. Make a real effort to overcome laziness once every day.
3. In the morning and before you go to bed, recall what your short-term goal is.
4. When the educator or teacher is not in sight, ask yourself

what you should be doing if the educator or teacher were there, and then adjust your behavior accordingly.

5. Before going to sleep, review your day, find one area that you have slipped up in, and make a firm decision to be better in that area tomorrow.
6. If you find you have offended anyone, even slightly, apologize before the day ends.

To cultivate good manners:

1. Do not reach across the table.
2. Serve another before you serve yourself.
3. Compliment one person once a day.
4. Compliment two different people twice a day.
5. Think of something you do that might be annoying to the others and avoid doing it. (The educator may have to suggest something based on the kid. It could be anything from shouting at others during sports to picking on a guy because he's fat.)
5. Open the door for your companions.

To cultivate initiative:

1. Help someone every day.
2. Come up with a way of being quicker at something you are presently rather slow at (getting ready in the mornings, doing your homework, getting a chore done)
3. Get interested in something new (ask a kid what he finds great about stamp collecting, join in a recess tournament in a sport you really don't care for and give it your best shot, sign up for some extracurricular activity that you

may have never tried).

4. Learn about another guy's family.
5. Invent and propose a competition.

To cultivate a spirit of hard work:

1. Finish your homework on time, and if you need extra time, ask for it.
2. Finish your chores on time and ask for extra time if need be.
3. Ask your educator to evaluate your work and ask him for suggestions as to how you could do it better.
4. Make sure you have everything you need for the job before you start (books, copybooks, pens for homework, and clothes for the morning ready the night before)
5. Take immediate action if you see you get distracted. During study, stand up if your mind begins to wander and only sit down when you're back on track, turn on the cold water tap if you find you are taking too much time in the shower.
6. Keep your things dust free (top of your locker, under your bed).
7. Be better at sports (be faster in the pool, be more accurate with your shots, be quicker in your reactions, or learn a new technique).
8. Leave a place better than you found it (your classroom, the recess hall, the shower area, or by turning off the dripping tap).

Glossary

Academy

A live-in school environment. (Language) Academies differ from boarding school in so far as students are not expected to be in a language academy more than one school year. The language academy curriculum covers all normal school subjects, although there is an emphasis on language learning. A language academy will usually offer a variety of courses: a full year course, a four-five month course and a summer course. These academies are single gender. They offer an ambitious human formation program and the present document speaks primary of this.

Base, or basic, quality

The quality that is at the base of all other qualities: our awareness of being children of God, brothers of our Lord, destined to eternity and our awareness that our destiny is determined by what we do here on earth.

Cause qualities

Qualities that lead to other qualities. Being truly concerned for others, for example, will lead us to be self-sacrificing with our time.

Dialogue, please see "Human formation dialogue"

Discipline

The two poles of discipline: external and internal

External discipline derives from the observance of norms of behavior, as in any educational institution... (for example, the schedule of group activities, the use of facilities). Internal discipline has two meanings. The first is the voluntary, convinced assimilation of external discipline... for example, following a schedule, punctuality...

The second meaning (of internal discipline) is self-mastery. This consists of the control of our interior world: thoughts, desires, passions, feelings. Self-mastery is not purely internal, it profoundly influences our external conduct. It is an element of personal maturity." (Marcial Maciel, LC, quoted from *Integral Formation of Catholic*

Priests, Alba House, New York, 1992).

Educator

An adult in charge of a kid or of a group of kids. His responsibility ranges from the personal well-being of the student to the student's personal development. This document details this responsibility in some detail.

Health qualities

Qualities that can only blossom when a person takes seriously the acquisition of other virtues. They are the true sign of sincere personal effort. Among these qualities we find joy and drive.

Human formation dialogue (dialogue)

A formal or informal talk between a kid and his educator in which the kid's personal formation program is reviewed and short term goals updated.

Kidspeak (also written "kidsspeak")

The medium of kid communication. The kid's world as he sees it. It includes concepts and ideas that kids can relate to. Youth fashion uses kidspeak. Successful music (and, yes, let's call it 'music' for the sake of the illustration) aimed at kids uses kidspeak. Not to be confused with kidtalk. Telling a kid that "he will die a slow and painful death at seventy if he continues to smoke" might be true, but it is not kidspeak. Kids really believe that, even should they "grow up," they will never 'grow old." Kids don't relate to being seventy. "Smoking smells," or "Smoking costs money" might be more in keeping with kidspeak.

Kidtalk (also written "kid talk")

The words kids use to communicate. Meanings of words tend to vary according to the age of the user.

Language academy

A live-in school environment. Language academies differ from boarding school in so far as students are not expected to be in a language academy more than one school year. The language academy curriculum covers all normal school subjects, although there is an emphasis on language learning. A language academy will usually offer a variety of courses: a full year course, a four-five month course and a summer course. These academies are single gender. They offer an ambitious human formation programme and the present document speaks primary of this.

Maturity

There are as many definitions of maturity as there are fast food outlets in down-town New York. However, in "genesis" when I speak of maturity, I mean that a person, no matter what his age, behaves as God would have that person, at that age, behave in a given situation. A sixteen year old who throws himself around a dance floor as if the victim of an onslaught of flees may be quite mature. Should a forty year old man do it, well, he'd be kind of overdoing it. A seven year old will cry if given a kick during a football game. A sixteen year old will not. But a ten year old will be expected to do as he is told in the same way a thirty-five year old is expected to obey his boss. So basically, "being mature" is "acting, or being, your age."

Measurable

The capacity to be quantified or evaluated objectively, as in "He walked seven miles the first day, eight the second..." as opposed to "He walked a good deal."

Prototype (God's)

The image God has in His mind of the perfect kid. Having a clear idea of what this is, is the starting point for an educator's work.

Regnum Christi

A movement dedicated to the Catholic apostolate. It was founded in the middle of the twentieth century by Fr Marcial Maciel.

Symptom qualities

Qualities resulting from other qualities. For instance, reliability is a symptom quality that will result from responsibility.

Study Guides

If you use **genesis** as a basis for study, we suggest you draw up a study guide for each section you read. Here is an example:

1. What are the four steps an educator should follow in his work as formator?
2. What is the first question an educator should ask when he is entrusted with the formation of a kid?
3. What are the causes, symptoms, and health qualities of God's prototype kid?
4. Apart from knowing what God wants of each kid in general and from each kid in particular, and apart from knowing how to help the kid attain this goal, there is an essential goal we must aim for in our work with kids. Without this element all our work will be nothing but superficial effort. What is this element we must strive towards?

Study Guide: Answers

1. Know what the God prototype of a kid is; know how your kid matches, or measures up, to the God prototype; draw up a personal formation program for the kid; guide the kid along.
2. How does God want this kid to be?
3. Cause qualities: generosity, willpower, responsibility, discipline, hard work, constancy, and initiative. Symptom qualities: self-sacrifice, discipline, and good manners. Health qualities: joy, serenity, drive, and optimism.
4. To get the kid to sincerely ask the question, "What does God want of me?" and then to give him the tools he will need to answer elegantly.

Topic Answers

Here you will find some guidelines as to how you could go about answering several of the topics posed.

From page 33

1. People are not trees. Just as a baby would die within hours after birth if not cared for, so too the growing child needs help. For every tree that "makes it" in a forest, tens, if not hundreds, of saplings die. A tree is not called to help others.
2. This is perfectly true. In our work we must be careful to avoid the kids "following the book" just to keeep out of trouble. External discipline must (repeat, must) go hand in hand with interior discipline.

5. A kid does not believe in God and is adverse to all things spiritual. Is his formation doomed to be unbalanced and unsurefooted? There is a difference between what a kid might say and what he actually believes. He might have a problem and feel that by saying "he doesn't believe" God will simply go away and free him of his hang-up. This can be a typical approach, especially in boys after they hit puberty. God—and his commandments—make certain demands that the kid cannot, or feels he cannot, meet. So this is one angle. A kid claiming not to believe in God might just be saying that he doesn't believe in the god he has been told about. So this would be another angle. An aversion to things spiritual may also be a carryover from earlier experiences of religious teaching or an overzealous family's approach to religion. We will not get into how to solve these problems here; let it suffice to say that opening up spiritual horizons for a kid

is certainly possible and indeed essential. But to answer that question, we must confirm that without the spiritual dimension, all formation will be weak; it will lack a true backbone and thus be ineffective in the long run.

6. In-depth spiritual formation by itself is sufficient to allow a person to attain complete and true happiness in this life and the next. Not true. Spiritual formation needs an outlet. And the better the outlet, the more a person will fulfill his life. Spiritual formation also needs a base. The stronger the base, the healthier the spiritual formation. Bout outlet and base are the other aspects of formation.

WHEN ALL IS SAID AND DONE, THERE IS MORE DONE THAN SAID.
Gaelic Book of Wisdom, revised edition

Endnotes

1. A readable, clear-cut, and well-worth-reading book on values is *Building on Solid Ground* by Father Thomas Williams, L.C.
2. In Spanish and Italian, "integral" can mean "whole (wheat)," and "integral bread" is bread made from whole—as opposed to refined— wheat.
3. Another meaning of "integral formation" is that all those who have contact with a kid in some way share in the mission of forming the kid. Teachers, instructors, and even the gardener have their role to play. While this is a valid interpretation of the term, it is not what we are referring to in this document.
4. Please refer to Group Management for ways of dealing with such cases.
5. By this we do not just refer to boosting the actual quality itself, but to use the confidence that this quality instills to help the kid venture into new realms of quality acquisition.
6. Cf also "Using the positive..." page 202.
7. These examples could also be due to other factors as well (the kid might be devastated by family problems, or he might be lacking iron or other vitamins), but the fact remains that his conduct indicates laziness. Such conduct will serve to help us get started.
8. See the note on "The workings of a goal," page 165
9. This is what some call "virtue": the ease to do, or to be, good.

10. see Glossary
11. We do not speak of personal tuition (private classes) in this section. Please see page 162 for this.
12. Obviously an invented text.
13. Some cultural differences may be accepted. It is perfectly normal for Italians, for example, to embrace and kiss both cheeks when meeting friends. Latins will often embrace as an expression of congratulations. Taking these cultural differences, and circumstances, into account, an educator should follow local custom without going overboard.
14. This sin has no forgiveness, because to be forgiven we must recognize our fault and ask God's mercy. If we feel that God will not pardon us, we will not even ask Him and therefore we will not receive pardon. Ask and you shall receive is what the Lord said. If we do not ask we will not receive.
15. The reader might like to refer to "Tips of the Trade" (page 210) where some of the elements used by this educator are mentioned with equally wonderful results.
16. And no, I have not.
17. Not to be confused with serenity which comes from knowing your place and how you fit into the bigger picture.
18. As in the case of sanctions that go beyond an educator's brief.
19. *Hacer. Hacer hacer. Dejar Hacer*, Marcial Maciel, L.C.
20. Mk 1, 21-39
21. Fr Javier Orozco, L.C.
22. For examples of this, you might like to go over the dialogues I mentioned beginning on page 70.
23. When the Old Testament David was leading a procession

with the Ark of the Covenant he was singing in a full, but out-of-tune voice. He was doing his best. His wife comes up to him and tells him to stop that he was making a fool of himself. His rebuke? "I'm singing for the Lord, not for you."

24. *respicere*, to look upon
25. If you have not read the previous pages, you might like to read up on "Vision" beginning on page 262.
26. Mathematical certainty is definite. If today is Wednesday, tomorrow will be Thursday. Moral certainty is not mathematical, but none the less valid. If you put the correct address on a letter and the correct postage and post it in the correct mailbox, you can be morally sure that it will get to its destination.
27. Words will vary according to ages. Never send a thirteen year old out on a "treasure hunt." Give it a different name. Call it an OAM (Objective Acquisition Mission) or something.